D0775801

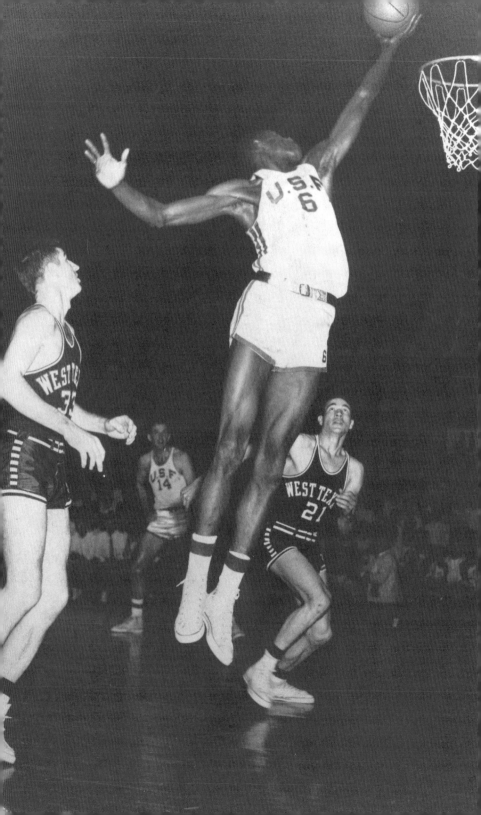

JAMES W. JOHNSON

# THE DANDY DONS

Bill Russell, K. C. Jones,

Phil Woolpert, and One

of College Basketball's

Greatest and Most

Innovative Teams

UNIVERSITY OF NEBRASKA PRESS

LINCOLN AND LONDON

Library of Congress
Cataloging-in-Publication Data

Johnson, James W.
The Dandy Dons : Bill Russell, K.C. Jones,
Phil Woolpert, and one of college basketball's
greatest and most innovative teams /
James W. Johnson.
p.   cm.
Includes bibliographical references.
ISBN 978-0-8032-1877-2 (pbk. : alk. paper)
1. University of San Francisco—Basketball.
2. Basketball teams—United States—
History. 3. College sports—United States—
History. 4. Russell, Bill, 1934–5. Jones, K. C.,
1932-6. Woolpert, Phil. I. Title.
GV855.4.J64 2009
796.04'30973—dc22      2008048163
Set in Scala by Bob Reitz.
Designed by Ashley Muehlbauer.

796.04
JOH
1995

*To Don Carson, the best friend anyone could ever have.*

# CONTENTS

# PREFACE
## The Changing Game

"We changed the game. I think you can say we developed a whole new philosophy of basketball. We attacked the offense and made it react to the defense."
—Bill Russell

One of the first things that new University of San Francisco (USF) coach Phil Woolpert did when he walked into his office in 1950 was open a filing cabinet that predecessor Pete Newell had left for him. "My God," he muttered, as he looked at folder after folder—each at least an inch thick—on high school prospects. Overwhelmed, he slammed the drawer, went home, and told his wife, Mary, "This is just beyond my capability." He wanted to resign. Woolpert's wife minced no words, calling him a quitter. He listened. And then he returned to work. "Frankly, she whipped the hell out of me that day, and I went back. She was right."

Had Woolpert called it quits, two extremely talented players might have been denied the opportunity to play basketball in college, let alone bring two national championships to the University of San Francisco, help the team set numerous records, help bring about social change, change the rules of the game, and usher in the modern era of basketball. Because he stayed, college basketball has never been the same.

Those talented African American players—Bill Russell and K. C. Jones—elevated basketball to a higher level, particularly with their defense. Theirs was an effort accelerated in the next four or five years by Wilt Chamberlain, Elgin Baylor, Oscar Robertson, and other black players. Through the efforts of Russell and Jones USF earned its place in college basketball lore with two championship seasons in 1955 and 1956. "The inclusion of black players at the college level . . . gave . . . more emphasis to defense," coach Pete Newell said. "Their athleticism, quickness, and speed created a tempo of play that brought basketball to heights the coaches of my time had never envisioned."

In one of the least recognized but perhaps most influential changes in the game of basketball, Russell and the Dons moved it from a primarily horizontal game, one in which players rarely left their feet except to rebound, to a vertical game, with more jump shooting and shot blocking. Neil D. Isaacs, in his 1976 book *All the Moves: A History of College Basketball*, said Russell "brought the fourth major element of modern basketball to the game; he was the intimidator of inside shooters, the rejecter of shots, and the quick releaser of outlet passes to trigger fast breaks after rebounding."

Until that time defense had been an afterthought. Russell and Jones changed the idea that defense was a time to rest while your team didn't have the ball. Before Russell and Jones came along, players relaxed on defense, hoping to get the ball off a rebound and race down the court for a lay-up. But Russell effectively stopped the lay-up, forcing players to pull up short when they saw him and his long arms waiting for them. Coaches had to develop new strategies to work the ball around the perimeter of the court to set up shots Russell couldn't reach. They used screens to get open for shots. This new game provided a greater challenge for players and more enjoyment for spectators.

Russell was the first player to help generate his team's offense by his defense. He and Jones saw defense as a positive transition of the game, the starting point of the team's offense. For example Russell would block shots toward Jones, who would start a fast break that often led to his scoring 2 points. "When you played Russell," Newell said, "nobody had really seen that shot-blocking technique. You were never ready for that hand coming out of the air. He made coaches look at big men in a different way." The Dons' two championship seasons "laid the groundwork for how basketball was to be played," said former USF coach Jesse Evans. "That style would still be productive fifty years later. You've got a big, mobile guy inside and guards that could run the floor." Said *Sports Illustrated* writer Frank Deford,

> Russell was so dominant in his last two college seasons that he can spot everybody else a year and still be, indisputably, the greatest player in the history of the collegiate game. . . . Russell changed college basketball more than any other player in the history of the sport. . . . Perhaps more significantly, Russell was the figure most important in establishing the black man's place in the game. . . . In a very real sense, it can be said that William Felton Russell changed the game defensively, offensively, and culturally. . . . Surely no college player has ever even approached Bill Russell as a force in the game.

In his 1998 book *The Greatest Book of College Basketball*, Blair Kerkhoff ranked Russell the fourth greatest college basketball player behind Lew Alcindor/Kareem Abdul-Jabbar, Bill Walton, and Oscar Robertson. He ranked K. C. Jones sixty-first. Kerkhoff placed Russell the fourth greatest in National Collegiate Athletic Association

(NCAA) tournament play behind Alcindor/Abdul-Jabbar, Walton, and Christian Laettner. Phil Woolpert was ranked the seventeenth greatest college coach. Kerkhoff called the USF Dons the third greatest team behind the University of California–Los Angeles (UCLA) team of 1968 and the Indiana team of 1976.

Another element was the racial issue, but if the impact on basketball were to be measured on a scale from one to ten, the team's play elevated its place in basketball history to at least an eight if not higher, while the racial issue would rank about a five. To be sure, the extraordinary play of that team with its five black players pointed to the realization that they could play the game as none before them ever had.

Before and during those years many great black college basketball players played at small schools outside of the NCAA against other black schools, games that attracted little attention from fans or newspapers. Certainly Bill Russell, K. C. Jones, and the other black players brought race to center stage by winning the NCAA tournament two years in a row and setting a record of sixty consecutive wins. "At first . . . black players' approach to the game was indistinguishable from their white counterparts," wrote Frank Fitzpatrick in *And the Walls Came Tumbling Down*. "Basketball was a mostly slow, patterned, and physical game as yet devoid of any great flair. It wasn't that black players weren't capable of more athletic and improvised style, it was just that most were reluctant to call attention to themselves in what was still an alien world." Until then perhaps the best black college player for a major school who preceded Russell was UCLA's Don Barksdale, who, like Russell, grew up across San Francisco Bay from USF. The six-foot-six-inch center became the first African American to be selected to the consensus All-American team in 1947. Jackie Robinson, also from UCLA, led the Pacific Coast Conference in scoring in 1940.

It was an unwritten rule that there existed a racial quota in basketball at that time, but USF coach Woolpert didn't care about a player's race; he wanted the best players on the floor. Regardless of whether Woolpert was making a statement about racial issues in a nation awakening to the plight of minorities, he was one of the first to recognize that the blacks were an untapped pool of outstanding basketball players. They were athletes who other coaches had not heard of or had refused to recruit despite their abilities. It was perhaps coincidental that the Dons became the first team to start three black players the same year—1954—that the U.S. Supreme Court issued the *Brown vs. Board of Education* desegregation decision. Woolpert started the three players after USF lost to UCLA. He inserted Hal Perry into the starting lineup, joining Bill Russell and K. C. Jones. The Dons never lost another game that year or the next. Perry later said, "[Woolpert] deserved as much respect as any coach, but even more than that, as much as any person in any phase of the civil rights movement. . . . He went through hell. Very few people knew it. As far as they knew, he was a coach and that was it."

People wanted Woolpert fired, Perry said, but because he was a winning coach, that wasn't going to happen. Woolpert received hate mail and was chided by opposing coaches, particularly those on the West Coast. Some called him Abe Saperstein after the owner/coach of the Harlem Globetrotters. Woolpert's son Paul, also a basketball coach, said, "He knew he was bucking the trend, but he never even considered the color of the guys. He said, 'These are the best players, and we're going to play them.' He definitely did everything he believed in." Bill Russell commented, "The most you can ask from a coach is a chance. Phil gave black players a real chance."

Woolpert also gave scholarships to the five blacks when many coaches refused to even recruit black players. At the time, black players failed to attract the attention of most newspapers, so few coaches outside of their immediate areas knew of them. And only a handful of coaches on the West Coast took chances on African American players. Woolpert was one of the first along with UCLA's John Wooden. "A lot of coaches talked about human rights," Pete Newell said. "Phil did something about it. Maybe he didn't break the color barrier, but he stretched it. There were very few black players getting scholarships before Phil. He opened the door of college basketball. He caused more programs to take a look at their policies." Said forward Mike Farmer, "[Woolpert] was color blind. That was his legacy."

The 1966 Texas Western NCAA championship win over the all-white Kentucky Wildcats with five black starters certainly was monumental, but USF indisputably helped pave the way for that Texas team. Farmer, who played as a sophomore on the 1956 title team, said, "Not to take anything away from Texas Western, but the [1955] USF [team] made the real breakthrough racially." *Sports Illustrated* writer Frank Deford has argued that Texas Western "was the end product of what Russell inspired—and what he had suffered through—a decade earlier." Carl Boldt, a forward on the 1955–56 national championship team, said that race was just as important on the court as off. "I think USF changed basketball by the quickness of its black players. That may have been the biggest thing I noticed about our teams."

Russell also brought an intimidation factor to defense that had rarely, if ever, been seen in college basketball—at least the way he did it. Said one coach, "With his incredible sense of timing, he'd leap with you and jam your best shot down your throat. The next time you raced to the basket, you looked over your shoulder, wondering 'Where's Russell?' . . . and miss your shot." Guard Hal Perry said, "Bill could put his hand on his hip and dare you like a matador. And he was like a ballet artist in the air." Blocking shots became Russell's signature on the court. He would say about his defense,

Playing good defense takes a lot of practice, sure. But I do a lot of thinking about it, too. Look, if I tried to block all the shots my man takes, I'd be dead. The thing I got to do is make my man think I'm going to block every shot he takes. How can I do it? Okay, here. Say I block a shot on you. The next time you're going to shoot, I know I can't block it, but I make exactly the same moves. I'm confident. I'm not thinking anymore, but I got you thinking. You can't think and shoot—nobody can. You're thinking, will he block this one or won't he? I don't even have to try to block it. You'll miss.

Pete Newell coached Russell on the West team in the Hearst Fresh Air Fund in 1956 in Madison Square Garden. Most of the eastern players had never seen the likes of the jumping jack from USF. "I have never seen players so openly dismayed by the ability of Russell to block any shot within sixteen to eighteen feet of the basket—and once from over twenty feet," Newell said. "The game turned into a rout as Russell would block the shot to K.C. [Jones], and K.C. would end up laying the ball in for 2 points. One East player had his first three shots blocked and refused to shoot again." Russell was so dominant as the Dons' center that his play led to rule changes that remain in place today. In one game Russell jumped over a UCLA player to dunk the ball after an inbound pass thrown over the backboard, a play later to be banned by the NCAA.

At the end of the 1955 season the NCAA changed the width of the lane from six feet to twelve feet in an attempt to keep players like Russell from camping under the basket. Some writers argue that the shot-blocking abilities of six-foot-ten-inch George Mikan, the National Player of the Year in 1947, led to the change as much as did Russell's shot blocking. There is an element of truth to that argument, but it was ultimately designed because of Bill Russell; the rule is often referred to as the "Russell Rule." Tom Heinsohn, who played against Russell in college and with him for the Boston Celtics, said Russell could move across the lane much faster than other big men. He said Russell "had an effective rebound range of eighteen feet. If he was nine feet off to one side of the basket, he could race over to pull down a rebound nine feet off to the other side. . . . That's the kind of athletic ability he had." No widening of the lane could slow down Russell's play.

The NCAA also adopted a rule the year after Russell graduated to prevent offensive players from touching the ball above the basket until it had hit the backboard or when it was within the cylinder, again because of Russell and Chamberlain. Russell often jumped high above the rim to guide in errant shots by teammates—the "steer shot" they called it. Russell scored most of his points that way. On several occasions, coach Woolpert would tell players not to worry about making a basket, but just to shoot it near the hoop so that Russell could funnel it in. "We weren't planning to make any changes [in the rules]," said Doggie Julian, Dartmouth coach and a member of the rules committee. "But after some of the coaches saw Russell's performance [in the 1955 NCAA tournament] they got scared."

Russell also brought the dunk to college basketball at a time when most players shunned it as hotdogging. He may have been the first to hook up on passes to teammates for alley-oops on fast breaks. The dunk became standard fare as black players began to dominate the game—players like Wilt Chamberlain, Elgin Baylor, Oscar Robertson, and others. In 1967 the dunk was outlawed in what "appeared to be aimed at a big, strong, threatening black man [David Lattin of Texas Western]," said Frank Fitzpatrick, author of a book about the all-black Texas Western team that won the NCAA title. The dunk was restored in the 1976–77 season.

In the view of at least one writer, USF's success also may have changed the focus of year-end tournaments from the National

Invitation Tournament (NIT) to the NCAA's. Said Peter C. Bjark-man: "With USF so clearly the cream of the collegiate crop of two seasons running, attention had now been focused squarely on the postseason NCAA event where the Dons continued to strut their magical game. For the first time, 1955 and 1956, it seemed absolutely clear that the NCAA event was indeed the tourney that was providing the nation's undisputed national champion."

In two thrilling seasons, the Dons arguably changed the game of basketball forever under the most unlikely of conditions. It all came about because of the hard work of an initially reluctant coach, a player who had started on his high school team for only half a year, another who thought about becoming a postal worker instead of going to college, a black high school student-body president at an all-white school, and a handful of players from a nearby Catholic school within walking distance of USF. Theirs is a basketball story for the ages.

# ACKNOWLEDGMENTS

Writing a book is isolating work. What makes it palatable is the many people who come into the writer's life to help with the research, the critiques, and the editing. They help keep you sane when you think you otherwise aren't.

First and foremost, thanks go to the players, coaches, and others who gave up their valuable time to answer my questions, especially Carl Boldt and Mike Farmer. Carl gave me telephone numbers and e-mails of many of the players, even informing them ahead of time that I would be calling. Mike helped me gain access to newspaper articles and many of the photographs used to illustrate this book.

It is unfortunate that I was unable to talk with Bill Russell or K. C. Jones, but Russell's three autobiographies and K. C. Jones's autobiography were immensely valuable, particularly because of their frankness about their early years at USF.

Another helpful person was Father Michael Kotlanger, who let me plow through the University of San Francisco archives. He cheerfully answered my numerous e-mails with useful responses.

Thanks, too, go to Ryan McCrary, USF's assistant athletic director for media relations, who provided photographs and written material.

An assortment of friends lent me their encouragement, including Wally Sparks, Don Carson, and Ron Navarrette. My wife, Marilyn, never ceased listening to my endless stories about the USF team and even helped with some of my research. Besides, she got a trip to San Francisco. Her thoughtful editing made this a far better book. I appreciate her help more than I can adequately express.

Librarians are always marvelous in their patience and help. What would we do without them? Thanks particularly to the several who helped me at the University of Arizona and the Tucson city library.

John C. Kelly of the *New Orleans Times-Picayune*; Dr. Michael Giorlando (athletic director and head basketball coach) and archivist Art Carpenter at Loyola University of New Orleans; and Lee Hampton and Shannon Burrell of the Amistad Research Center at Tulane University provided invaluable help in researching USF's visit to New Orleans in December 1955.

My special thanks go to Rob Taylor, acquiring editor for sports at the University of Nebraska Press. It was a pleasure to once again work with Rob. His patience with an impatient author is greatly appreciated, as were his helpful suggestions that improved the book. Ann Harrington was an exacting editor, just what this sometimes-awkward writer needed to smooth his syntax and to ferret out his errors of fact.

Thanks one and all. You made my job a lot easier.

# INTRODUCTION

I was twelve years old when my father took me to see my first college basketball game—the University of San Francisco against whom I can't remember. But I do remember that it was during the 1949–50 season, the year after the Dons won the NIT, then the biggest college tournament in the country. Don Lofgran, Rene Herrerias, Ross Guidice. What a night.

If I saw another college game in the next five or six years, I can't remember it. But I do recall seeing the 1955 and 1956 Dons play during the years they won the NCAA tournament. As a youngster I just appreciated good basketball. I wasn't able to recognize the historic and cultural significance of the excitement on the court. Perhaps it has taken me fifty years to gain that perspective, but I've never forgotten the game Bill Russell and K. C. Jones brought to the hardwoods in those years. They changed basketball in terms of race, rules, strategy, and even popularity.

Fifty-one years later while watching the grainy, black-and-white highlight films of games I saw as a teenager, I recalled how different the game was back then. It was slower and much less physical. Over the years officials have allowed players to become more aggressive. Basketball is no longer a noncontact sport.

In the 1950s you didn't see palming of the ball, pushing and shoving, or high levels of turnovers. Nor did you see tattoos, headbands, T-shirts under jerseys, or baggie pants. "We weren't trash-talkers and in-your-face the way a lot of players are today," said Mike Farmer, a forward on the 1956 championship team. What you did see were set shots when players' feet rarely left the floor. The same was true on the defensive end, where teams took defense to mean a chance to rest up for their offensive. And then there were those underhand free throws.

With the USF Dons several things stood out. Gene Brown's skills rivaled those of Michael Jordan with his twisting jump shots. Bill Russell jumped higher above the rim than anyone I had ever seen. K. C. Jones was inside his opponent's jersey on defense. Opponents rarely got off set shots against the tenacious Dons' defense. Only once in the highlight films did I see an opponent make a set shot, and that was Bernie Simpson of Cal, who drilled one from at least thirty feet away, far beyond today's pro three-point line.

The game in the mid-1950s had more finesse—almost like slow-motion ballet—compared with what we see today. Athletes are more athletic and much bigger now, there's no doubt about that. And coaches play a much greater role during a game as well. USF coach Phil Woolpert just let his team play. No plays were called out from the bench, and there were no special plays for Bill Russell. Coaches didn't call repeated time-outs to tell the team what to do. Money and television have changed the game. During a game in the 1956–57 season, Cal's Pete Newell and UCLA's John Wooden entered into a psychological battle to see who would call the first time-out. Wooden gave in first, calling a time-out with four minutes left in the game. That time-out gave Cal a psychological lift that enabled the Bears to pull ahead and win. Today television demands a break every four minutes for commercials; coaches often hold out for those commercial time-outs to avoid using one of their own. At times teams resume play after a commercial time-out, run up and down the court a couple of times, and then abruptly stop playing again when the coach calls a time-out. Where's the rhythm? Where's the momentum? Whatever happened to just letting the players play?

The word "revolution" is tossed around far too loosely in the world of sports. Revolutions come in stages and don't happen very often. The USF years did indeed constitute a revolution—and in my mind one of the most significant—although I'm sure to provoke arguments with that statement. In winning the championships in 1955 and '56, the Dons also set a record for the most consecutive victories with fifty-five—extending it to sixty the following year—a record the Dons held until the fabulous UCLA teams from 1971 to '74 won eighty-eight in a row.

CBS basketball analyst Billy Packer in his 1989 book *College Basketball's 25 Greatest Teams* listed the Dons as no. 4, behind UCLA's Alcindor/Kareem Abdul-Jabbar teams from 1966–69 as no. 1. Despite the passage of nineteen years since Packer wrote his book, it is unlikely any team would now have moved above the no. 4 spot in his rankings.

Boston Celtics coach Red Auerbach once questioned the rankings though. He doubted whether Abdul-Jabbar's team should have been ranked higher than Russell's Dons. "I don't know," he said, "I like Kareem. . . . He's a hell of a guy. . . . But Bill (Russell) came out with the greatest statement of all. The media once asked him, 'Well, how do you think you'd do against Kareem?' Russell said, 'You've got the question wrong. The question is, how do you think Kareem would do against me?' And that's right."

Packer is expert enough about basketball to avoid having used the word "revolution." But consider what he did say: USF's

"defensive machine . . . ultimately changed the face of basketball."
Eddie Einhorn, founder and chairman of the TVS Television Network, who was responsible in the early 1960s for the increased popularity of college basketball on television, recalled that the first final four (it wasn't capitalized until 1978) he saw was when USF walloped Iowa for its second NCAA championship. He praised USF, "which I still think is the most dominating team I've ever seen in the NCAA finals."

This is the story of a relatively ignored chapter in basketball's evolution, told through the chronology of two championship basketball seasons at a small Jesuit university that was relatively unknown outside the West Coast. This is a story worth hearing.

# THE DANDY DONS

# ONE

## Russell's Coming of Age

"I saw that head of his appear above the multitudes."
—Hal DeJulio, who recruited Bill Russell

During the summer of 1953, Phil Woolpert, thirty-eight-year-old basketball coach at the University of San Francisco, traveled to Lawrence, Kansas, to learn about the pressure defense the Kansas Jayhawks had used to win the national championship in 1952. Kansas played a man-to-man defense that cut off the passing lanes and made it difficult to move the ball down court.

Dean Smith, who later rose to fame as the coach of the North Carolina Tar Heels, was a substitute player on that team, one of eleven lettermen. "This was unheard of at the time," Smith said, "really the first instance of man pressure as we now know it."

Woolpert wanted to get firsthand knowledge of the press from Kansas coach Phog Allen's astute assistant coach, Dick Harp. He told Harp, "I have a guy named Bill Russell coming in, and he's going to be a great shot blocker."

Bill Russell was six feet two inches tall and weighed 128 pounds when he walked into the McClymonds High School gym during his sophomore year in Oakland, California. He looked like a scarecrow, with long skinny legs sticking out from the bottom of his shorts, and long arms and hands dangling below his shorts. "I was so skinny I had to keep moving in the shower to get wet," he would say. He tried out for the varsity basketball team at a school he once called "one of those integrated-segregated schools," which was 90 percent black.

Russell had hoped to go to Oakland Technical High School like his brother, Charlie, but he wasn't a particularly good student. School officials told him to enroll at McClymonds High School, in Oakland's flatlands, or so one story goes. Another said Russell found himself in the shadow of his brother, a talented athlete, and wanted to go to a different high school so he would not be compared to Charlie. Russell never clarified the story in any of his three biographies. But if he did try to escape his brother's shadow, it didn't work. The McClymonds coach showed no patience with the gangly and awkward Russell. One day he heard the varsity coach, a man who he only identified as Fitzpatrick, say in front of the whole team the day the coach had cut him, "Why is it that if there are two brothers in school, we always get the bum?" It left him shaken and nearly broken.

He tried out for the football team and the cheerleading squad but failed in those endeavors, too. A widely reproduced picture shows him wearing an Indian headdress and clothing to depict the McClymonds mascot, the Warrior. One day as a sixteen-year-old walking in the school halls he decided he was okay with who he was. He could see no reason to believe there was anything wrong with him. This realization turned Russell's life around. From that day on, whenever he felt hostility from someone, he assumed it to be that person's problem rather than his. He turned his cowering look into a glowering one. "My father always told me that the most important thing is what you think of yourself," Russell said almost sixty years later. "He had an expression about there being all these little red wagons that get pulled around and that it's got nothing to do with me."

His athletic fortunes began to change then, too. He met George Powles, McClymonds's white baseball and basketball coach, and "For the first time in my life I came in contact with a white person who brought things down front, who talked to us realistically," Russell recalled. Russell would say over and over again through the years, "I have never met a finer person. I owe so much to him it's impossible to express. This is a compassionate man, honest in the truest sense of the word."

Powles saw something in Russell and urged him to try out for the junior varsity (JV) basketball team. For one thing, he noticed the awkward boy's huge hands—hands that would eventually measure ten and a half inches from wrist to fingertip. In addition Russell's skinny legs had plenty of spring, and he had square shoulders. After his experience with the varsity team, Russell was reluctant to subject himself to yet another tryout. "I dragged my feet, but I came out. I didn't break any records. I was terrible. But Powles had faith in me as a person and didn't want to break my spirit."

Powles, a respected baseball coach, over the years had coached high school players such as hall of famers Frank Robinson and Joe Morgan as well as Curt Flood and Vada Pinson. But Powles knew little about basketball. He only took over the JV team after the principal demanded it. He didn't particularly like basketball, either, but he did know how to mentor athletes and how to get the best out of them.

On the first day of practice Powles brought the game rulebook with him. "Our very first practice there was no running, no jumping, no shooting," Russell said. "Just, we were going to learn the rules." One of the things that came in handy in later years was what the rulebook didn't say. It said nothing about a player leaving his feet to block a shot. "I had never seen a shot blocked when I was learning basketball," Russell said. "I didn't even know what it was."

Russell didn't even make the JV team, but Powles somehow came up with a sixteenth jersey that Russell would wear every other game, sharing it with a boy named Roland Campbell. "I could run and jump all right, but if there was a basketball within twenty feet of me, I went to pieces." One of his classmates, Frank Robinson, who led McClymonds to a city championship, said Russell "couldn't even put the ball in the basket when he dunked."

Powles put Russell in to play once in awhile when a game was out of reach. Fans would chant, "We want Russell," and he would play his heart out only to receive hoots, laughter, and catcalls from spectators. Russell wanted to quit, but Powles wouldn't hear of it. "[Allowing me to share the sixteenth uniform] was an act of kindness on Powles's part," Russell said. "He used to tell the guys I'd be a pretty good basketball player. But George was the only guy on the planet who thought that," Russell said. "I couldn't even make the homeroom team. He gave us a sense of self-worth that it was okay to be ambitious, okay not to be afraid, and really okay to find out how good you could be."

Powles said he kept Russell on the team because "he had nothing else, nowhere else to go." One of Russell's problems was that he was too easygoing and wouldn't stand up to another player. Then Powles asked one of Russell's teammates, Bobby Woods, to "get on him. Stir him up. Make him aggressive." Russell had difficulty getting angry with anybody. He didn't understand why Woods was all over his back, hacking away at him. "I couldn't get angry at anybody," Russell said. "I couldn't understand [Woods] sometimes because he would get on my back and really hack me. [I was] anything but a killer." Finally, Russell began to get the picture, that Powles had told Woods to foul him and stir him up.

In time Russell turned his embarrassment to anger and finally to determination. "I believe that man saved me from becoming a juvenile delinquent," Russell said. "If I hadn't had basketball, all my energies and frustrations would surely have been carried out in some other direction."

Powles gave Russell two dollars so he could join the Boys Club and play every day. "It was frustrating," Russell said. "Most of the kids wouldn't let me play. I had to play with the little kids, and who wants to play with them when you're six-feet-two?"

Russell also practiced at DeFremery Park in Oakland. "What really attracted me to Bill was his smarts," playground director Bill Patterson said. "He not only had the gift of gab, he liked to investigate. He was inquisitive about everything and anything. He was very outgoing, very outspoken." Russell attended youth workshops at the park that dealt with such topics as narcotics, alcohol, police relations, and race relations. Patterson believed Russell's strong social views grew from his attending those workshops.

Powles once told Russell, who complained that he wasn't as good as the other players, "Son, remember this: If you think the other guy is better than you, he will be." Russell said he never forgot that. Powles also told Russell and his teammates that they had to play clean and be good sports, particularly because they were black and the referees might be laying for them. "We're going to be typed, so play clean. No matter how unfair a call may be, keep your temper. Anyone who gets mad gets pulled out of the game." Then he added quietly, "In order to be good at anything, you have to be a gentleman at it." He also told the boys, "If you play like the rest of the teams, you're going to be called roughnecks, dirty, and worse. If you get into a fight, it's a riot. So we're not going to get into any fights. We're going to play good, clean basketball. You are a Negro team, and the second there's any trouble everyone is going to blame you, whether it's your fault or not. You'll be guilty. The slightest trouble and everybody will claim it was a riot.

Remember that. You've got an extra burden here. But we can carry it. We'll play with it and win, right?" Russell and his teammates took the advice to heart and stayed out of trouble. "There were times when we were pushed to the brink but, you know, we had a good team," he said. Three years in a row McClymonds won the Keyes Memorial Trophy, an award given to the school that had demonstrated the best sportsmanship.

Powles repeatedly admonished the team to play harder and embarrass the other team with the final score. "And that's what I did, whenever somebody bothered me, I'd just play harder," Russell said.

During high school Russell began shooting up in physical height. At the beginning of his junior year he was six feet five inches tall and weighed 160 pounds. Nonetheless, he was cut from the JV by a new coach. Powles had moved up to coach varsity, which was Russell's good fortune. Although Powles had persuaded him to try out for the varsity team, he sat on the bench through the season and played very little. Russell often wanted to quit, but Powles wouldn't let him. By his senior year, the team's other two centers had graduated so Russell inherited the job. "[Powles] may not have known too much about basketball, but he taught me a lot of other things, how important your heart and your attitude [are]," Russell later said when he was playing for USF.

Now as a starter but certainly not the best player on the team, Russell discovered he was in love with basketball. He read every article about basketball he could get his hands on, a habit he continued in college. "I had stacks and stacks of magazines. I studied what players said, learned about their habits and idiosyncrasies, and I remembered all of them." He pored over photographs of players, particularly ones he thought he might later play against or ones he simply admired, who he believed had something in their game he might be able to use.

Good fortune was about to come Russell's way.

USF freshman forward Dick Lawless had been playing a three-on-three pickup basketball game at a Boys Club in Oakland against Russell during the summer before Russell's last year at McClymonds High. Lawless told USF coach Phil Woolpert and assistant coach Ross Guidice about the "string bean" who, when he jumped, towered over the six-foot-four Lawless. This player had successfully rejected virtually every shot the Oakland All-City player had taken. "I couldn't believe it," Lawless said.

After the game, Lawless asked Russell if he was interested in college. Russell responded that he was, so Lawless told Woolpert that he should keep an eye on him. Woolpert sent one of his scouts, Hal DeJulio, who also had recruited Lawless, to check out Russell. DeJulio, who played on USF's NIT championship team in 1949, attended a game between Oakland High and McClymonds. It was Russell's last game. (Russell played only half of his senior year. As a "splitter" he had started school in midyear when he turned five years old and had then attended "split" school sessions throughout school. Russell graduated in January.)

Russell played the game of his life, scoring 14 points. It was the only game so far in which he scored more than 10 points. What impressed DeJulio was that Russell scored 8 points in a row at the end of the first half and 6 in row at the close of the game as McClymonds won. He particularly liked Russell's sense of timing. Russell had a knack for going after the ball even though he often got tangled up in his own ungainly arms and legs. He saw Russell as a game-winner and liked the way he played defense, jumped, hustled, and ran the floor.

"All the players could jump," DeJulio said, "but Russell excelled at it." DeJulio was mesmerized by the gangly center. He couldn't take his eyes off him the whole game. "I could see great speed, great quickness. He had great timing. He was all over the ball. The tighter the game, the tougher Russell got. I could feel the electricity."

After the game DeJulio went down on the court to talk with George Powles. "You know that kid, that Bill Russell, is a fantastic prospect. If we can teach him, if we can train him, I think we can make him great," DeJulio said. "Is he as good as I think he is?" Powles responded, "He's good." "Is he intelligent?" "Yes, he is." "Can he make Division I?" "He's got a long way to go."

Powles told DeJulio that no college yet wanted Russell. "But I wanted him," DeJulio said. "I could feel the magnetism of the kid. He was raw—couldn't shoot—but he was all over the court, tenacious, tough in the clutch. He was *there*."

# TWO

## A Road Trip to Discovery

"The very idea that I could innovate in basketball thrilled me."
—Bill Russell

Things seemed to be going Russell's way. He was asked to join a group of California All-Stars—also "splitters"—on a tour of the Pacific Northwest, playing local teams. Some of the top basketball players in California graduated midyear, but most of the good players didn't graduate until June. McClymonds had the best team in northern California that year, and the sponsors—the Oakland Jaycees and the Mohawk Athletic Club—wanted someone from McClymonds to join the tour. Russell was the only one available. "I was happier than if I had found a thousand dollars under my pillow," Russell said. He saw the tour as a way to improve his basketball, get out of Oakland, and not have to look for a job. He had been prepared to begin a job as a sheet metal worker to save money for college.

His new touring team traveled by Greyhound bus, lived in host families' homes, and ate in restaurants as they toured towns in Oregon, Washington, British Columbia, and Idaho. Russell's life took another good turn on the tour thanks to his coach, Brick Swegle, who allowed the team to do just about anything on the court. Basketball at that time had strict coaching rules. One of the unwritten rules was that you didn't take jump shots as they were considered "hot dog" shots. "If you have to jump to shoot, you didn't have a shot in the first place," was the standard line. Coaches also told players not to jump unless rebounding. This was difficult for a player like Russell to buy into, especially because, for him, jumping was "one of the purest pleasures I know." At McClymonds High the players preferred, as Russell called it, "Negro basketball," including the jump shot. "We never jumped on defense, but we loved to go up in the air on offense," Russell said. "It was more fun—and it worked."

Swegle was willing to let the boys have their fun. Swegle gave Russell the green light to use his curiosity and experiment on the court. They played "Negro basketball," even though only two black players were on the team. "We ran and jumped on that team, and we wore most teams out," Russell said. Most of the opposing coaches complained to Swegle about their tactics, but he just shrugged and said his players were having fun. One coach told his players not to guard the All-Star players when they tried a jump shot. The final score of that game was 144–41.

Russell said that within a week after the tour began, "something happened that opened my eyes and chilled my spine." He was sitting on the bench one night watching one of the team's best players go through his moves. He closed his eyes and tried to see the play in his mind. Eural McKelvey, the only other African American on the team, grabbed an offensive rebound and took the ball to the basket. It was a shot Russell didn't do well. "Since I had an accurate version of his technique in my head, I started playing with the image right there on the bench, running back the picture several times, and each time inserting a part of me for McKelvey," Russell said.

When he went back into the game he grabbed an offensive rebound and put it in the basket just like McKelvey did. "It seemed natural, almost as if I were just stepping into a film and following the signs," Russell said. "Now for the first time I had transferred something from my head to my body." It was his first dose of athletic confidence. But it was most likely more than that, something Russell and perhaps few others realized about what scientists now call "the power of intention" or, in other terms, "mental rehearsal," "mental practice," "implicit practice," and "covert rehearsal." It is a practice modern coaches widely use to separate elite athletes from second-division players. Russell's mental rehearsals show how far ahead of other athletes he was in more than just athletic skill.

Mental rehearsal was a technique that boxer Muhammad Ali used when he said, "I am the greatest." Ali has claimed that he used this statement as a message to himself—as a mental rehearsal—rather than as a boast.

Russell would practice his defensive maneuvers in his mind over and over and then apply them on the court. He built his own private basketball laboratory in his mind, where he created mental blueprints for himself. "It was effortless; the movies I saw in my head seemed to have their own projector, and whenever I closed my eyes it would run. . . . With only a little mental discipline I could keep myself focused on plays I had actually seen, and so many of them were new that I never felt bored."

Once during practice, he blocked a shot on one of the team's best players, Bill Treu. He was ecstatic, not because he matched Treu's standard of play, not because he had a premonition that defense would become his calling card in basketball. "I was happy because those defensive moves were the first that I invented on my own and then made real," he said. "I didn't copy them; I invented them. They grew out of my imagination, and so I saw them as my own." Early in his burgeoning career Russell learned that he would never be an offensive force as a shooter, and that he would have to earn a name for himself with his defense. "I couldn't do what [other players] did offensively. My game was defense first and feed the offense off my defense," he said.

Russell discovered one reason he was good at blocking shots was that he was left-handed, which put his strong hand directly across from the shooter's right hand. His natural left-handedness was one of several factors that pushed him toward defense. He also learned that he could jump much higher than other players, snaring rebounds high above the rim. He loved to jump and look down at the rim. When he was a sophomore at USF some friends gave Russell a test to see how high he could jump. They covered his fingers with chalk. Then Russell got a running start, jumped, and left his chalky fingerprints fourteen feet above the ground. That's four feet above the rim and a foot above the top of the backboard. "It scared me the first time it happened," he said, "and I had the same strange feeling the other two times as well. I leaped up for a jump shot and was—well, let's say I was shocked to find myself looking down into the basket."

Even so, blocking shots often came under criticism from coaches who believed that defense was a time for players to rest up so they could play better offense. Blocking shots usually led either to fouls or to the blocker knocking the ball out-of-bounds, allowing the offense to get the ball back. Russell soon learned that he could intimidate players who tried to put shots over his long reach. They also discovered that even if they did fake him into the air and drive by him, he could recover quickly and—with his long arms—reach back and still block shots.

The key to Russell's success in blocking shots was his quick leap. Because he flexed his knees, if a player gave him a pump fake and he went up, his feet often stayed on the floor. Moreover, Russell didn't bat balls out-of-bounds; he would direct them toward one of his own players, who then would start a fast break down the court. Sometimes he would snatch the ball out of the air with one of his huge hands.

Russell also realized that he felt awkward handling the ball with his back toward the basket before turning to shoot. Although he worked hours on his shot, he was far from being a good shooter. On defense, however, he was confident and would use his extraordinary jumping ability and speed to rebound and block shots. He had found his niche. "I was nearly possessed by basketball. I was having so much fun that I was sorry to see each day end, and I wanted the nights to race by so that the next day could start."

Because he was jumping to block shots he was inventing moves, not copying others. "What I really liked about the game were running, jumping, grabbing rebounds—just being out there." Russell would make an acrobatic move to block a shot that would draw "oohs" and "aahs" and handshakes from his teammates. "This was before the palm slap. Black players never slapped each other on the ass back then, and we were shocked when we saw the white ones doing it," Russell said.

The Northwest trip provided a big step in Russell's maturation as a basketball player. "My commitment to basketball and eventual love of the game came directly from taking advantage of this opportunity," Russell said.

When Russell returned from the tour, he told his father, "I can play now." His father was delighted, and he had some news for Bill. The USF scout, Hal DeJulio, had stopped by the house while Russell was on the tour and wanted to talk to him about going to college. Finally DeJulio telephoned Russell to ask him if he was interested in going to USF. "What's that?" Russell asked.

DeJulio seemed irritated that Russell had not heard of USF.
"The university," DeJulio replied.

"You mean San Francisco State?" Russell asked.

"No," he said. "The University of San Francisco."

"Oh," Russell replied.

# THREE
## On Catholic Schools and Race

"For many American colleges basketball is the outward
and visible sign of Catholicism in the United States."
—*Sports Illustrated* writer Frank Deford.

In the mid-1950s the University of San Francisco was a small
Jesuit school with about three thousand students—98 percent
of them men—that sat just north of the Golden Gate Park pan-
handle. The fifty-one–acre campus on the southern slope of Lone
Mountain—which gave the school its nickname of "the Hilltop,"
hence the students became known as the Hilltoppers—was one
of the oldest institutions of higher learning in California, having
been founded in 1855 when California was in the midst of the gold
rush. That was more than a decade before the state's first public
institution—the University of California—opened its doors.

Until 1930 the USF team name was "The Grey Fog," an apt
choice because of the fog that swooped in through the Golden
Gate and engulfed the nearby campus along with the rest of the

city. USF was also known then as St. Ignatius College. As the school marked its seventy-fifth anniversary, it changed its name to the University of San Francisco and adopted the nickname "the Dons." The chamber of commerce instigated the change because of the poor impression the word "fog" gave to the city. The new name came from the early swashbuckling Spanish dons who explored California.

Across the street, St. Ignatius High School, a prep school of sorts for USF, provided a fertile ground for attracting basketball players. USF's history in sports remained rather lackluster until 1949, when thirty-three-year-old Pete Newell coached the Dons to a title in the NIT, then the largest and most prestigious year-end tournament. No team from the West Coast had ever before been invited to the NIT. The Dons earned a no. 8 seed with a 21-5 record. Pete Rozelle, who later became the commissioner of the National Football League (NFL), marketed the Don's national championship season into a national media event while he was a student at the university that year. The NIT invited the Dons the following year, but they lost in the first round.

Two years later USF's football team went undefeated but received no invitations to a postseason bowl game because the team refused to play without its two black players, Ollie Matson and Burl Toler. Many rate that team as one of the greatest college teams of all time. Matson, along with Bob St. Clair and Gino Marchetti, was later named to the Pro Football Hall of Fame. Toler became the first African American NFL official. NFL teams drafted nine USF players from that team, five of whom played in the Pro Bowl. Rozelle also earned induction into the Hall of Fame.

In 2006 USF honored the 1951 team for its bold stand against racism. "The team members exemplify the values that remain at the core of USF's identity as a Jesuit Catholic university: dedication to a common good, rather than the interests of any one individual; respect for the dignity and worth of every human being; and an unwavering commitment to excellence on the field, in the classroom, and in one's personal and professional life," said Bill Hogan, the university's athletic director.

Matson provided at least some inspiration for a freshman basketball player named K. C. Jones. During his first year on campus Jones was walking to class with Matson, who told him, "Well, we've done it, now you guys go ahead and do it." Jones gave him a quizzical look and asked, "What do you mean?" "Go undefeated," Matson said. "The football team was undefeated. Now let's have that basketball team go undefeated." Little did he know.

Football at Catholic universities was a big-time sport in the 1940s and '50s, with teams like Santa Clara and St. Mary's from the Bay Area being invited to prestigious games such as the Cotton and Sugar bowls. But the huge expense of operating a football program took its toll on small Catholic schools. At least seventeen Catholic colleges and universities have dropped Division I football. USF dropped football in 1952 because of the heavy expense. Today only two Catholic institutions of higher education remain in Division I-A football—Notre Dame and Boston College.

Basketball was another story. It was a relatively inexpensive sport with twelve to fifteen players and no more than two coaches in the mid-1950s. Throw on a pair of sneakers and find a high school basketball gym, and you have it—at least as far as USF was concerned. The Dons lacked a gym so they practiced at St. Ignatius across the street. They played their home games at the drafty Kezar Pavilion and the Cow Palace. The relative low cost of a basketball program still holds true today. In 2005 Gonzaga player Ronnie Turiaf said, "All you have to have is two hoops, twelve guys, twelve uni's and a basketball. That's all you need. And a coach, too. Just in case."

That's the way it was for many of the Catholic colleges and universities at that time and even years later. Basketball became the sport of choice for Catholic schools. Although those schools are relatively small compared with public institutions and other private colleges, they have held their own. For example, Villanova of Philadelphia was in the first final four in 1939, and by 1986 seventeen different Catholic schools had achieved that distinction. Only three—Seton Hall, Marquette, and Georgetown—have made it since then. In 1947 Holy Cross, another school without its own gym, was the first Catholic college to win the NCAA title, and five more—including USF—have won it since then. La Salle, with a student population of one thousand, won the 1954 national championship and was runner-up to USF in 1955 behind the stellar play of superstar Tom Gola. Catholic schools won eleven NIT titles when the tournament was ranked above the NCAA tournament.

Writer Frank Deford noted that Catholic schools' sign of outward recognition too often is their basketball programs. "And because private schools of any stripe tend to be smaller and more focused than the sprawling public mega-universities that they play games against, basketball has become even more the cynosure of the Catholic campus."

Deford pointed out that most basketball players at Catholic schools today are black Protestants, although the schools' students are predominately white males. That also was the case in the mid-1950s at USF when none of the five black players was Catholic. In 1986 the Reverend John Lo Schiavo, then USF's president, pointed out that Catholic schools accepted black students long before public institutions did. Catholic schools are often at the forefront of social justice.

Certainly USF took a risk with Russell, who came from an academically poor and predominately black school in Oakland, but Russell proved to be up to the task. Gene Brown struggled with his schoolwork. Perry was a good student who became a lawyer. Questions arose about Jones's likelihood of graduating, but he did—and in four years. Coach Phil Woolpert saw to that. Jones commented, "I know Phil once said that my getting a diploma at USF was one of the most satisfying things that ever happened to him because he knew how hard I worked for it. . . . If it weren't for [him] there wouldn't have been any diploma because I wouldn't have had the courage to stay without [him] there."

That was the setting for USF's national championships, both of which came after the U.S. Supreme Court's *Brown vs. Board of Education* decision, which marked a turning point in the history of race relations in the United States. On May 17, 1954, the court ruled against constitutional sanctions for segregation by race and made equal opportunity in education the law of the land. It was a decision that marked the beginning of the civil rights movement. "We were right in the middle of that, Dr. [Martin Luther] King and Rosa Parks," guard Hal Perry said.

The decision touched off anger throughout the South. "Name one field of endeavor that has been taken over by Negroes and succeeded. Name one," a 1961 editorial in the Jackson, Mississippi *Daily News* cried. "The same group that killed boxing and is dooming baseball will soon take over professional football, and it too will perish." Not a chance.

In 1956 Harvard, which had no black players, canceled a four-game trip to the South to protest segregation while several large midwestern schools said they would not play in the South if southern schools prohibited black players from playing. USF's black players experienced racism when they traveled to play southern schools on at least three occasions. In 1955 Loyola of the South, a Catholic school, invited USF to play a game in New Orleans as a statement against segregation.

At home in the Bay Area, the players and school officials regularly received racist letters and comments about whether the school was playing too many blacks and whether they should be limited to having no more than three on the court at any one time. Yet through it all, the players kept their cool and dealt with it in a classy manner. They were young men and they were primarily interested in playing basketball. That was their bond.

They were right in the middle of the 1950s movement to improve race relations across the country, although it seems a stretch to rank them with Rosa Parks and the Montgomery, Alabama, bus boycott, which began the civil rights movement. But in the years during which the Dons won national championships no major college or university had anywhere close to four or five African Americans on its team.

Big-time sports have played a role in the advancement of civil rights dating back to Paul Robeson, Jesse Owens, Joe Louis, Jackie Robinson and others, who in their own way protested the exclusion of black athletes from the arena. It certainly didn't help the cause against racism that several of the athletes who were accused of point-shaving in the late 1940s and early '50s were black. There may have been three causes for this: the black players were from lower-class backgrounds and needed financial assistance, they were blue-chip athletes who were highly sought after, and racism.

As Russell matured, he became more aware of his ability to use his position both as a college student and professional basketball player to advance improvements in race relations. It wasn't always easy. Despite the liberalism of the Jesuit school, the black players encountered stereotyping and racism on and off the court. When Russell was a freshman, he, another freshman Hal Perry, and K. C. Jones were among the few African Americans on campus. Russell's height also made him stand out. The student newspaper, *The Foghorn*, wrote a feature about him in the first issue of the year, calling him a "future Globetrotter."

He heard the talk behind his back about race; he heard about some of his white teammates' objections to their inclusion on the team; he heard that the other coaches opposed their presence on the court; he heard about the high school priests who complained that the black players were keeping white Catholics from getting scholarships; he heard about the alumni who told Woolpert they never wanted more than two blacks on the court at the same time.

K. C. Jones remembered that when he and Russell were in their room, "We talked about life, of being black in a white society." They spent long hours discussing people's attitudes toward black student-athletes. "I guess we weren't supposed to be smart enough to understand remarks that were degrading to us."

They met the racism head-on when they traveled to colleges in the South, like in Oklahoma City and New Orleans where they were denied housing and food because of their skin color. Through it all, the black players met the racism with style, class, patience, and tolerance. But in their after-college years, particularly for Russell, the racism also set the tone for activism that grew during the civil rights movement.

# FOUR

## Another Surprise Recruit

"There's something that gives you confidence. That's what basketball did for me. In it, I could escape into my own little world of being good at something."
—K. C. Jones

His coach at Commerce High School in San Francisco laughed at his defense. The coach was just trying to be funny. But the shy black player didn't take it that way. He decided to show his coach that defense was his game. He concentrated on playing man-to-man defense and learning all he could about defending his opponent. That alone wasn't enough. He used hustle and determination to put the clamps on opponents. He liked playing defense because it made him a more complete player. He was a good shooter, but like Russell, he saw defense as his game. It was a good thing he did because his shot soon disappeared and never returned. In fact he may be the lowest-scoring player ever elected to the Hall of Fame with his 7 points a game during nine seasons with the Boston Celtics.

K. C. Jones—that's his full name, and he is named after his father—was a good athlete from the day he became fascinated with sports. His interest in basketball began when he picked up a soccer ball in eighth grade in a San Francisco park in the Bayview District in San Francisco and shot some baskets. Soon he began playing three-on-three basketball.

By the time he enrolled at Commerce High School in San Francisco, he had developed a deadly set shot. Five-foot-nine-inch Jones broke the league scoring record and developed into a ferocious defender. One year Commerce played its rival Galileo and its six-foot-six star Don Bragg, who later went on to a stellar career at the University of Southern California (USC). When Bragg didn't guard Jones, he felt disrespected. Jones was so motivated that Commerce won the game 26–23, with Jones scoring 18 points.

While Jones excelled in sports—he was also a star on the football team—he wasn't much of a student. "The world of books was still a foreign world in our house," he said in his autobiography, *Rebound*. He thought the best job he might get after high school was working as a postal carrier. College? Out of the question, especially as an African American in those days. "There was a ceiling where I came from, and you just didn't bother or even expect to go up into the attic. It was: This is me, this is where I am, and this is where I'll stay."

Jones had been selected to the all–northern California All-Star basketball and football teams, but no college showed interest in him. While it may be understandable that Russell wasn't pursued after his lackluster high school career, the fact that Jones was not recruited gives rise to conjecture that universities in those days never gave serious consideration to offering black players scholarships. Until Jones joined USF a year ahead of Russell, Carl Lawson—who played from 1949–53—was the only black player to have worn a Dons uniform.

A white history teacher named Mildred Smith stood up for

him, a fact he didn't learn until five years later. She made repeated calls to USF coach Phil Woolpert, but he showed little interest. One day Jones was talking with Al Corona, a sportswriter for the *San Francisco Examiner*. Corona asked him what colleges were recruiting him. "None," replied Jones. Corona stared at him and then said, "Okay, read my story tomorrow." The next day Jones read in the *Examiner* that he was being recruited by UCLA, USC, Stanford, Washington, Oregon, and Cal. Woolpert began to show some interest.

On the day that Jones and his Commerce teammates—who were almost all black—played in a city championship game against St. Ignatius, Jones reached one of the low points of his young life; he fouled out at halftime and he believed it was more than just his aggressive play that led to it. It was the only time he had fouled out in his high school career. Later he only fouled out of two games in his entire college career.

"There was some racism [by the referees] in that stuff," Jones said. "Bing, bing, bing, bing, bing, I'm out, and I was the star of the team." He was guarded by future USF teammate Bill Bush. Jones retreated to the locker room, where he began "crying like a baby." In walked Woolpert, who introduced himself and offered Jones a scholarship, the only one he was to receive. Five opposing players from that St. Ignatius team would wind up as Jones's teammates at USF.

Like Russell, Jones had to take an entrance exam. He got lost looking for USF even though it was just a fifteen-minute bus ride from his house. He never did find the school. The next day Woolpert had Jones picked up by car and taken to the exam, which he passed.

When Woolpert gave scholarships to the black players, several Catholic high schools in San Francisco complained that he was taking scholarships away from white players, not to mention that neither Jones nor Russell was a Catholic.

The summer between his senior year and the start of college Jones grew four inches, but strangely his shooting drastically dropped off. "To this day I can't understand what happened," he wrote in his autobiography. Jones went from being one of the highest scorers in northern California high school basketball "to an All-American brick thrower," he said. "I didn't know it then, but I would never shine on offense again."

College changed Jones's life. "If you're black and started in the Jim Crow South (he was born in Tyler, Texas) and lived on welfare with no dad around, you'll understand that I was coiled as tight as a spring when I started at USF," Jones said. "There was a frightening feeling of unreality as I walked around the campus. I was awful lonesome. I felt the glances and heard the racial wisecracks, and it didn't exactly boost my confidence level, but it surely fueled my determination to succeed." About thirty-five African American students attended USF, which had an almost all-male enrollment of three thousand in the early '50s.

Woolpert, he said, made all the difference. "From the first, I knew he was color blind—when you're black you can tell. . . . With Phil we were the same, all of us on the team. He was for us—black or white." Any success he had as a player started with Woolpert and ended with the Boston Celtics' Red Auerbach—"two of the classiest men that ever walked on this earth."

Jones started for the USF freshman team. Freshmen couldn't play varsity then because it was felt that first-year players needed to be acclimated to college academics before they moved up to the varsity, which played many games on the road, causing them to miss classes during a season. Jones discovered almost immediately that year that his shot was still missing. He wound up scoring an average of 5.6 points a game on a team that finished 7 and 14. Bill Russell was still in high school that year. Jones figured that he would never again be a scorer and decided to focus on being a playmaker and tenacious defender. "The team would be the talent. From now on the points I would score wouldn't show up in the box score under my name, but my teammates would score more and play better because of my efforts on the floor," he said.

He was also determined to play as hard as he could for the entire game. He set his mind to hustling and scraping every minute he was on the floor. Nobody would outhustle him. Not for one minute or any part of a minute.

But Jones also began to question whether he should continue with college and go off playing basketball while his mother struggled to feed four children at home. Being born black, he said, is the quickest way to learn that life is not fair. "I knew it was time for me to do something to bring some fairness to my mom's life. I was the oldest in the family, the man of the family. I had to start helping take care of the family." So he decided to quit school and get a job.

When he told Woolpert, the coach became upset, telling him he shouldn't pass up the opportunity to attend college. Woolpert asked Jones if he had told his mother. Jones said that he had not. Woolpert said he wanted to talk with Jones's mother himself. Afterward, Woolpert found a job for her as a chambermaid at the St. Francis Hotel, which allowed the family to get off welfare. Jones then promised his mother he would stay in college.

In Jones's sophomore year, life became better. A tall, rangy freshman was assigned as his roommate. His association with Jones became "one of the most meaningful of my life." The roommate's name was Bill Russell. Here they were, two future basketball Hall of Fame members starting off their basketball careers not only as teammates but as roommates, and as friends.

# FIVE
## A School He'd Never Heard Of

"I was determined to make the most of it."
—Bill Russell on his scholarship to USF

It is not surprising that a young African American who was raised in the flatlands of Oakland and who attended a predominately black school might not have heard of USF. Russell said that before he came to USF he felt like he was a captive of his ghetto life in Oakland. "You know, it was only twelve miles from my home to the USF campus, but there was a whole world in between that I didn't even know existed," he said.

To Russell, the City by the Bay was an exotic land. "The [San Francisco–Oakland] Bay Bridge spanned a cultural gap so wide that the two sides had a language barrier," he said. "I used to joke that I never knew the word 'mother' could be used by itself until I got to San·Francisco."

Russell saw USF as his chance to go to college. He thought before meeting Hal DeJulio that he would either go to junior college, which was free in California, or go into the army "and get it over with." But he had taken the physical and was classified 4-F because of his height. "To me, San Francisco was my one chance. The one chance I'd ever get."

DeJulio said that when he met with Russell, he told him, "From what I saw, I think you can be an All-American basketball player and go into the pros and make more money than you've ever seen." Russell was shocked. No one had ever talked to him in such an encouraging way. He hadn't thought anyone cared. DeJulio told Russell he would arrange a workout with coach Phil Woolpert. When DeJulio hung up the phone he said, "I called [Woolpert], and he damn near died. But I was going with Russell all the way. You've got to have a little guts."

Russell was surprised by the attention he was getting. He didn't think he was good enough to play college ball. But it was the only scholarship he was offered, and he took it because he knew he couldn't have gone to college any other way. In those days less than 2 percent of African Americans attended college.

If Woolpert offered him a scholarship, it would consist of tuition and room and board but no spending money the first year. And he would be required to wait tables and wash dishes. "We had nothing to offer a high school boy in a competitive bidding situation," Woolpert said. "Our only inducement was a sincere approach that the boy would get an excellent college education and that he would be able to play on what we hoped would be an excellent basketball team."

A few days later Russell crossed the Bay Bridge to work out for Woolpert. He had never been to San Francisco and became lost. When he found the campus, he couldn't find the gym because the school didn't have a gym of its own. When Russell arrived he was frustrated and nervous. "I don't remember anything about that workout except that I ran and jumped without the ball a lot," Russell said. After the workout Woolpert thanked him and was noncommittal. But he did ask Russell to take the entrance exam just in case he was offered a scholarship.

Woolpert clearly remembered that day years later. "My God, the first time I did see him at a workout, I couldn't believe my eyes," Woolpert said. "He could jump—oh, how he could jump—but he was so ungainly. Still, there was something about Bill then that you just couldn't ignore. He had this rare, wonderful confidence in himself." Russell told Woolpert and freshman coach Ross Guidice, "Gentlemen, I want you to know that I am going to be the University of San Francisco's next All-American." Woolpert remembered that moment. "He was as fiercely competitive, as proud as any athlete as ever appeared in any sport." Years later Russell said, "That was mostly bravado. I never really felt I was any good until my junior year."

A future teammate and lifelong friend was on hand to watch the workout as well. "I had never heard of Russell," K. C. Jones said, "and I was only a year ahead of him. He came over to talk with the coach, and that was the first time I had ever seen him. . . . His tenacity was off the charts, and the intelligence was Oxford."

Another onlooker at the Russell tryout was John Lo Schiavo, who was then a philosophy teacher at USF. Lo Schiavo had once been an assistant to Woolpert at St. Ignatius. He later went into the priesthood, returned to USF, and eventually became its president. Lo Schiavo saw Russell shooting some baskets and asked Woolpert who he was. "He's from Oakland," Woolpert said. "He's as green as grass, but I think I'll take a chance on him."

The Dons' starting center, Frank Evangelho, a junior, was also present when Russell worked out with the varsity. He didn't think much of Russell as a player. "Woolpert asked me what I thought of him, and I said, 'I don't think he's going to make it.'" Evangelho recalled saying that Russell "can jump well, but he doesn't shoot that well."

Russell told Evangelho that he someday would be a better

player than the talented six-foot-nine Kenny Sears of Santa Clara. "I sort of laughed and said, 'Sure, Bill.'" Seven games into the 1953–54 season, Russell was leading the California Basketball Association (CBA) in scoring with 21 points a game while Sears was averaging 16 points a game. In a head-to-head battle on January 16, 1953, Russell outscored Sears by 22 points to 11 points, although Santa Clara won 54–52. Russell said Woolpert didn't think much of the way he played the game. "No one had ever played basketball the way I played it, or as well. They had never seen anyone block shots before. Now I'll be conceited: I like to think I originated a whole new style of play."

He didn't know it at the time but he fit in perfectly with the kind of team Woolpert was trying to build, one that stressed defense. Woolpert's philosophy was that if a team couldn't get off a shot, it couldn't score. Russell said, "A good defensive team never has a bad night, and a shooting team does. Defense is nothing but hard work. It's digging, digging, digging, especially when you don't feel like it. Offense is much easier, because it's fun." For Russell—the poor shooter—defense was fun, and his meeting up with Woolpert was a match made in heaven.

After his tryout Russell worked in the shipyard and played basketball every waking minute of his spare time. Finally, he received a letter from USF telling him he would be given a scholarship. Russell was ecstatic. "I was not even a star high school player, and here I was being selected at a time when blacks were simply not given scholarships to prestigious four-year schools." To Russell, San Francisco was his one chance—the only chance he might ever get.

Russell became the third black player to earn a scholarship to USF. UCLA was also at the forefront of giving scholarships to blacks, but only if they attended junior college for two years first. "You could count the number of black players on West Coast teams on the fingers of one hand," Coach Pete Newell recalled.

The way Russell was "recruited" was indicative of the times. Coaches pretty much stayed out of the process. Friends and alumni recommended players to the coach. UCLA coach John Wooden said he would have been interested in having Russell and/or Wilt Chamberlain playing for him, but "I was not contacted by them or anyone else speaking on their behalf." A small athletic department with a small budget, which forced him to recruit in the Bay Area, further restricted Woolpert. Undoubtedly such restrictions led Woolpert to take chances on players no one else wanted whether they were African Americans or undeveloped players with incredible potential.

When Russell arrived at USF he was six-seven and weighed 158 pounds—"a real mass of muscle," he would joke. To say that he was a late bloomer was a vast understatement. Two years later Woolpert was asked how he developed such a great basketball team at USF. "It was like this," he said. "Under my coaching [Russell] improved so much that he is now a six-foot-ten-inch player. You understand now what coaching genius is."

Bob Feerick, the coach of Santa Clara, another Jesuit school in northern California, didn't think much of Russell. "He was a kid over at McClymonds. He was small. He was nothing. He grew up after he got to college." Feerick no doubt later regretted this slight as USF and Russell dominated Santa Clara in the years to come.

When Russell arrived on campus as a freshman, he found he wasn't the only black player on the team. An All-City player from the now-closed Commerce High School in San Francisco was a sophomore on the varsity. That player, K. C. Jones, would become his roommate and best friend, a relationship that lasted throughout their lifetime. K.C. already had spent a year on campus. He knew what to expect and he was willing to share that experience with Russell—after a time.

# SIX

## Roommates and Friends Forever

"[Russell] and I became inseparable."
—K. C. Jones

K. C. Jones was sitting in his dormitory room on the USF campus when Russell walked in to announce that he was Jones's new roommate. They quickly discovered similarities in their lives. "He was black, and his family had left the South for the Bay Area," Jones said. (Russell was born in Monroe, Louisiana, and Jones in Tyler, Texas.) "He was almost as cautious and watchful and quiet as I was. He was just as shy as I was."

For a whole month after that, Jones didn't talk to Russell. "Nothing," Russell said. "Not a word. Not hello. Not goodbye. Not a single word." Russell slept on the top bunk, Jones the bottom. Jones would get up to an alarm while Russell would hunker down under the covers. As Jones left the room, he would slam the side of the bunk and shout, "Russell." Russell would jump out of bed, throw on some clothes and head to the cafeteria for breakfast. There the two of them would eat in silence before heading off to class.

When the ice had been broken and they had finally begun to talk, he and Russell "talked of everything, of the school and the people in the school," Jones said. But most of all they talked about basketball. Jones and Russell often talked into the early morning hours about basketball. "[Russell] had a gift for mapping out plays and strategies." Jones said. "He focused on details: how to position your body, how to find a player's blind spot, how to anticipate the shot. The details made up the big picture." Which was to win.

Jones became like a big brother to Russell. Everywhere K.C. went, Russell tagged along. To Russell, Jones was rich. Although they both received room, board, and tuition, Jones also received thirty dollars a month from USF while Russell was given nothing. Jones shared his largesse with Russell, once buying him a pair of shoes when his wore out as well as meals, movie tickets, and books.

When Russell arrived on campus, tradition dictated that he had to wear a freshman beanie, which the proud young man didn't particularly appreciate having to do. But he got through it. He often felt out of place on campus. Yet Russell said that with few exceptions he was treated as a human being, not just as a basketball player. "I think I knew 90 percent of the students on campus," he said.

But some of the white Catholic students didn't care for African Americans—and said so to his face. "There were always a few guys around who thought it was okay to say or do what they wanted," Russell recalled. "But it wasn't all right."

Russell took advantage of the opportunity offered him at USF to become educated, starting out as a business major and later switching his major to transportation.

But morality and values also piqued his interest, so he took a course in political science during which the students studied communism. The priests brought in communists as well as brainwashed soldiers from the Korean War to talk with them. "The Jesuits felt the way to fight communism was to learn about it firsthand," Russell said.

Once in a philosophy class on logic, a priest was leading the students down a path of thought by asking questions designed to develop their ability to analyze. Russell realized what he was doing and yelled, "Hey." The priest smiled and told him, "Congratulations, Mr. Russell. You have just had your first real and complete thought. How does it feel?" Russell never forgot the lesson the priest was trying to impart—to think.

Still Russell kept his classes to a minimum so that he would have time for basketball in addition to his studies. This led to his falling sixteen credit hours short of graduation at the end of his senior year. K. C. Jones enjoyed school and did not miss more than three or four days of classes during his entire college career. He took great pride in getting a college education. Jones said he was no "wizard" with the books, but with tutoring and hard work he was able to remain eligible to play basketball. Carl Boldt, a forward on the 1956 team, said none of the coaches put pressure on them to maintain good grades in order to remain eligible to play. On the other hand the priests demanded academic excellence, especially during a student's first two years. But when it came to studying on trips—forget it. "No one ever took a book on a trip," he said. The players were by and large good students who were very intelligent. Five team members went on to become lawyers and five became teachers or administrators.

But during those college years when Russell and Jones talked it was mostly about basketball. And when Russell wasn't talking basketball he was in the gym working on his game. The freshman coach, Ross Guidice, worked countless hours with Russell to improve his skills. When Guidice once asked Russell, "What do you want out of basketball," Russell replied, "I just want to be the best basketball player in the world." Guidice, playing guard, sank the game-winning free throw when USF won the 1949 NIT championship. But he may have been the most unlikely candidate possible to teach the lanky, awkward Russell how to play center.

Guidice had solid training under then-USF coach Pete Newell. Newell had turned out two other well-known college coaches, Rene Herrerias, who became head coach at Cal, and John Bennington, head coach at Michigan State. All three played for Newell's NIT team. In 1950 when Newell left USF for Michigan State, Phil Woolpert moved over from St. Ignatius High School to become head coach. Twenty-six-year-old Guidice heard that the school was looking for a freshman coach and an assistant to Woolpert.

Guidice, at the time he decided to apply for the job, was teaching at Riordan High School in San Francisco. Woolpert had no input in the USF hiring. That was done by a group of USF officials and backers including Charles Harney, who later built the San Francisco Giants' home at Candlestick Park, and athletic director Jimmy Needles, who had been a USF coach and had coached Woolpert and Newell at Loyola of Los Angeles (now Loyola Marymount). The year Guidice got the job, his freshman team racked up an 18-3 record. The next year he coached the junior varsity to a 19-7 record. He proved to be a valuable asset to Woolpert because of the way he prepared his players for the varsity and because as a scout he picked up ways to exploit opposing teams' weaknesses.

Russell said Guidice always supported a player's love of the game, and "he did so with a generosity and good spirit that I've never seen since." Guidice would stay as long as a player wanted to work, as much as four hours at a stretch—just the two of them—including Saturdays, nights, and holidays. As long as Guidice was willing, Russell would work with him. "He was excited over every bit of progress I made," Russell said. Guidice taught Russell how to set screens and how to pass the ball. He showed him how to shoot the hook shot. "Without him," Russell said, "it would have taken me years to catch up with what other players knew about basketball." Guidice never accepted credit for developing Russell's game. All he would say was that "it was fun." Guidice said he tried to give Russell a foundation, "But make no mistake, he taught himself how to play like a champion." Russell never forgot the unselfishness that Guidice showed him. He noted that Guidice left the university years later to operate a furniture store. "I used to think that if a kid were to walk into his office and ask for coaching help, Guidice would go right down to the gym. I'd have bet that he'd walk right out on the customers in his store in his street shoes, just to teach basketball. He was that unselfish."

Many nights Russell would work alone on his game, sometimes until midnight or one in the morning, often putting up five-hundred shots left-handed and five-hundred right-handed, mostly hook shots. He couldn't get in enough hard work. He learned how to move his feet, when to plant them, how to shift them, when to take small steps rather than big ones, and when to turn, angling his body toward the basket. "I taught myself to have 'smart feet' by running and moving, whenever I could, like a guard rather than a big man. Smart feet are the result of both brains and endless work," he said. The fact that Russell was a late bloomer after so many years of struggling no doubt lead to his determination, his focus, and his will to win that guided him throughout his college and professional basketball careers.

When Jones and Russell were in their dorm room, talk always turned to basketball. They would think, talk, and then try out what they had talked about. "Most of the [college] players weren't interested in strategy," Russell said. "The prevailing strategy was that you went out, took your shots, and waited to see what happened. It was not considered a game of thinkers." The barest mention of basketball "would throw [Jones] into a Socratic dialogue that would go on for as long as anyone would carry his half of the conversation," Russell said. He and Jones decided that basketball was a game of geometry—with lines, points, and distances—and that the horizontal distances were more important than the vertical ones. Horizontal meant how they moved side-to-side; vertical meant how they played up and down. "K.C. and I spent hours exploring the geometry of basketball, often losing track of time," Russell said.

"If I were playing against someone a foot shorter, the vertical distances could be important, but in competitive basketball most of the critical distances are horizontal, along the floor or at eye level," Russell said. "Height is not as important as it may seem, even in rebounding." Russell discovered early in his college career that 75 percent of rebounds were pulled in at or below the level of the basket. With his long reach and tremendous jumping ability, he realized he could grab rebounds high above the rim.
He said years later,

> Ever since my freshman year I have looked at the game of basketball as a vertical and horizontal game. For example, jumping is a controlled asset or skill. Sometimes I jumped to touch the top of the backboard, sometimes I hardly left my feet. I have noticed that many highlight films of me show me catching so and so from behind to block his shot and get the rebound. I am always asked how I was able to do that. The answer is in merging of the horizontal and vertical games. It all starts with imagination. As a player with the ball moved down the court, I visualized the angle that I would need to block his shot. Then, trailing him, I would take a step to the left so that I would then be coming at the shooter from an angle, allowing me to block his shot with my left hand while landing to the player's side rather than on his back. Not only

did it turn out to be an intimidating move, but also by arriving on the opposite side from where I'd blocked the shot, what I had done might even have seemed a little mystical.

Russell also recognized the psychological impact that blocking shots had on opposing players. "By blocking shots without fouling I forced the opposition to react to the defense. . . . From that point forward, this would also help me in a practical way, because I would always be in their psyche, blocking shots I might physically never have been able to get to," Russell said.

His ability to block shots gave him an intimidation factor that served the Dons well, too. Hal DeJulio said, "Russell would study you. He would figure out how to beat you psychologically as well as physically. He always told me, 'The first thing I try to do is block a man's first nine shots [laughter]. Just to get his attention. After that, I figure out how to get the other four guys. I would pick out guys here and there and try to stuff shots right down their throats.' So what happened is that when you played USF, you had to come in with a Russell offense. It was never yours."

It didn't hurt that Russell had extremely long arms and huge hands. His hands measured ten and a half inches from heel to fingertip, while someone six inches shorter in height, for example, might have seven- to eight-inch hands. In addition, not many players were left-handed, which gave Russell more of an element of surprise. He became left-handed as a toddler when a relative gave him a chicken leg and other food and forced him to use his left hand to eat. The idea was that maybe when he grew older he might become a left-handed pitcher in Major League Baseball.

Jones said it was difficult trying to describe the conversations he had with Russell. "I find it curious that I can't easily explain those conversations because they were easy and endless. We invented our own court language to describe plays, moves, counter-moves, and strategies."

Russell and Jones continued to talk plays and strategies and they tested them on the court in practice. Jones developed techniques to guard a taller, stronger player by guarding Russell, and Russell learned how to defend a quicker, smaller player like Jones. For example in practice Russell and Jones would battle each other furiously. One day while scrimmaging, Russell brought the ball up court with Jones guarding him. Russell was sure he had Jones beat. Russell looked at Jones and could see he felt Russell had him, too. Then all of a sudden Jones started to improvise. He started jumping around and moving one way and the other—movements Russell had never seen him do before. Russell began wondering what Jones was going to do next. All of a sudden he got his feet tangled up and fell to the floor. "That's right—one minute I'm sailing along, confident, and the next minute I'm sprawled all over the floor, and K.C.'s taken the ball away from me and dribbles down for an easy lay-up."

As defense-minded players they tried to make the opponent take a shot they wanted him to take at a spot on the floor from where they wanted him to shoot. "I guess by the time we graduated from USF Bill Russell and I had talked, studied, worked, practiced, and played as much defensive basketball as any two people ever had," Jones said.

In 1981 Russell said, "To this day I've never had a conversation with anyone that had a clearer understanding of winning than K.C. Other people taught me to play. He taught me how to win."

Jones couldn't wait for the day that Russell moved up from the freshman squad to the varsity. He had noted that while the varsity players were good, they were underachievers who didn't win. "Some of those talented players felt they were above their teammates," Jones said, "and this superior attitude kept us from being a team because a team is a group of players who support one another on the court and who think of the group before they think of themselves. . . . But I figured the big freshman sitting on the bench would help change things around for us in my junior year." They almost didn't get the chance.

Russell had been told he, too, would receive thirty dollars a month for "laundry money" if he made the varsity. Instead Woolpert confirmed that the school's administration had decided against giving him the stipend. When he heard this, Russell went back to his room, got down his suitcases, and began to pack. Jones came into the room and asked Russell what he was doing. When Russell told him, Jones said, "You're leaving because they're not paying you thirty bucks?" "No," Russell said. "I'm leaving because they told me one thing and did another." Jones left Russell and went directly to the athletic department to tell Woolpert what was happening. Woolpert and Jones returned to the dorm room and wanted to know why Russell was leaving. "Because I was lied to," Russell replied. "The school made a choice to go back on what it promised me, so I'm making a choice to leave school."

Woolpert asked him not to leave until he talked with the university president. The coach told the president what Russell had said, adding that if Russell left, the school would lose a very good basketball player. The president responded that he had no funds available in the athletic department, but asked if Russell would take twenty-five dollars from an academic scholarship? Woolpert took the compromise back to Russell, who—after some thought—agreed to accept the money.

It was the right decision for Russell as well as for USF. Russell would say more than thirty years later, "Before [USF], I'd felt like I was a captive of my environment. USF freed me."

"It wasn't always easy for Bill at USF," Woolpert said thirty years later. "There were very few blacks on campus at that time." Russell was unaccustomed to being in a predominately white world. Because he felt out of place, Russell sometimes acted like a clown and antagonized people. The student body president at one point told Woolpert that unless Russell "shaped up" they didn't want him on campus. Woolpert tried to explain to the student what Russell was going through, but it fell on deaf ears. "I talked to Bill," he said, "and, as far as I know, there were no other incidents."

# SEVEN
## Time to Produce

"If you can't shoot, you can't score."
—Phil Woolpert

Woolpert looked forward to the 1953–54 season because of the talented freshmen moving up to the varsity. Guidice had groomed them well. The freshmen had put together a 19 and 4 season. Russell scored 461 points or just over 20 points a game—a freshman record. The freshmen had a better team than the varsity, which they beat regularly in practice.

Russell had frustrated some of the varsity players with his defense, especially center Frank Evangelho. Evangelho found that during scrimmages he was getting his hook shot blocked again and again. "Nobody can do that to me," he said to himself. He began to lose confidence. He expressed his concerns to Woolpert, who told him not to worry; Russell was an exceptional player.

Woolpert thought he had the nucleus of a good team—a solid, veteran team with a number of promising freshmen moving up.

He knew he had to produce. The alumni were breathing down his neck for more years like the 1948–49 season when the Dons won the then-prestigious NIT at Madison Square Garden under coach Pete Newell. From the time he took over from Newell, who left after the 1949–50 season to coach Michigan State, Woolpert's record had been less than spectacular. Woolpert's first USF team went 9 and 17, and in the 1951–52 season his team finished 11 and 13. The following year showed little improvement—11 wins and 12 losses.

After three losing seasons one alumnus called Woolpert a lousy coach to his face. Woolpert threatened to quit. But after further thought, he instead went to the university's president and asked, "Does my employment depend on a win-loss record or an effort to integrate athletics into the university's academic program?" The president reassured him his record was not a consideration, and Woolpert headed back to his office.

With such pressure to win, Woolpert's recruitment of blacks might be considered an act of desperation. It was very difficult for small schools like USF to attract top players. Indeed, many of his recruits came from nearby St. Ignatius High School. But it is unclear whether Woolpert was making a social and cultural statement by recruiting black players when no one else did. He certainly had the liberal leanings to have given some thought to such a radical move. The players he brought to the team could withstand the pressure of integrating basketball, much as Jackie Robinson had in baseball. It was no coincidence that Russell, Jones, and the three other African Americans had the character and mental toughness to take the heat that was to come with playing against mostly white players. They certainly had the athletic and academic ability to succeed as well.

An additional difficulty for Woolpert must have been trying to recruit players when the school didn't even have a gym. The bigger public institutions could offer better facilities, transportation, and accommodations for their players. Why should athletes go to USF when they could attend Cal, UCLA, or Stanford, which could offer perks that the Dons could ill afford? That Woolpert could develop such teams from a group of "nobodies" is impressive.

Moving up from the freshman team with Russell was the fourth black player in school history, Hal Perry, who also carried out a key role in helping the Dons elevate their level of play. "I didn't know who Bill Russell was," Perry said. "But he was the biggest person I ever saw."

Bill Bush, who had sat out his sophomore year, and senior Rich Mohr joined Perry at guard. Bush, an All-City player from St. Ignatius High School, injured his back late in his freshman year and rested for the entire season. Two forwards—Jerry Mullen and Stan Buchanan—returned as well. With Russell's arrival, Woolpert moved Evangelho from center to forward where he joined backups Bob Wiebusch and Dick Lawless.

Buchanan and Bush were two of five teammates who played at St. Ignatius High School when Woolpert had coached. After Woolpert left for USF St. Ignatius went on to win a championship in 1951. It's not difficult to see why Woolpert would recruit players who knew his style of coaching, but forward Dick Lawless always wondered if Woolpert didn't tend to favor those former St. Ignatius players over others. In addition to Buchanan and Bush, the other three on the team from St. Ignatius were All-City forward Bill Mallen, Rudy Zannini, and Bob Wiebusch. Zannini was forced to sit out his junior year because of family problems but returned for his senior year when the Dons won their first championship.

Mullen attended St. Mary's in Berkeley, walk-on Tom Nelson graduated from Serra in San Mateo, and Gordon Kirby matriculated at St. Joseph's in Alameda—all Catholic high schools. Other players from the Bay Area were Lawless, an All-City player at Oakland High School, and Steve Balchios, a second-team All-City player from Lincoln in San Francisco.

Kirby may have been the least likely to join the team. After being named second-team All-City in his junior year, he tried out for Woolpert but was turned down for a scholarship. Nevertheless, he attended USF where he kept active by playing recreational basketball. In his junior year he walked on at USF, and Woolpert told him that if he made the team he would receive a scholarship. He did.

College basketball wasn't the popular game it is today, nor did the pressure to raise money rival today's levels. In the mid-1950s the players were students first—ones who played basketball while they went to school. There was no pressure to leave school early to play for the National Basketball Association (NBA). Most of the players attended USF primarily for the education.

On the two national championship teams, only one player was from out of state. Most were from the Bay Area and northern California, and only one—Carl Boldt—hailed from Southern California. Most had high school sports careers that would not attract attention from schools outside the Bay Area, and maybe not much from within, either. Nor was recruiting as widespread as it later became. Undoubtedly, the St. Ignatius players wound up at USF because it was a Jesuit school, just like their high school, and it was right next door. It didn't hurt that Woolpert was their former coach. The players from San Francisco received scholarships for tuition and books and lived at home. The out-of-town players lived in former army barracks that had been moved to the campus. Lawless, for example, lived in the barracks and had a fifty-dollar-a-month job answering the telephone from midnight to 8:00 a.m. at a mortuary.

Like Russell and Jones, Perry wasn't recruited by USF. He chose USF after Cal and Oregon State turned him down. Perry was a star athlete in four sports in Ukiah, although the competition in rural northern California was less than competitive. He played quarterback on the football team, but basketball was his best sport. One of his high school opponents was future teammate Jack King, who played for a small Catholic school in Petaluma, California.

Perry—the only black in his high school—was elected student body president as well as president of the school's marching band. Even with all his honors, though, he doubted that he would go to college. Then in the fall of 1950 he traveled to the University of California at Berkeley for Band Day. Numerous schools had been invited to play during halftime of the Cal–USF football game, Perry's among them. Perry, who played saxophone, looked down on the field during the game and saw two blacks, Ollie Matson and Burl Toler, playing for USF. "Good Lord," Perry said. That's when the five-foot-ten guard decided he was going to attend USF on a scholarship.

Accompanied by his father, Perry made the 125-mile trip to San Francisco to work out for Woolpert. The coach asked him to play against K. C. Jones, whose defensive prowess shut him down. "He reversed everything I tried to do," Perry recalled. "I don't think I got a shot off." Woolpert ran off a list of seven or eight reasons Perry wouldn't be offered a scholarship.

Undaunted, he countered Woolpert's arguments. And then Perry, a Baptist, made an unusual request: "Before you make this decision, please pray for guidance." On the ride home Perry's father tried to soothe his son and prepare him for a letdown. "It doesn't matter," Perry replied. "I'm still going to get the scholarship." Two days later he did, just about the same time Russell got his. Years later, Perry said, he heard that some Catholic high school officials complained that black players took scholarships that USF could have awarded to white players.

Perry never regretted his decision, saying, "I was always comfortable at USF." Nor did Woolpert regret his decision to give Perry a scholarship. Toward the end of Perry's college career, the coach called him his "rapier" and "gambler" because he would parry like a sword through defenses and he would gamble on defense, knowing that Russell was behind him. "He gives us a lot of mobility," Woolpert said. "He's a buzz saw who likes to do the unexpected. He has a lot of hustle. He is a fine dribbler, fine passer, and has as good a shooting touch as any man on the team."

When practice opened in the fall of '53, Woolpert was ready. So were the players, but they didn't know what the coach had in store for them—in practice or during games. They dressed in their dorms or at home and walked over to the St. Ignatius gym. There was no weight training, and there were no dining halls or study halls just for basketball players. Conditioning amounted to jumping rope and running one-on-one drills. Woolpert had a plan: First he was going to use defense to break up the opposition's attack before it could get set. On offense he wanted to use a balanced floor, with his players working the ball around the court until they got the right shot.

Woolpert had always been a strong advocate of defense and he saw an opportunity to develop his players into an aggressive defensive squad. "I can't see just standing around and letting the other fellow shoot. To me, it is common sense to try to stop him from scoring. There is a science and a skill to defense. It's what makes the game interesting, not a race from one end of the court to the other for one more basket." He was also fond of saying, "We figure to have the ball only about half the time in a game, so in practice, we work on defense half the time."

He taught the Dons to play at their own pace, to force opponents who had been trained to get off their shots in ten seconds to get out of their patterns, out of their rhythm, and to shoot long shots rather than lay-ups. Woolpert also told his players not to worry if their opponents got past them because Russell would be lurking behind them.

Woolpert was without a doubt a defense-minded coach. In Woolpert's system, if you couldn't defend, it was unlikely you would get much playing time. He disdained "jackrabbit basketball," once remarking about the up-tempo offense becoming popular then: "It just isn't good basketball. I wouldn't know how to go about coaching it. You can't expect to execute scoring plays when you're running up and down the court like madmen."

Although Woolpert was a high-strung coach, he didn't take himself too seriously, once cracking with his deadpan humor: "There are two ways [to guard a tall man]. The first way is to assign your tallest man to guard the opponent's tallest man. The second way, if you don't have a tall man on your team, don't schedule an opponent who does."

Practice included what Woolpert called the "hands-up" drill. The players would line up with their feet in position, bend their knees, and put one hand high above their heads and the other one out to the side. Then they moved quickly forward or backward, to the left or to the right, at Woolpert's direction. One of his players, Hal Urban, who played for the Dons from 1958–62, described it as the team's "time in hell" because it was sheer pain and seemed to last an eternity. "But we always played good defense because we were ready; our feet, knees, and hands automatically went into the right position." It was the same drill that Hall of Fame coach Pete Newell used when he was at USF and in 1959 when his Cal team won the NCAA title. Most players introduced to the hands-up drill lasted about three minutes before they begged for mercy, but eventually they could go twenty minutes nonstop. That kind of stamina paid big dividends during the season.

Woolpert was also a stickler for making his players pick up the fundamentals of the game—dribbling, passing, footwork, and shooting. "A basketball player sent on the court with rusty fundamentals," he said, "is a good bet to fail in his operations."

In addition to sound fundamentals a team needed talented players and a simple offense and defense. Woolpert believed that regardless of what offense a team used, "the essentially important need is for simplicity and efficiency of operation. If the players know what they are doing, and why, and are impressed with the importance of each move in an overall pattern, the chances of that pattern creating good shot opportunities are excellent."

Woolpert believed in balancing the floor and passing the ball to create shots. He recognized that with the guards' quickness and Russell's shot-blocking ability the pressure defense might work to perfection. He was ready to put in the pressing defense that he'd learned in Kansas. Should a team get by Jones and other pressing defenders, there was Russell waiting like a windmill to bat away shots. "In those days they always tried to challenge Russell," Lawless said. "They came out second best."

Many coaches argued against attempting to block shots—including Woolpert initially—for three reasons: players would pick up fouls; the blocked shots more often than not went out-of-bounds so the offense got the ball again; and defensive players left their feet for the blocks, leaving them open to fakes that allowed the offensive player to drive around them.

"Woolpert wanted me to play in the same fashion as his former center [Evangelho], who had been six-five," Russell said. "My style was defense, plus shooting. We established a détente of sorts." Evangelho, Russell said, was big, slow, and could barely get his hand over the rim. "I could run faster backward than he could run forward," he said.

Sometimes, just for fun, Russell would try to see how high he could jump. He stunned himself when he could get his eyes higher than the level of the rim. He was also able to kick the bottom of the net. "But [Woolpert] insisted that I play just as [Evangelho] had. [He] wanted me to position myself, rebound, plant myself in the middle, just like [Evangelho]." Russell refused, setting off arguments with Woolpert. During his entire college career, the headstrong Russell and the disciplinarian Woolpert argued constantly over how Russell should play his game.

"He was brought up in the old school," Russell said. "When he saw me leave my feet on defense, he believed I had overcommitted myself; when he saw me move the ball like a guard, he thought I was taking unnecessary chances. I wasn't." It is probably fair to say that Woolpert came around to appreciating Russell's defensive prowess. "I admit," Woolpert said, "that at the time I was coaching him I was kind of old school. The coach had to run the show. But not through intimidation, through persuasion. Sometimes, I just couldn't persuade Bill." About Russell, he would say twenty-five years later: "He was a hard one to handle. He's not a simple man, that guy. He's different—intelligent, though, I'll tell you. Smart as a whip." Russell said, "I studied the rules. Most people say the rules say what you can't do. I saw that they also tell you what you can do," and that was to leave his feet to block shots.

Russell and Woolpert clashed many times. Russell was stubborn, and Woolpert had a short fuse and was quick to show his temper and impatience. "Bill was a man of many moods," Woolpert said. "We had a lot of run-ins." Although he recognized Russell's special talent, Woolpert wouldn't let up on molding the team according to his own style. "I always considered myself more a leader than a driver, and I attempted through logic and example to indicate to the players what I wanted done. But I did want it done my way."

Russell had other problems with Woolpert. The coach, he said, never complimented him on the way he played and failed to see the positive things he accomplished on the court. Russell craved a good word from his coach. "Woolpert never said anything. . . . It hurt me plenty that Woolpert didn't," Russell said in his 1966 autobiography, *Go Up for Glory*.

Two years after Russell's autobiography, Woolpert told a *Sports Illustrated* writer, "Okay, my judgments are as imperfect as anyone's, but as a coach I have to make them. In those days I wasn't about to help give Bill an inflated sense of his own importance. As a sophomore, he was a lazy player; I kicked him out of the gym many, many times for loafing during drills." Woolpert noted that he had fewer problems with Russell when he was a junior and none during his senior year.

Woolpert also kept after Russell if he slacked off in his schoolwork. Early in his career Russell was lackadaisical about his classes. Woolpert almost dropped him from the team because of it. He talked with Russell and even had football star Ollie Matson talk to him. But it didn't do much good. "He was that close to being out," Woolpert said. The coach summoned Russell's father, Charlie, who as Woolpert put it, "gave Bill the business." Russell never got into academic trouble again.

Fellow sophomore Hal Perry thought that Woolpert "was simply trying to toughen up Bill, to get him mentally ready for professional ball. And I think he did get him ready. The record shows that. But, at the time, Bill wasn't mature enough to understand what Phil was trying to do."

One thing happened to Russell that despite his disagreements with Woolpert he never revealed to his old coach until more than thirty years later: Four schools asked him to transfer after his freshman year. "Many colleges came around with offers which were considerably more than washing dishes and gassing cars. I laughed them away. USF and I were together. I was with them as long as they were with me."

Although he could be hardheaded, Russell still wanted to learn everything he could about basketball. Woolpert taught him that players could put their peripheral vision to better use, and Russell had extraordinary peripheral vision. He could see on either side of himself when he went up for a ball. "People have a line of focus on whatever they're trying to see, and objects outside that line are blurry," Russell said. "In fact, they lose sight of the objects within their peripheral vision unless they train their eyes to pick them up."

Jones and Russell practiced using their peripheral vision by standing near each other, focusing at different distances while trying to keep track of each other peripherally. "Eventually we discovered that under certain conditions you can hide on a basketball court," Russell said. "With no one on the floor but ten players and two referees, you can still position yourself so that a player facing you will not see you. It's possible because everyone has a blind spot in each eye, about fifteen or twenty degrees on either side of straight-ahead. This enables defensive players to apply pressure without being seen for a brief moment, enough to knock a ball away or come up with a steal. He won't lose sight of you completely, but his impression might be so dimmed that he won't react the way he should."

"I concentrated on developing 'split vision,'" Woolpert said. "There is no medical authority for the term. But the quickness of a boy's visual reactions can be accelerated. Most of us do not use our eyes efficiently. We neglect the fringe area of lateral vision."

Russell and Jones also figured out one of the reasons why officials called so many fouls on defensive players attempting to block shots—players would lunge forward trying to swat the ball away soon after it left offensive players' hands, often running into the offensive player. But a player wouldn't lose as much reach toward the arc of the ball, they decided, if he jumped straight up and reached out instead. That way he could avoid running into the shooter and prevent injuries, too, because the defensive player would be off-balance. "The vertical technique—jumping straight up and reaching out with your arm—puts a premium on long arms and high jumps; it was made for people built the way I am."

Russell also learned that even though he might be shorter than some centers, he still could block their shots. Early on he figured out that an offensive player tended to jump about half as high as he could when he shot, but a defensive player always jumped as high as possible—and Russell could jump much higher than most players, even those taller than him.

Even when Russell left his feet when faked out—and he often was—he was so quick he could recover by reaching back with those long arms to block the shot from behind. Russell spent countless hours on the court with the super-quick Perry trying to guard him to improve his reactions. Perry told Russell, "If you can catch the flea, you can catch the elephant." Perry said he "saw something—a person who manifested destiny. He lifted himself, and he lifted me. He became my leader."

Russell, in addition, learned to steer blocked shots to a teammate to start a fast break. When Russell blocked a shot, his teammates tried to determine which way the ball was going to go. "And then we were off to the races," Jones said. Russell would come tearing down the court, and Jones and Perry would lob the ball up to Russell for a dunk. "It would make for a ballet," Perry said.

Said Jones, "The fast break and defense—we'd box out and set great D—was the thing that really killed teams." Sometimes Russell would find defensive players dropping off him after he rebounded to cover the outlet pass. When that happened, Russell would use another move that drove coaches to early retirements— he dribbled the ball down the court. No coach wants his center taking the ball down the court. A video of Russell doing just that after a rebound under the basket showed him taking only eleven— that's right, eleven—giant strides and then leaping toward the basket over the top of a defender to dunk the ball.

Russell learned a psychological side to defense, too. He wanted the offensive team to deviate from its habits. "What I try to do on defense is to make the offensive man do not what *he* wants but what *I* want. If I'm back on defense and three guys are coming at me, I've got to do something to worry all three. First I must make them slow up or stop. Then I must force them to make a bad pass and take a bad shot, and finally, I must try to block the shot." As Russell's reputation grew, coaches had to figure out how to deal with his defensive ability. It was not, "How do we stop Russell?" but "How do we avoid Russell?" They had to find a way to score.

Russell pointed out six years into his career with the NBA that "defense is a science, not a helter-skelter thing you just luck into. Every move has six or seven years of work behind it. In basketball your body gets to do things it couldn't do in normal circumstances. You take abnormal steps, you have to run backward almost as fast as you can forward. On defense you must never cross your legs while running, and that's the most natural thing to do when changing directions. Instead, you try to glide like a crab."

It all started with practice. Woolpert tweaked the pressure defense somewhat, coming up with a three-quarter-court press. He was blessed with quick guards in Jones, Perry, and—a year later—Eugene Brown and Warren Baxter. "Each of these players," Woolpert said, "was able to recover from a mistake as quickly as anyone I've ever seen."

Woolpert noted that a pressing defense is tiring work and requires a great deal of stamina. Newell, who was a mentor to Woolpert, said nobody played the press defense better than USF during its two championship seasons. He attributed that to the quickness, speed, and athleticism that the black athletes brought to USF's defense. The black athletes who were starting to make their presence felt in college basketball, Newell said, "brought basketball to heights the coaches of my time had never envisioned."

He later remarked that Russell was "the single most dominant defender, I believe, that the game has ever known." He called Russell "the perfect center." In addition, he said, "few players were as adept at playing the ball baseline to baseline as K. C. Jones.

He possessed very quick feet and even quicker hands." Jones, he said, was "the best defender from baseline to baseline I have ever seen." And if those weren't enough superlatives, Newell added, "Bill [Russell] and K. C. Jones anchored the most effective defensive collegiate team I've ever seen."

Woolpert developed two methods of playing the three-quarter-court press. One was to force the offense to bring the ball down the middle of the court where the ball handler could be double-teamed just before the midline. The other tried to force the dribbler to the outside of the court where he could get trapped along the sideline.

Woolpert also used an offense that Newell had employed. Both had picked up the complex "reverse action" play from their college coach at Loyola of Los Angeles. The strategy, which required countless hours of practice, spread the defense around the court. It meant reversing the ball so that the defense moved from one side of the court to the other. The system called for reversing the ball from forward to guard to forward, with people rolling outside to the corner and a lot of cross-court passes. It also proved to work as a defensive strategy because rolling an offensive guard into the corner put the opponents' guard in the corner as well. When in the corner the defensive guard was out of position to receive an outlet pass that would start a fast break.

Woolpert pinned high expectations on Russell's play, but he had numerous run-ins with his talented center, who also had difficulty fitting in with the older—and white—players, although Russell never used race as an excuse for dissension on the team. It started before Russell played his first college game. In his autobiography *Go Up for Glory* Russell said a starting guard, who he did not name, told Woolpert in front of other players that he thought giving Russell a scholarship was a mistake. A starting forward told people he was going to be an All-American and he considered Russell a lousy basketball player. "Russell," he said, "next week you're gonna be playing with the men, and I don't think you can cut it." Russell was undaunted. He was confident in his ability and wasn't going to let anyone get him down.

Although Russell denied any racial problems among that team, more than one player said Russell had a chip on his shoulder about race. It goes without saying that Russell might have been sensitive to racial matters that the white players would not understand. In addition some of the players were more interested in individual statistics than in developing teamwork that led to wins.

While Woolpert was battling with Russell over how to play the game, he was also making changes in Jones's game. Unlike Russell, Jones more willingly complied. The flashy behind-the-back passes that Jones had used in high school and playground basketball were as anathema to Woolpert as was Russell's leaving his feet to block shots. Jones toned his game down to meet Woolpert's wishes, and his game didn't suffer.

Like Woolpert, Jones was confident that "[Russell] would change things around for us in my junior year." While they did improve, it was not as much as Jones expected, possibly because of a misfortune that befell Jones after the first game of the upcoming season.

# EIGHT

## A Disappointing Season

"We were worse than awful."
—Stan Buchanan

At the start of the 1953–54 season the Dons expected to unseat Santa Clara as champions of the CBA. The Broncos had made it to the final four in 1952 as well as to the Western Regional finals in 1953, and several players returned from that team in the fall, including powerhouse forward Kenny Sears.

USF's season started off with a formidable opponent—the tenth-ranked California Golden Bears, a team that included All-American Bob McKeen, a six-foot-seven, 225-pound center. The last time the two teams met, Cal had overwhelmed USF 64–33. The prognosis wasn't good this time, either. A reporter for the *San Francisco Chronicle* commented, "Some observers have said that Russell, who is six-nine and 200 pounds, will be outwrestled by good pivotmen. This remains to be seen. The long boy from Oakland's McClymonds High is mostly muscle and bone."

McKeen was backed up by sensational playmaker Bob Matheny, a sophomore who had been northern California's Player of the Year while at Lowell High School. K. C. Jones was well aware of Matheny's talents, having played against him when Jones was at Commerce.

The Dons had some firepower of their own alongside Russell. K. C. Jones was beginning his second varsity season, and his running mate at guard was senior Rich Mohr. Forwards Frank Evangelho and Jerry Mullin flanked Russell.

The game was played before a standing-room-only crowd of sixty-four-hundred fans at dingy Kezar Pavilion, about twenty blocks from the USF campus at 755 Stanyan Street, the "home" court of the Dons. More than two-thousand people were turned away. The pavilion, which was built by the city in 1928, was rocking to see Russell's first varsity game. "Before that," Jones recalled, "we wouldn't have much of a crowd. I guess they anticipated something great . . . or wanted to see Cal." Said the *San Francisco Chronicle*, "Those lucky enough to find a seat or a place to stand will not forget the night."

Woolpert was asked why the game drew so many fans, especially when basketball attendance had been down for Bay Area basketball. "Maybe that kid [Russell] started us off. A lot of people were curious to see him, after what he did as a freshman. Russell didn't disappoint on the varsity. It takes a name. He's got it. I haven't seen a better coordinated tall man."

The Dons took the court in their green and gold warm-up suits, which included flaps on the back like a sailor's uniform with "Dons" printed in big letters. Pompon girls wearing below-the-knee skirts and long-sleeved sweaters greeted them. The Dons wore tight-fitting shorts and jerseys with no T-shirts under them. Nary a tattoo was in sight. Nor a headband. The nervous Woolpert—unable to light up a cigarette—chomped on a piece of gum.

Watching the game that night was a five-foot-eight guard, Warren Baxter, who played for City College of San Francisco and was a friend of K. C. Jones and Bill Russell. Baxter joined the Dons the following year and provided a strong backup to Jones and Hal Perry in the Dons' two championship years.

As play began Jones tenaciously guarded Matheny—eventually holding him to a single field goal for the game. When Matheny passed to McKeen, he found Russell right there to reject shots. Russell smacked the first shot McKeen took into the third row of seats with his big left hand. In later games, as Russell gained experience, he learned how to steer blocked shots to his teammates, which often lead to a fast break. But in that game, "He blocked three shots into the stands," McKeen recalled. "And he stayed a foot and a half off me. I'd never run into anybody who could play off you like that and control the game. I never had trouble with any other centers. He was the only guy to block my hook shot."

The Dons had scouted McKeen and discovered that the bulky center could not move well to his right, preferring to spin left and throw up a right-handed hook shot. Russell was waiting for it and, being left-handed, swatted the ball away with ease. Russell recalled, "His first seven shots, I blocked. They called a time-out. I walked back to the bench with my chest puffed out. [Woolpert] said, 'You can't play defense that way. A defensive player never leaves his feet.' Basically, we fought for three years. And when I played the way he wanted, we got our butts kicked."

Russell said Woolpert told him during the Cal game that he wanted him to deny McKeen the ball. "So I try that, and his point guard [Matheny] takes two dribbles to his right and drops a bounce pass, [McKeen] catches and turns, I'm on his back out of the defense, and so he shoots three lay-ups in a row. I said this doesn't make sense. I do it this way and I stop him. I do it that way and he goes in for lay-ups? And this is how he wants me to play?"

Russell said what he did for the next three years was to play it Woolpert's way "enough to keep him from kicking me off the team, and still [play] the way I thought I should play. So I had to play it with a disguise so it looked like I was playing the way he wanted me to play."

The Dons opened a 21–11 lead that the Bears narrowed to 23–19 at halftime. At one point during the second half, USF scored twice as many points as the Bears, and the team wound up stunning Cal with a 51–33 victory. Russell scored 20 points and blocked 8 of McKeen's shots, 13 overall. Russell's rebound totals aren't available, but based on his yearly average of 19 rebounds a game it is likely he registered a triple-double in his first college game. Russell "covered the backboard on rebounds like fly paper," the *Chronicle* wrote. And he held McKeen to 14 points. "His defensive play left Bob McKeen so frustrated that the lanky Cal man had his best look at the basket from the bench," the *Alameda Times-Star* said.

Russell set the tone by blocking McKeen's first field goal attempt. Said Jones, "When you take a little five-footer and it's blocked, you take a lay-up and it's blocked, and you take a hook shot and it's blocked . . . McKeen may have been shell-shocked."

Two years later, Woolpert called Russell's defense against Cal "the best defensive job he ever did, I guess. . . . It's difficult to measure Bill's defensive value because much of it is psychological—a shooter hurrying a shot he shouldn't take in order to avoid him or not taking one he should take." Cal's Bob Albo said, "It was a rude awakening for [McKeen]. I don't know that he'd ever had a shot blocked. Bill Russell was absolutely phenomenal."

The Dons even dominated in the preliminary game. Guard Gene Brown, a strong player soon to move up to the varsity, scored 22 points as the freshman team beat Cal 60–54.

The northern California basketball writers and sportscasters selected Russell as their player of the week for his performance against Cal. Five days after the game Russell sat down with *San Francisco Chronicle* artist Howard Brodie, who sketched a portrait of him, a common newspaper practice in those days. Russell told Brodie, "I got a break so far . . . if it continues and I can play pro ball after graduation, I'm going to buy my father a home." After an hour of posing, he credited Jones for his play. "You know, K. C. Jones's passes . . . make me look better than I am. I've got plenty to learn, couldn't make the glee club unless I was so tall."

While a star was born that night against Cal, another one almost died. K. C. Jones took the floor against the Bears with a pale and drawn look. He attributed it to nerves. But he played the entire game occasionally clutching his stomach and wincing in pain. He had felt that pain once before, during his senior year in high school when he spent two weeks in bed unable to eat and almost unable to move. His family had no money for a doctor or a hospital, but Jones managed to get through it. He thought he could do it again. But it was not to be.

The pain became worse while he was on a bus bound for the Dons' next game against Fresno State. "My stomach was doing flips," he recalled. Student trainer Vince Briare sat next to Jones trying to comfort him, but his limited medical skills provided no relief. It was Thanksgiving weekend, and Jones thought he'd eaten too much. By the time they got him to a hospital, he was in agony. His appendix had burst, and he was near death. Doctors said that Jones's appendix might have ruptured three or four days prior to the Cal game. Jones had not said anything about the pain because of the importance of the Cal game. "We almost got to him too late," a doctor at the Fresno hospital said. "Very likely, impossible though it seems, Jones played the California game with a burst appendix. One more minute of basketball might very well have killed him." While Jones was in a coma for four days, students at USF held a special service to pray for his recovery. Fresno State held a vigil for him. "I never saw anything like it," Woolpert said.

Woolpert was also touched when players from Santa Clara, which was playing Fresno State a few days after Jones fell ill, stopped by the hospital to visit him. When they learned that they wouldn't be allowed to see him, they chipped in and bought Jones a loud pair of pajamas. St. Mary's players sent him a bouquet of flowers, while the Stanford and Cal teams sent him Christmas cards.

Jones lost twenty-five pounds and could barely get out of bed. His basketball season was over. He spent six weeks in the hospital. Woolpert and teammate Carl Lawson spent hours with Jones. But most telling of all, even while he was recovering, Jones continued a detailed analysis of opponents with Russell.

With Jones out, Russell became the only black starter on the team, which drew resentment from some white players. Criticism that started before the season began continued. One player chastised him for not being tough enough. Russell said he would have preferred encouragement rather than disapproval of his inexperienced play. Other players began to pick up the negative attitude, although the team overcame the dissension enough to come away with some quality wins during the season. "It was not a very homogenous team," forward Stan Buchanan remembered. Russell never openly called his teammates racists, but on one occasion he pointed out that while the Jesuits at USF generally had a progressive attitude about racial matters, "not all the students took them to heart, especially on the basketball team." Hal Perry wasn't quite so diplomatic. "We ran into the racial issue," he said. "They didn't see the need to have us in the school."

Cliques tended to split the team, forward Gordon Kirby noted. But Kirby also said he felt that 1953–54 was the year the team started to jell, even though it would have had a far better record with Jones in the lineup. Kirby also thought that some players sitting on the bench should have been starting.

A turning point for Russell came when the Dons traveled to Provo, Utah, to play Brigham Young University (BYU). On the first play of the game, BYU's quick six-four center spun around Russell for a lay-up. As they ran back down the court, USF's team captain hollered at Russell, "Why don't you try playing some defense?" That did it, Russell said to himself. "He wants defense? He'll get defense. That center won't get any more points tonight." Russell shut him out the rest of the game. "At USF, you weren't supposed to dance with girls as close as I was playing that guy," Russell said.

But Russell had gone overboard. He so concentrated on defending his man that he didn't shoot, set picks or pick up anybody else's man, especially the captain's man. "Guys would go by for lay-ups, but I was playing torrid defense on my guy—exclusively. I'd step out of the way when any other player went by me." The BYU player had 2 points and 2 rebounds. The Dons trailed by 25 points at halftime. During the break, Russell stalked around the locker room in anger. Woolpert laid into Russell. "What's the matter with you, Russell? You've been reading your press clippings?" For ten minutes, Woolpert ripped Russell up one side and down the other. Russell was deeply hurt that Woolpert had not asked what was troubling him.

After the blistering, Russell thought, "This is not a very good team and we're not going anywhere. But I want to be a good basketball player and I'm going to play as hard as I can for as long as I can with no regard to what these people—my teammates—can do. We're not going to win, but I'm going to be the best basketball player any of these guys ever saw."

Russell scored 22 points in the second half and the Dons cut BYU's lead to three before eventually losing. "[Woolpert] walked away from this game thinking that what he had said had motivated me. . . . All it did was to make me want to be the most dominant player ever," Russell reflected.

While the season failed to meet expectations, the Dons posted a 14-7 record overall, finishing second to Santa Clara in the West Coast Conference with an 8-4 mark. An impressive record, considering Jones was out for the year and forward Jerry Mullen dislocated an elbow that kept him out of action for six games. Student trainer Vince Briare knew little about those kinds of injuries, but a doctor in the stands popped the elbow back into place. Bob Wiebusch and Dick Lawless also suffered minor injuries that slowed them down. Without those injuries, Lawless said, the Dons could have won the national championship that year as well.

Russell averaged almost 20 points and 19 rebounds a game. In one stretch, he scored 25, 32, and 31 points as his improvement continued. Despite this record, though, he was largely unheard of outside northern California.

Russell, decidedly unhappy with the team's performance, thought the Dons had enough talent to be one of the top teams in the country. Something was missing. He blamed it on some of the players' "elitist" attitudes, saying it kept them from being better than the two teams that won national championships that year. "We [the younger players] were just considered beneath them. It showed in our performance. We had wall-to-wall jerks on that team, and we couldn't win," Russell said. "I played my heart out, but our team was riddled with dissension, and I was part of it. I was not strong enough to change the atmosphere for the better, and the team wasn't strong enough to change me, so we feuded." Russell admitted he was wrong, that he was part of the team and that never again would he allow himself to concentrate on individual goals at the team's expense.

All the ill feelings of that season did an about-face for the upcoming 1954–55 season, thanks to Russell's growing up, the "jerks'" graduation, and K. C. Jones's return. But the team ran into more racial dissension when Hal Perry moved into a starting role and Warren Baxter transferred from junior college. The discord came more from off-campus than it did from teammates. One USF alumnus complained, "They are scarcely representative of the school. Perhaps a rule should be established that only three can be on the court at one time." Woolpert—livid—decried such racist comments time and time again. "Anyone who claims there should be discrimination toward a Negro or a Protestant or a bricklayer's son on an athletic team or in a classroom is not representative of this school, either."

# NINE
## An Unlikely Coach

"He could make coffee nervous."
—Forward Mike Farmer

Phil Woolpert may have been the luckiest and yet the most reluctant coach ever to head a major college basketball team. When he graduated in 1940 from Loyola University—now Loyola Marymount—he planned to become a social worker. Instead, he went to work in a prison. Then, while in the army during World War II, he was assigned to serve at the "disciplinary barracks" in Hawaii, a hellish experience. At that time, he said, "Coaching was the farthest thing from my mind."

Woolpert—born in Danville, Kentucky—lived a nomadic lifestyle until age ten, moving over and over from Kentucky to Ohio to New Jersey and finally to California. He lived in an integrated neighborhood in Los Angeles where his southern-raised but politically liberal father influenced his social conscience. After graduating from Manual Arts High School during the depths of the Depression, Woolpert attended Los Angeles Junior College hoping to get a degree that would allow him to help people. "I didn't quite know how. Just helping them," he said.

At six-two, weighing 135 pounds, Woolpert looked like "the results of an X-ray," said Pete Newell, who later became his teammate at Loyola. Woolpert played a decent enough game of basketball that after his freshman year of junior college he came to the attention of coach Jimmy Needles. Needles offered him a scholarship to the Catholic university. Woolpert considered himself an agnostic, but he saw the offer as his chance to get a college education. Thus began a lifelong connection with Catholicism, even though Woolpert never embraced religion. During his years of coaching, some of the players he recruited would say, "But Coach, I'm not Catholic." Woolpert would respond, "Neither am I."

At Loyola under Needles's guidance, Newell, Woolpert, and a third player—future Loyola coach Scott McDonald—learned how to play and, more importantly, how to coach. Newell called Needles the most important influence on his coaching career. Needles had been the United States' first Olympic coach in 1936. He taught Newell and Woolpert how to play defense and how to run the reverse-action offense that both used so well in their careers. During his three years at Loyola, Woolpert exhibited a competitive streak. It caused him to get booted out of four games for fighting.

When the California state prison system hired Woolpert, it had just instituted a reform plan at Chino using unarmed guards, cells without locks, and an honor system for inmates. Woolpert was one of thirty-five applicants selected out of a field of fifteen hundred to be supervisors.

Two years later he was drafted and sent to Hawaii where he was assigned to the disciplinary barracks staff because of his prison experience. The barracks were the infamous Stockade, made famous by the 1951 book and the resulting movie *From Here to Eternity*. He said that the author, James Jones, "If anything . . . underwrote the scenes. God, how grotesque and sordid and brutal men can be." He was called on to witness executions. "Your view of life is never the same after being around that kind of thing," Woolpert said.

After the war Needles, who was by then USF's athletic moderator, asked Woolpert to consider taking the job as basketball coach at St. Ignatius High School, then a prep school for USF. His former teammate Pete Newell had hired on as USF's coach. "I suppose none of us really knows—for certain—whether we're making the major decisions of our lives because we truly want to ourselves or because of what other people expect us to do," he said in a 1968 *Sports Illustrated* interview. But whatever his reasons, Woolpert said he was interested, and with Newell's blessing he was hired.

The St. Ignatius team won the city championship after Woolpert's first year, and he ran up a 63-29 record over the course of his four years there. Woolpert loved high school coaching and recalled no desire to move up to the college level. Then Michigan State lured Newell away by offering him almost twice what he had been earning at USF. Newell practically had to beg Woolpert to take the USF job, telling him, "You know damn good and well you don't want to be a high school coach all your life."

Not only did Newell have to talk Woolpert into taking the job, he also had to persuade USF to hire him. Woolpert's presumed political views worried school officials because during the Depression his parents had been proponents of California's Townsend Pension Plan, a radical social security program. "Only when I told them that Phil wasn't a communist would they hire him," Newell recalled.

Thirty-five-year-old, chain-smoking, high-strung Woolpert took over coaching the Dons in 1950 at a salary of $3,600 a year. When he wasn't coaching basketball, he served as golf coach, tennis coach and supervisor of the school's intramural program.

Athletic programs were simpler then. Most, particularly at Catholic institutions, had low-budget operations, which often made it difficult to meet alumni expectations. USF was no exception. In the championship years the athletic department consisted of five employees: the athletic moderator, a secretary, ticket manager, publicity director, and team trainer. Coaches, as in Woolpert's case, often had to oversee more than one sport. In the athletic moderator's case, the Reverend Ralph Tichenor carried out his ministerial duties while overseeing sports activities and serving as chaplain for the athletic teams, as academic enforcer, and as counselor. He also traveled with the team to all of its games.

Woolpert coached USF's basketball team to a 9-17 record his first year and then told Needles he was resigning. "I figured I'd had my exposure to the big time, and I just was not cut out for the pressures." Needles talked him out of it, but coaching took a physical toll on him. Before and during games Woolpert—who looked like a bookkeeper—chain-smoked, developed a facial tic, and generally became a nervous wreck. His intensity on the bench was legendary. "There's always this gnawing in the stomach," he said. "It's almost the same whether it's a national championship or the last game of a losing season. Somehow, I've got by all these years without getting an ulcer. If I did, I'd quit. But the pressure is always there. The pressure you put on yourself." The pressure eventually did get to him, driving him away from USF after the 1958–59 season. Nonetheless, his ten-year career posthumously earned him Hall of Fame honors in 1992.

Needles had to do some fast-talking to get Woolpert to stay after that first year. "Phil felt guilty because he didn't think he was doing justice to the kids," Needles said. "It was typical of Phil to blame himself. But he had poor material, and I finally made him believe that he did have the technical mastery, that it wasn't all his fault." Woolpert had two more lackluster years before Russell arrived.

Woolpert brought Jimmy Needles's techniques to USF. He also brought discipline to a simple offense, and he stressed tenacious defense. He had the players during the two championship years to pull it off. Above all, Woolpert's strong point—defense—set the tone for the offense, which didn't have any great shooters, only great scorers. Woolpert's motivating technique, 1955–56 forward Mike Farmer said, was a "funny sarcasm," although Farmer said the team didn't need to be motivated. "We were determined that we could not be beat no matter what." Woolpert was fortunate to have strong leaders on the floor. K. C. Jones brought focus to the team—Woolpert called him a coach on the floor—while Hal Perry provided the rah-rah.

Woolpert also saw to it that his players played as a team. He wouldn't let egos get in the way. This perhaps explains why Woolpert didn't sing Russell's praises as much as the star center would have liked. He didn't want Russell to get a big head. "There was not much individuality on the team," guard Rudy Zannini said. Woolpert treated everyone the same. "You always knew where you stood with him," Zannini said.

Woolpert rarely allowed his team to run up the score. His bench players received a good share of playing time because the first team quickly opened up big leads, allowing Woolpert to freely substitute. "We held our own against other teams' starters," said forward Jack King. If the opposing team began to narrow the point margin on the Dons, Woolpert put his first team back in to assure the win. Woolpert also pulled a player if he started racking up a lot of points—except during close games, which wasn't often. He tried to avoid letting individuals stand out, preferring team play over individual play. "Russell could have scored 35–40 points any time he wanted," said Carl Boldt. "But Phil didn't want to run up the score. He never really let us loose."

"[Woolpert] was very innovative," Farmer said. "He and Ross [Guidice] got together and just decided that the team, as athletic as it was, we would just start the game in a full-court press. And that was really not done back then. We used to run up some very large scores at the beginning—32–2, 21–1."

Jones said that while Woolpert taught the team defense, "We took it a step further with our creativity." But Woolpert didn't care much for fast-break basketball. He liked to have the guards bring the ball up slowly and pass it around until someone was open for a good shot. Russell, however, liked to smack an opponent's shot into the hands of players who would take off down the court. Woolpert, Russell said, "believed about the fast break like Woody Hayes thought about the forward pass—that three things could happen, but two of them were bad. We never practiced the fast break. But, of course, we used it from the start of every game."

There was never any question who was in charge. Woolpert did what he had to do to maintain control, taking difficult disciplinary action when he had to, including throwing Russell out of practice for not following his instructions. Although Russell was the coach's "fair-haired boy," he was not immune to Woolpert's discipline, said Mike Preaseau, who played on the 1956 championship team. Preaseau said that on a goodwill trip to the Philippines in 1958 some of the players complained that the slow style of play Woolpert was using wasn't working well. They asked Preaseau to talk to the coach about speeding up the offense. Preaseau gave his pitch and then was kept out of the next seven games on the trip.

While Woolpert helped bring USF's basketball program to national attention, he always felt his job entailed more than coaching. He considered himself to have an obligation to prepare athletes for life after college as well. "Phil wouldn't take a kid unless he was positive—absolutely certain—that the boy could make it through college and would be able to make a success of something other than sports as a career," Needles said. A player's grades were as important to Woolpert as his athletic ability. He suspended team members who failed courses. Woolpert once threatened his meal ticket—Russell—with suspension if he didn't improve his academics. Woolpert "didn't have to have a dean or anybody in the administration to tell him. That's what he believed, that they should be students first," said Lo Schiavo.

Woolpert often wondered if he would have made a more lasting impact as a social worker than a basketball coach. But in reality he did both as a coach. Hal Urban, one of the 1958 team members, gave an example of this when he paid tribute to Woolpert in his book, *Life's Greatest Lessons*. When Urban was a sophomore he took a shot at the basket that was easy to defend. Woolpert took Urban aside and showed him how to get off the shot against a defender. "He said that developing little habits like that could make a big difference in my overall effectiveness. Then he added, 'Good habits make the difference, not just in the gym but in everything we do.' Here was a man I greatly admired teaching me about a game I loved. And in the process, he gave me one of the most valuable lessons in life. Phil was respected because of the principles by which he coached and lived. . . . His high principles were actually his own habits, the successful things he did every day."

The cerebral, bespectacled coach, who earned the nickname "Socrates" once remarked, "People say to a guy, 'Hey, John, you're not working up to capacity. You could be making another $100 a day. What's the matter with you, John?' But what if John wants to improve in something intangible? Human communications, maybe, or loving his neighbor or studying sunsets? By our simplistic measures of success, a man like John doesn't count." In 1968 Woolpert told *Sports Illustrated*, "I have enormous empathy with the hippies. I might have been an extraordinarily good hippie. The best of what they stand for—love, peace, compassion for other people, individualism unobstructed by artificial values of the establishment—these are things I'd like to think I stand for at my best."

Woolpert could talk as philosophically about coaching as he could about life. "Coaching is the product of the macho mentality," he said years after he left USF. "When we were kids, winning was everything. Always has been. There is something wrong when winning becomes the motivating factor. We come to believe that the only measure of accomplishment is victory. There has to be something more rational."

Said K. C. Jones in paying tribute to the only coach who offered him a scholarship,

> Phil was his own person and an innovator, starting . . . black players when advised otherwise. He was honest and cared about his players, both on and off the court. Phil had a great sensitivity to what we were like as individuals, what our strengths were, how we best worked together, and he capitalized on this. He listened to our personal problems and showed concern for racial issues at the time. He was an extremely bright person and recognized the same high intellectual level in Bill Russell. Bill and Phil had a special appreciation for one another. He treated us all like we were members of his own family, and Bill, like the rest of us, gave Phil his best effort. Phil was truly an exceptional person. He was like a father to all of us. I owe Phil Woolpert everything.

Despite what Jones said about Russell's relationship with Woolpert, Russell had a different take on his coach. He was much harder on Woolpert in his younger years, but they patched up their differences years later and became good friends. In Russell's autobiography *Go Up for the Glory*, written ten years after he left USF, Russell was critical of Woolpert, calling him "a strange man" and saying,

I was not fond of Woolpert as a coach, but I liked him as a man . . . sometimes. I believe then and I believe now that he played favorites. I think he injured the team in the manner in which he played his favorites both during the practice sessions and in the games. I do not believe Woolpert did this because of prejudice. It was just the way he was. . . . But though I gained my first fame with him, I could never be close to him as a man. I can't believe he was prejudiced, yet in those days I felt certain that he was. In my freshman year a player named Carl Lawson was starting guard on the varsity. He had earned the job. Now, the next season, a white boy named Rich [Mohr] joined the team, and Woolpert automatically gave him Lawson's starting job.

He said the same thing happened during his junior year with Hal Perry when Woolpert gave his job over to Bill Bush.

In another instance, Russell thought K. C. Jones should have been captain, but Woolpert named Jerry Mullen. "I don't think to this day Woolpert knows what he did was wrong." Russell was also puzzled that Woolpert gave little or no credit to his assistant and freshman coach Ross Guidice. "When we gained . . . national prominence and the round of banquets and testimonials began, Woolpert never thought to thank Guidice, which hurt him terribly. Woolpert would thank his wife, the dean, this person and that person. But never his assistant, who did so much. [He was] a strange man."

At least one other player, Carl Boldt, said Guidice "was really the coach, not Woolpert." He said that Woolpert was jealous of Guidice and his relationships with the players. Woolpert didn't praise Guidice, Boldt said, because he was insecure in his role as head coach. Posed team pictures never included Guidice although the team manager was often included. "He had a lot of problems with people," Boldt said, but "nobody disrespected Phil."

Said guard Hal Payne, "[Guidice] never got the recognition he deserved." Vince Boyle agreed with Boldt. "There's no question [Guidice] was a better coach." He said Guidice was more personable than Woolpert and was more of a mentor to the players—a teacher rather than a coach. Boyle said Woolpert could be distant, and he had a veil around him that was difficult to penetrate. He said Woolpert was reserved and hard to get close to—"a philosophical man." Others said he taught at an intellectual level. Several of the players, especially those who played for Guidice on the freshman team, praised Guidice's teaching ability. "He was there to help you," Boyle said. Guidice would not be drawn into a discussion of whether Boldt or others were correct, but did say, "I thought I knew more about basketball than [Woolpert] did." Nonetheless, Woolpert was the coach, and the team was going to do things his way. While Guidice may have been strong on technical skills, Woolpert was more of a tactician.

After Russell became a coach at the end of his playing days, he thought differently of Woolpert's coaching ability. "I was thinking as an individual," he said. "Phil had to be thinking in terms of layers." He said Woolpert taught him discipline. "I could never have made it with the Celtics without that."

The years have tended to mellow Russell even more. As late as 2004 Russell said, "I have thrown down some of my psychological baggage. Phil Woolpert saw something in me nobody else did. He gave me my chance."

Woolpert was blessed with an unusual collection of unselfish players with a complete lack of jealousy over the acclaim Russell received for his play. That perfect combination proved difficult to beat.

Despite achieving two national championships, Woolpert's name today is hardly as recognizable as Adolph Rupp's, John Wooden's, Dean Smith's, Bobby Knight's, or a dozen others. K. C.

Jones once called Woolpert the invisible coach. Yet Woolpert is as responsible for making basketball what it is today as any of them. He took a group of talented players, instilled discipline and technique, and then let them play their game—a strategy that soon gained wide acceptance in the world of basketball.

# TEN

## A Surprising Move

"Like the big left hand of God."
—Teammate Stan Buchanan's description of Bill Russell's shot-blocking ability.

At the start of the 1954–55 season Russell reached the announced height of six feet, ten inches. But Russell said that wasn't so. "I'm only six-nine and five-eighths of an inch," he said. "Don't call me six-ten. I'm enough of a goon already."

Russell and Woolpert continued to battle in practice and during games over how he should play. It bothered Woolpert that Russell would leave his feet while guarding an opposing player. "And here I was, airborne most of the time," Russell said. Woolpert told Russell he was "fundamentally unsound," and that "you can't do that." Russell responded, "But I just did."

Junior guard Hal Perry almost didn't play that season. Had he not, the whole outcome might have changed. The athletic moderator, the Reverend Ralph Tichenor, called him into his office in the spring of 1954—Perry's sophomore year—and told him if he didn't improve his playing he would lose his scholarship. Perry thought Tichenor was a racist. That was unlikely, but Tichenor was a tough administrator and may have been trying to motivate Perry.

He thought to himself, "He wants to get me out to get another white kid to take my spot." Perry got up, shook Tichenor's hand, and said, "I will do it." If Perry was struggling on the court, it wasn't because he didn't work at improving. He, Russell, and Jones played one-on-one at St. Ignatius, learning from each other during the off-season and whenever else they had the chance. Russell got Perry to pull him into the corners and then try to drive on him to the basket. "This is how we practiced defense," Perry said. "He (Russell) was always trying to get better. He knew his strengths and limitations." Russell told Perry and Jones, "Look, guys, don't ever do what you can't do. Just do what you can do— and do it well."

USF began the 1954–55 season without its no. 2 and no. 4 scorers from the previous year. Forward Frank Evangelho and guard Rich Mohr had graduated. Jones noted that they were replaced by "no-talent guys like myself, [forward] Stan Buchanan, and Russell . . . then all of a sudden we came alive with this total team thing." Jones may have downplayed his talent as well as Russell's, but he wasn't far off on Buchanan. At six-foot-three, relatively small for a forward, Buchanan's strength lay in boxing out opposing rebounders. He also played strong defense. "He just ran and hustled and did the best he could," Jones said. "That's what we all did. We were more into blue collar than talent. If we happened to score, fine. Our defense was so good, it took pressure off us offensively."

Besides Russell, who was a scorer but not a shooter, USF had six-foot-five forward Jerry Mullen, who averaged 13.6 points a game for the season. Russell finished with 21 points a game, Jones with a little over 10, Perry with almost 7 and Buchanan with just over 5. Over the course of the season, their opponents made fewer than 32 percent of their shots while the Dons' margin of victory was 15 points a game.

During this season Jones and Russell pulled off a number of times what became known as the "alley-oop"—a play where, on a fast break, Jones would throw the ball high and near the rim. Russell would fly through the air, grab the ball and slam it through the hoop, all in one motion. The alley-oop helped further the evolution of basketball, elevating it to a higher level.

Russell's ability to guide errant shots before they hit the rim into the basket was another move no one had seen before. With his great leaping ability and his huge hands, he could tap the ball in from high above the basket. The shot, outlawed as goaltending the year after Russell graduated, was called the "steer shot," "funnel shot," or "convoy shot." Woolpert often told players to just fire the ball toward the basket and let Russell take over. This steering of shots didn't go over well with some players. Forward Dick Lawless once chided Russell, "Hey, that shot would have gone in without your help." Nonetheless, Russell got credit for the 2 points.

Woolpert said about his starting lineup after the third game of the year:

*Mullen*: "Jerry has as much or more desire as any player I have ever had the pleasure to coach or see. He's a forever sopho-more, doesn't know what half speed is—always putting out everything he has." Woolpert named Mullen captain, which irritated Russell, who thought Jones should get the honor. Usually the players voted for the captain, but this time Woolpert made the selection. Russell wondered whether racial prejudice motivated Woolpert.

*Russell*: "His outstanding trait is that he has subordinated himself to the team. Bill realizes that if he were the lone scorer, opponents would concentrate on him and hurt the team. Also, many is the time he has sacrificed position on a rebound to move over and cover up a defensive gap left by a teammate."

*Jones*: "The team has a world of confidence in him, and I find him the most coachable player I have ever taught." Woolpert recognized Jones's leadership later in the year, but Jones didn't become captain until the following year. Woolpert said that even though Jones wasn't the captain, "He is the man the fellows look to when they are in trouble. He is the playmaker. He is the 'come-through' guy when we desperately need a basket to get under way. I can't explain to you how important a man he is on the team."

*Perry*: "He is not only a great hustler and team man, but is also the fastest man on the squad." Perry covered as much ground during a game as any man, Woolpert said, and he also worked as hard as anybody during the forty minutes of game time.

*Buchanan*: "Stan is a court opportunist, and he likes the rough going. An excellent student, he has the capacity to anticipate his opponent's actions on the floor. Additionally, Stan has mastered the difficult art of screening. He has good strength on the boards. Most important, though, he is a complete hustler and never slows down." Woolpert described Buchanan as a self-made player who often practiced alone six to eight hours on the court. Woolpert had coached Buchanan in high school.

Bob Wiebusch had been penciled in as the starting forward in place of Buchanan, but he suffered a shoulder injury in a preseason game against the alumni and was out almost six weeks. He never got back in the starting lineup.

Jack King had been a four-sport star at the 120-student St. Vincent's High School in Petaluma, but he had no intention of playing basketball when he enrolled at USF. That changed after a priest watched him play intramural ball and suggested he try out for the freshman team. King had grown four inches since high school. At King's tryout Guidice decided he liked the player's speed but that his fundamentals were lacking. The freshman coach went on to teach King techniques he did not learn in high school.

The Dons also added a transfer from the City College of San Francisco (CCSF), Warren Baxter, who played an important role by coming off the bench to fill in when players tired from the strain of pressing for the entire game. Baxter, who was five-foot-seven, had a deadly outside shot and was the best dribbler on the team. He had been widely sought by other colleges, including Cal and San Jose State, but chose USF "because I liked the courses that the college offered. And also because I figured that it would be more fun playing on a winning team."

Baxter was a solid player who averaged about 23 points a game while at CCSF. He could have started for almost any team in the country but never complained about being a substitute. When he played he made the most of his opportunities. According to forward Vince Boyle, who played with Baxter on the second championship team, the Dons were unselfish players, "and that was the reason for their success."

This team got along much better than did the previous year's lineup, although Russell didn't particularly like Mullen, a player he said he "held in low regard." Jones said the men "were quick to pat a teammate on the butt when he made a mistake to let him know mistakes were another thing we had in common. We never criticized one another's play. Our goal was the team's success. Everyone on the squad, black and white, believed the team came first. . . . Woolpert made every one of us feel valuable and important to the team. He gave us a pattern to follow and let us use our skills to modify or change that pattern as we needed to, and that told us he believed in us."

The Dons opened the season at Chico State, a small college in northern California. Chico State was no match for the Dons, who won 84–55, and Russell, who was guarded by a six-foot-one center, set a school record with 39 points. Then the Dons headed to Los Angeles to play Woolpert's alma mater—Loyola—and UCLA. USF beat Loyola 54–45. In that game Russell and Jones cooked up a plan that the pair still used in later years when they played for the Boston Celtics. The strategy was to confuse a player driving the length of the court toward the basket. When the player broke for the basket, and neither Russell nor Jones could catch him, Russell would holler out, "I got him, K.C." Jones would yell back, "No, I got him." The player would look over his shoulder and miss the lay-up.

Loyola coach Bill Donovan had nothing but praise for Russell. "Russell is the most valuable player to any one team I've ever seen," he said. "He probably blocked 10 of Bobby Cox's shots and 10 more of the other fellows'. And he ruined about 50 more because my guys were arching their shots to the rafters trying to keep them out of Russell's reach."

Then came the game against UCLA, in the sweaty, cracker-box Westwood gym. The same night that USF had played Loyola, their rival Santa Clara had been blown out by UCLA 74–39. "They demolished Santa Clara, our best competition," K. C. Jones said, "and when we read about it we almost soiled our pants. UCLA was ranked sixth or eighth, and we were eight-hundredth. We thought they'd beat us by 30, but it was only by like 6 [actually 7]."

USF lost to UCLA 47–40, and Russell was pushed and shoved all over the court by the Bruins' Willie "The Whale" Naulls. Jones later called guard Morris Taft the toughest man he'd ever had to guard next to La Salle's superstar, Tom Gola.

Russell took the blame for the loss. "It's my fault," he said, weeping in the locker room after the game. "It's not your fault," his coach Phil Woolpert replied. "It's everybody's fault." It may have been then that Russell learned a lesson that would follow him the rest of his career—you win or lose as a team.

But Jones saw some good come out of the game. "There was a transformation in our mental approach." That the Dons stayed close to the Bruins "just flip-flopped our minds," he said. "Almost overnight, we became arrogantly confident, and we just rode that confidence." Jerry Mullen talked with a couple of UCLA players after the game and told them, "We're going to get you in San Francisco." Mullen said they replied, "We know you are."

After that game Woolpert made a decision that changed the Dons' fortunes. Having seen Perry's play against UCLA, Woolpert elevated him to a starting position in place of Bill Bush. "Bush had a bad back, and it was hampering him some, so I put in Hal Perry . . . and got an extremely good game out of him." Woolpert said the move "was not all that inspired, [but] it was a move that ended up being as successful as a move could be."

He concluded that he had listened too long to alumni and other coaches who warned him about starting three black players. Forward Jack King said the move was not well accepted by the coaching fraternity. But by this point Woolpert had decided to play his best five players regardless of skin color. It was a bold move and it turned the season around for the Dons.

"He wasn't supposed to play more than two [blacks]," Perry said. "That's what Phil told me in my junior year. He said there were certain members of the alumni who said he couldn't have three on the first string. He said. 'I don't give a damn. I only care about talent.' He was a man of great principles."

Russell was overjoyed. He'd never been happy that Bush had been given the starting job ahead of Perry. "[Bush] didn't have to fight for the job," Russell said in his first autobiography. "Perry was heartbroken."

Fourteen years later, Perry said Woolpert's move saved the USF team from racial strife at a time when he, Russell, and Jones were skeptical of the coach. They remembered when a white player had started ahead of Carl Lawson, a black player who they thought was better. "We were waiting to see what would happen, giving Phil the benefit of any doubt about who should play," Perry said. When Bush started, Perry said, "It looked like prejudice to us because Woolpert wasn't playing his strongest team. . . . We wanted to win so we wanted the best five players going for us."

Guidice said he and Woolpert also wanted to play the best five players, and that's why the change was made—not because of any pressure from the black players. In Lawson's case, Guidice said, he "was a good player, but not a great player. (And) Bush was a capable guard" who had severe back problems that caused him to miss the following season. When Bush returned he stayed on the bench behind Perry.

Toward the end of his senior year, Bush told the school newspaper, *The Foghorn*, that it was no disgrace to play behind Jones and Perry. "I'm just happy to be on the squad and contribute what little I can for the team."

Woolpert made the right decision because the team never lost another game—fifty-five in a row—when the three black players started. It can't be discounted, either, that the black players' attitude toward their coach and conditions on the team led to improved play.

Said forward Dick Lawless, "We never thought about it in the least that we even had three black guys in the starting five. Most of us, being from the Bay Area, we were used to playing with black players. We just got along great. We didn't have any fighting or calling names or anything that I can remember." Jones agreed. "We were a close-knit team, and we just played basketball," Jones said. "It was no big deal to us, because we didn't look at our team as being made up of black players and white players. We were just players."

The next game, with Perry starting, USF beat Oregon State 60–34, but the Beavers were without seven-foot-three center Swede Halbrook. The Dons would play the Beavers again later in the season in the NCAA tournament when Halbrook returned from academic problems.

The following week USF had a rematch with UCLA, which ranked sixth in the nation. The Dons and the Bruins played at the Cow Palace, which opened in 1941 and is operated by a state agency of the California Department of Food and Agriculture's Division of Fairs and Expositions. The Cow Palace has extensive stables and facilities used for the annual Grand National Rodeo and other events. It received national attention when the 1956 and 1964 Republican national conventions were held there.

Two stories are told about how the Cow Palace received its name: One has it that a newspaper wondered how such a building could be constructed when the country was in the last throes of the Depression. "Why, when people are starving, should money be spent on a "palace for cows?" the editorial asked. The other was that an advertising company gave it the name after a man named Willard S. Anderson said, "They are just building a palace for cows." The building has been used for hockey, boxing, and basketball; it seats more than fifteen-thousand spectators. In addition to using the Kezar Pavilion, the Dons played at the Cow Palace on several occasions.

In the second game the Dons whipped the Bruins 56–44 behind Russell's 28 points and 21 rebounds. The game wasn't as close as the score indicated. At one point the Dons led 52–29. UCLA didn't score a field goal until ten minutes were left in the first half, and the Dons limited Willie Naulls to 12 points for the game.

UCLA coach John Wooden said after the game, "That Bill Russell is the key. He discourages opposing teams on defense, and even though he isn't the smoothest offensive center around, he still manages to average over 20 points a game. He's worth more than that on defense, however. He simply ruined my kids, and they are pretty good shots. We only hit about 20 percent of our shots against them, and it was mostly because the kids just got a bit frantic at seeing ordinarily easy shots blocked by that Russell."

"We played a lot of teams that were better than we were outside of Russell," Mullen said, "but we weren't going to lose. If someone told us we had to do a one-and-a-half off the Golden Gate Bridge to win we would have gone out and done it."

Ten days after USF beat UCLA, Scott McDonald, Woolpert's former teammate at Loyola of Los Angeles, described Russell as better than Clyde Lovellette of Kansas, the best big man he had ever seen. "Clyde was never better than this USF center," McDonald said. "[Russell's] effectiveness on the boards is unmatched. His blocking surpasses anything I've ever seen. There is something of romance about the way he plays." McDonald predicted that Russell would take the Dons to the national championship.

The Dons traveled next to the All-College Tournament in Oklahoma City, where the team's African American players encountered the first of at least three incidents of discrimination. Woolpert left Warren Baxter at home. Baxter was never told why, nor did he ask. Baxter wondered whether Woolpert thought four black players were too many to take on that trip. Baxter surmised that Woolpert took the three starters he needed to make sure USF won the tournament.

When the players and coaches arrived, hotel employees told Woolpert that the black and white players would be unable to stay together. The whites could stay but not the blacks. A visibly upset Woolpert told the team that the black players would have to stay in a college dormitory that had been closed for the holidays. When the players learned about the housing situation they just looked at each other. They talked about it, and then a white player—Rudy Zannini—said, "I move we all stay on campus, as a team." Perry said, "All in favor, say 'aye,'" and the vote was unanimous. They were the only ones in the building. It was so cold in the dorm that the players slept in their warm-up suits. Woolpert and Guidice stayed in the dorm as well.

"Up to that point, we had been a team that was looking for unity," Zannini said. "When we came back from Oklahoma City, we knew we had it. It was the greatest psychological injection of confidence. You could feel it. We knew nobody was ever going to put us in a position where we felt like beggars or second-class citizens."

"That was when we bonded," said Bob Wiebusch. "We realized we had something special." Woolpert kept Perry in the lineup even though the game was in the South, and he was "aware of the quota thing of never allowing more than one or two blacks on the floor at the same time. . . . We had enough confidence in ourselves not to be bothered by the aura of the situation, and I was no longer color conscious."

When the Dons took the floor for practice at the Oklahoma City campus gym, people started throwing coins on the floor and calling them Globetrotters, which was "about the nicest thing they called us," Jones recalled. Jones became upset, but Russell picked up the coins and asked Woolpert to hold them for him. Russell told Woolpert, "Save this money for us, Coach, and we'll spend it on a victory party." Regarding that incident, Woolpert said, "That may have been the toughest part of the tournament for the cool Dons." When he was inducted into the college basketball Hall of Fame in 2006, Russell remarked about such incidents, "Those were times when you grew up fast."

In the All-College Tournament the Dons methodically destroyed previously undefeated and favored Wichita State 94–75 (Mullen scored 28), Oklahoma City 75–51 (Russell scored 25), and George Washington 73–57 (Russell scored 23 and grabbed 30 rebounds)—three victories that boosted their confidence and made them believe they could play against anyone in the country.

Against George Washington, Russell dominated Joe Holup, whose best shot was a left-handed hook. Russell rejected it almost every time Holup took a shot. "The guy couldn't believe it, the tactic was so radical," Woolpert said. Mullen also held high-scoring Corky Devlin to 12 points. ✴

A *Daily Oklahoman* sports writer described Wichita State's defeat this way: "The fabulous Russell, who has springs in his feet and perpetual windmill arm motion packed into his six-nine frame, had the crowd bug-eyed with his slapping in of follow shots, stealing the ball in midair, deflecting a raft of Wichita pokes, and all the while stowing in the points with a wide variety of pitches." That wasn't what Wichita State coach Ralph Miller had expected. According to Russell, Miller's brother had scouted USF in its game against UCLA. His brother told Miller, "This team cannot give you a game. They can't shoot, they're not very good defensively, they have a tall black kid who jumps but can't really do anything." The Dons opened up a 25–3 lead in the first ten minutes and led Wichita 53–26 in the third quarter. Then Woolpert removed his starters. Although Woolpert was happy with the way his first team had played, the reserves fell short of Woolpert's and the first team's standards. "The first string was upset, not because they didn't play the fourth quarter, but because the reserves allowed too many points."

After the win over Oklahoma City, one of the team's players turned to Jones and said, "You guys are really terrific. What a great team you've got." Jones said he never forgot that piece of unexpected sportsmanship. The Dons also received some unexpected praise: A spectator—legendary coach Hank Iba of Oklahoma A&M—called Stan Buchanan, "the most finished ballplayer from a coach's standing" he had ever seen. The praise verified that USF was more than a one- or two-man team.

After routing George Washington, the players drank beer and goofed around in their dorm to celebrate their victories. Five-foot-six Rudy Zannini even donned Bill Russell's overcoat, put on his homburg, and paraded around the room to the laughter of his teammates. "Tonight," Perry said, "is the beginning of the dynasty." Little did he know.

It's realistic to remember that these were young men who may not have understood the ramifications of what was happening to them. They just wanted to play ball. "Our thoughts didn't get that far (to be aware of their ultimate impact on the game)," Jones said. "I didn't consider it any big deal. We were teammates, white and black."

Russell sat out a total of twenty-five minutes in the three games. Still he gathered almost as many rebounds by himself as the three opposing teams' total rebounds. In a stretch of four games dating back to the UCLA matchup, Russell committed only one foul despite blocking numerous shots.

After the tournament Russell commented that he was disappointed in the defensive play of the opposing teams. "I had heard so much about their great play and their fine defense that I guess I expected something spectacular. Actually, most of the teams didn't have much of a defense. All they thought about was shooting."

"During the course of our record-winning streak," Guidice recalled, "we often were criticized for playing a 'soft' schedule. I think the Oklahoma City tournament . . . [was] a solid rebuttal. The USF team felt it could handle anybody." The pollsters thought so, too, as USF moved up from seventeenth place to seventh place after the tournament.

"The country wasn't really ready for us," Perry said. "People who didn't know our team did not understand the tremendous human relationship we shared. Whenever we got into crisis situations, we'd call time-out and Russell would say, 'All right, let's go do it!' So, we'd start shooting and he'd stuff our missed shots into the basket. He'd block shots, and we'd run off 8 points, and the other team would say, 'My God! What happened?'" Perry gave himself the job of building up Russell's confidence, calling out for his teammates to get the ball "to the big man" and constantly praising Russell for his efforts.

In USF's 10-1 record so far that season, Russell made 54 percent of his field goal attempts, scored 244 points for an average of 22 a game, and averaged 21 rebounds a game. Woolpert got on his guards to step up their defense. "Go after that ball," he said. "Make some blind stabs. If you miss, just remember you have the big guy parked under the basket as a second line of defense." The guards—Jones, Perry, Bush, and others—became even more aggressive in their defense. Often, too, that gambling defense gave the guards an opportunity for a quick release down court to get a pass from Russell after a blocked shot or a rebound.

Perry's job was to be the disruptive influence on the court. He raised havoc with opposing players bringing the ball up court, customarily clapping his hands to distract them. "I'd get in the way of people," he said. "I didn't score much, but I kept people from scoring." Said Jones, "Our confidence came from being able to disrupt the other team."

The Dons still were primarily recognized only on the West Coast where they played most of their games, traveling up and down the state by train or bus. For longer trips the team flew. Meeting travel expenses was difficult for a small Jesuit college playing big-time basketball. The team often carried only the essential number of players to get them through away games. It helped that they didn't have to worry about Russell fouling out; he averaged just two fouls a game. One team manager is said to have joked that he had to hide in the train bathroom during trips because the school couldn't afford his ticket.

Back home the Dons waltzed through the first of three rounds of the CBA schedule—even a sprained ankle that kept Mullen out for two weeks didn't slow them down—and they moved up in the national polls. Russell had nothing but praise for Jones's play in those games. "You know when he is going to pass, but not where the ball is coming from, over either shoulder, behind his back. That's the mystery." Woolpert complimented Mullen: "Jerry has as much or more desire as any player I have ever had the pleasure to coach and see. He has a quick mind, good hands, and top mobility." Guidice told Woolpert after the Dons began winning by double figures, "The only thing you've got to do is to get a couple beers and a cigar, and sit down and enjoy the game."

Stanford and California from the Pacific Coast Conference were next up for the Dons, both games being played at the Cow Palace. While USF had dominated other teams, during this home stand the Dons discovered their ability to go on runs of 10–20 points while holding the other team scoreless. The Dons had moved up to no. 2 in the rankings, while Stanford was 12-3. Almost fourteen-thousand fans filed into the Cow Palace—the largest crowd in Bay Area basketball history—to watch what the *San Francisco Chronicle* called "the game of the year." USF jumped off to a 31–12 lead, substituted heavily, and wound up winning 76–60.

Stanford coach Howie Dallmar said after the game that the Indians (they didn't become the Cardinal until 1981) had used three defenses against the Dons—the zone, man-to-man, and panic. "[Russell] plays at seven-foot-ten. He can jump higher than any man in basketball. [George] Mikan would get 4 field goals a game off Bill. He might get the ball, but he just wouldn't get the shots." Dallmar said teams need fifteen minutes just to adjust to Russell's presence. "It takes at least that amount of time for the opposing players to fully comprehend what they are up against in Russell."

During the Stanford game Russell made what he considered "the best single play I ever made in college." A Stanford player stole the ball at half court and was on his way for a lay-up. He was so far ahead of everyone that nobody decided to chase him. As the player went loping down the court, Russell left the center position near his basket and ran after him as fast as he could. The player's lead was so big that he wasn't hurrying. When Russell reached half court he was flying. He took one long stride off to the left to change his angle and then went straight for the bucket. When the player went up to shoot in the lane, Russell jumped from the top of the key. The player lofted the ball so lazily that Russell was able to slap it into the backboard before it started down. The ball bounced back to Jones, who was trailing the play. The key to the play was Russell's step to the left. Without that maneuver he would have fouled the player by landing on him after the shot. By stepping left he had just enough angle to miss him and land to the player's right without a foul.

The next night, against Cal and Woolpert's former teammate and predecessor Pete Newell, USF scored the first 20 points with fans chanting, "We want a shutout." Again, however, Woolpert substituted freely as the Dons won 84–62.

The Dons, who were now on a fourteen-game winning streak, moved up to no. 1 in the polls in early February after Kentucky, the previous top team, lost to Georgia Tech. "If we hadn't made it, our kids' disappointment would have been worse than the added pressure [that] the no. 1 rating carries," Woolpert said. The Dons had not received a single vote in preseason polls.

"There shouldn't be any question about the rating if the polls mean anything at all," Woolpert said. "This is the first time I have said publicly that we should be on top. I realize the pressure will be terrific. Still, the boys have been dreaming and working toward this goal. They think they are entitled to no. 1, and I agree with them." He said the team was hungry. "Their appetites are such that they can do a lot of eating before they're filled up." Woolpert also answered critics who said the Dons had played a weak schedule. "We've met some top teams, and we seem to play our best game when the opposition is tough. I wouldn't call UCLA, Oregon State, George Washington, or Stanford weak sisters."

K. C. Jones received a surprise in mid-February when the Los Angeles Rams picked him in the thirtieth round of the NFL draft. The Rams remembered Jones from his days as an All-City player at Commerce High School before he gave up the game for basketball. Had USF not discontinued its football program in 1952, Jones might have achieved fame on the gridiron instead of the basketball court. Jones said that after graduation he was going to enter the army where he might get a chance to return to football. "Then I'd like to give the professional game a whirl before trying pro basketball."

USF's style of play often forced its opponents into a slow-down game to try to keep the game close. "No matter what they tried," Jones said, "we were going to pounce on it, then smother it. That became our foundation of confidence."

In mid-February Hank Luisetti, who became a legend for developing the one-hand shot at Stanford, weighed in during an interview on the state of basketball in the 1950s. He didn't like what he saw except the way USF played. "Today the players just want to shoot," he said. "They lack defense and team play, but USF is a notable exception. Phil Woolpert obviously spends a lot of time on defense. But name me another team that has each man playing with left hand kept high and weaving to bother the offense." Luisetti said the Dons brought back the "good old days [when] basketball was played tough. And all of us old-timers are coming out from under the rocks to see them. They make you play an entirely different game from what you want to. . . . It's a throwback to the old-type defense, the kind where it was tough to get a shot away, let alone make one."

A week later retired California coach Nibs Price voiced the same opinion. "I really enjoy watching the Dons if only for their defense." Price also railed against the seven-minute stall carried out by UCLA against Stanford that week. "It's not a game when you do that," he said. A similar stall by Price's successor at Cal, Pete Newell, in the 1955–56 season against USF lives in infamy in the Bay Area.

USF raced through the remaining CBA schedule allowing no team to come closer than 10 points. Tom Meschery, who played for St. Mary's across the Bay in Moraga, said about the Dons, "We all knew how great USF was defensively. Russell and K.C. couldn't hit the ocean if they were standing on the beach. They were terrible shots, and they still could beat you." Russell was named a first-team All-American and Woolpert was named Coach of the Year by the United Press. Woolpert outpolled Kentucky's Adolph Rupp by 140–28.

Russell was denied the honor of being the best player in the CBA. That award went to Santa Clara's Kenny "Big Cat" Sears, a six-foot-nine senior, who edged Russell by one vote of sports writers and broadcasters. Sears, who showed speed, agility, and a good outside shot, averaged 21 points a game and shot 52 from the floor. The award to Sears came despite the fact that Russell's team beat Sears's team twice, that his team won the national championship, and that Russell had outscored him 31–19 when the Dons beat Santa Clara 66–52 on February 14, their last meeting of the season. Fifty years later, when Santa Clara retired his number, Sears remembered that he was shocked he had won the award. "I couldn't believe it," Sears said. "Bill Russell was a great player and he had some amazing numbers. I didn't know what to say when they called my name. It was nice to be honored and to even be compared to a player like him." The choice of Sears opened up another wound between Russell and Woolpert. Russell thought he should have been named Player of the Year and blamed Woolpert for failure to praise him in the press.

Russell complained that Woolpert "never once in all the years said that I did a good job, a bad job, or a mediocre job." He wrote in his first autobiography that Woolpert told him years later that he never praised him "because I had too much going for me to need that sort of thing. The hell I didn't. Anyone wants to be told they are doing a good job. . . . It hurt me plenty that Woolpert didn't." Russell was further incensed when a sports writer called and told him that he was okay and that if he would try harder next year, maybe he'd win it then.

Russell told Woolpert that he wouldn't show up for the presentation banquet. "Bill, that'll demean you as a man; it's beneath you," Woolpert said. Russell refused to go until the day of the dinner. Once there, he was called on to make a speech. "Honest to God, he was wonderful," Woolpert said. "He made a great, laudatory talk about Sears. [Russell is] a fine, unpredictable guy."

Russell said he was offended that he was a runner-up to Sears after the year he'd had. "It was then and there that I determined, 'If my team wins a championship every year, there's no quarrel anyone can come up with to deny me that.'"

Years later Russell adopted a more mature outlook toward awards. "Winning is the only thing I really cared about," he said after he retired from the Boston Celtics, "because I found that when I left the cocoon of my childhood I came into the world and found that individual awards were mostly political. But winning and losing, there are no politics, only numbers. It's the most democratic thing in the world. You either win or lose, so I decided early in my career that the only really important thing was to try to win every game because when I got through, no one could say, 'Well, he was the best athlete at this or that.' The only thing that really mattered was who won—and there is nothing subjective about that."

USF's success in basketball drove a campaign to start raising funds for a gymnasium for the school. There was no question a gym was needed. The 1949 NIT champions had practiced in an old barn with a leaky roof on Page Street. The current Dons shared time with high school players, practicing in the St. Ignatius High School gym. The new $700,000 gym was to be called the San Francisco Memorial Gymnasium. It wouldn't be built until after Russell left USF and would be nothing fancy by modern standards, but it is still being used today.

A backer named J. T. O'Connor wrote to the *San Francisco Chronicle*, "I was amazed to find our 'number one' Dons have no gym. It would be a fitting reward for the Dons who have brought much prestige to Bay Area basketball to start a 'Dollar for the Dons' gym collection." He enclosed his dollar. The hope was that the gym could be built before the next season started, but it wasn't completed until the 1958–59 season. K. C. Jones said years later, "Russell built the gym we never played in. He's the main reason any of us got anywhere, with his attitude and ability, how he played."

Before the Dons could worry about a new gym, they had business to take care. They had to get ready for the NCAA tournament to test themselves against the best teams in the country.

# ELEVEN
## The Trail to the Title

"K. C. Jones was the best defender baseline to baseline I have ever seen."
—Hall of Fame coach Pete Newell

Until 1950 the NIT dominated college basketball. Many of the top teams at that time were not members of the NCAA. If a school wanted national exposure for its program, the best place to get it was at the NIT in Madison Square Garden in New York City. The best teams—many of them independent schools—played in the NIT while the also-rans took the court in the NCAA, which was scheduled after the NIT instead of going head-to-head with such a prestigious tournament. Some teams played in both, such as Utah, which was eliminated in the first round of the 1944 NIT and then went on to win the NCAA title.

The tournament began to lose its luster after 1950, the year CCNY won both tournaments and big-time college basketball subsequently became threatened with extinction. This happened because CCNY and players from three other New York schools were indicted for point-shaving by keeping the winning margin of scores down to benefit gamblers who gave them money. Between 1947 and 1950 thirty-two players from seven schools around the country were implicated in fixing at least eighty-six games. The scandal erupted in 1951. Much of the point-shaving had taken place during NIT games.

As a result many schools decided to stay away from the NIT and opted for the NCAA tournament, which drew a bigger field and was spread throughout the country, with sixteen teams representing two districts—East and West. The NCAA set the date of its tournament to coincide with the NIT so that no school could play in both tournaments. As the *San Francisco Chronicle* noted, "The . . . winner of the NCAA is America's champion basketball team, and the winner of New York is champion of Madison Square Garden." In addition, by the mid-1950s the NCAA made it virtually mandatory for any team winning its conference to participate in the NCAA playoffs. Today the NCAA operates the NIT, and it is relegated to also-ran territory, even allowing teams with losing records to compete.

With a 23-1 record, USF had to choose between playing in the NIT or the NCAA. USF received some feelers from the NIT, and Woolpert put a vote before the team: Did they want to play in the NCAA or the NIT? A vote of the players was split 7–7. USF administrators and the Board of Athletic Control, not the players, decided to play in the NCAA, which was Woolpert's preference.

Before the decision Woolpert noted, "Neither the players nor myself have a thing to say about it. While a trip to New York would be nice, my personal feeling is that we should keep faith with the CBA [the new conference USF had joined] by accepting an NCAA bid if offered. The CBA champion has gone to the NCAA regionals during the two years of the league's existence, and I don't think we should break the precedent."

The Dons' performance in 1955 and the following year gave new luster to the tournament, sending it on its way to today's level where it is as important a sporting event as the World Series, the Super Bowl, and the Olympics. The big difference is that in 1955 the take from the game was $12,000 for the Dons—far below the millions of dollars teams earn today.

The NCAA tournament got its biggest boost when television began broadcasting games among the final four teams. Superstar Tom Gola attracted the first television coverage of the championship game in 1954. Undoubtedly the luster of USF's exciting brand of basketball also brought TV's attention to the game.

As the 1955 NCAA tournament opened, USF drew West Texas State (now West Texas A&M) in a matchup at the Cow Palace. The Buffaloes (15-7) had won a coin flip with Texas Tech after the two teams tied for first in the Border Conference.

Utah coach Jack Gardner complained that the NCAA gave USF an unfair home-court advantage by allowing the team to play at the Cow Palace, which was ironic in that USF lacked a home gym. Playing close to home wasn't unusual. Oregon State, for example, met USF in a later game on its home floor. Certainly in today's tournament no team would be allowed the home-court advantage.

Gardner may have been trying to distract the Dons, who might become Utah's opponent in the second round. A cry of home-court advantage had a hollow ring to it. The Dons never got to practice in the Cow Palace, relegated as they were to St. Ignatius or at times to the Boys Club's Page Street gym.

If Gardner distracted the Dons, it didn't show as they ran up a convincing 89–66 victory over West Texas State behind Russell's 29 points. During the first three minutes of the game, a Buffaloes player submarined Russell, knocking him flat on his back. Two minutes later, it happened again—this time by a different player—with Russell hitting his head on the floor. Neither

foul hurt Russell, but he went to the bench for some rest. Referees warned the players that another such move would get them
ejected from the game. "I was quite upset about it at the time,"
Woolpert said, "and let the [other] coach know I didn't like what
happened. . . . This ended up arousing our team, and we turned
what was a close game and a game of concern to me into quite
a rout." Mullen thought the Texans were trying to scare Russell,
but it only fired him up. Jones said, "It was rough out there. What
they were trying to do with the physical style of play backfired,
because it angered us and made us play harder."

The next step in the West regional play promised to be more
competitive. In the second round the Dons faced Gardner's Utah
Utes in Corvallis, Oregon. Utah had beaten defending national
champion La Salle earlier in the year. The Oregon State Beavers,
who had the home-court advantage, were to play Seattle (22-5),
which beat Idaho State 80–63. Utah was ranked fourth in the
nation with a 23-3 record, and Oregon State was ranked eighth,
based in part on the Beavers' handily beating UCLA in two straight
games in a Pacific Coast Conference best-of-three playoff.

Before the Utah game the Dons learned that a Salt Lake City
paper had published a scouting report saying that Perry shouldn't
be in the starting lineup and that Russell's only weapon was a
tip-in. The report also described Buchanan "as just being out
there to fill out the team," and "if you have to get the ball, foul
Buchanan first, as he is not used to shooting, and Russell second,
as he doesn't seem to be good at the foul line." The scouting report
proved to be the incentive the players needed.

Russell had a habit of vomiting before most games. "Sometimes I'm a total wreck," he said, "but I don't let the other guys
know it." Guard Hal Perry said he would yell at Russell before a
game, "Hey, Bill, it's time to do your thing."

If ever there was a game in Russell's career that could give
him the heaves, this was it. *San Francisco Chronicle* columnist Art

Rosenbaum wrote that Woolpert often would get a premonition of what was to come based on Russell's behavior before a game. "If Big Bill is extremely fidgety, if he can barely lift himself to his feet when the call to court arrives, all will be well. . . . Russell has his own special kind of tenseness before a big game. Imaginary aches overwhelm him. He discovers his socks are bunched under his shoes. Then his shorts chafe against his skin. Suddenly he notices that one shoulder droops lower than another, accompanied by iron-hot pain. He arises, barely, from the bench, but his left knee buckles under him. He looks down to see if his knee is attached to his leg, but he can't see because his eye is twitching." Then, miraculously, Russell would recover just as the game began. Guard Gene Brown also threw up once in 1956, but he had drunk some Pepto Bismol before a game.

The Dons took the floor on March 11 against the Utes and blew the game open in the first half, leading 41–20. Russell didn't start the second half because he apparently vomited blood in the locker room at halftime. The Dons didn't have a physician traveling with the team, so Woolpert sought advice from an Oregon State doctor, who recommended against Russell's resuming play. With Russell out, Utah rallied to within 8 points. "Russell called over to me a couple of times," Woolpert said, "and said he felt fine." A frantic coaching staff was looking for another opinion on whether Russell could play. Perry said they shouldn't have worried, that Russell was suffering from emotional stress, and that he always vomited before games. "And he always snapped out of it," Perry said. "I told the coaches to let him play. I knew him well enough that he could play."

The coaches found a doctor in the stands—Dr. Ed Duggan, a USF alum—who was traveling with the Dons' booster club. The doctor told Woolpert that Russell had eaten some raw steak in a pregame meal and that was what he had coughed up—not blood. "We put him back into the game. Bill was a wild man, and we ended up coasting," Woolpert said. USF opened a 15-point lead and rolled to a 78–59 win. Forward Gordon Kirby had another explanation. He said flu had swept through the team the week before the tournament began. In fact, Kirby missed the next game against Oregon State because of the illness. Al Brightman, the Seattle coach whose team was beaten handily by Oregon State, watched the USF–Utah game. "After what I've seen, maybe it's just as well we didn't win and don't have to play this gang tomorrow."

Up next was Oregon State—with its seven-foot-three giant Wade "Swede" Halbrook—which had beaten Seattle 83–71. Would Russell be up to the task? He'd never faced anyone of that size. UCLA coach John Wooden wondered whether Russell might well be meeting his match. "Russell's the greatest defensive man I've ever seen," he said, "but I don't see how he can cope with Swede Halbrook. Russell is the only man capable of playing Halbrook man-to-man, but Halbrook is easily 50 percent improved over last year. I don't believe that Russell will be able to block Halbrook's shots or control him like he does smaller men."

The Dons received a morale boost before the game when a *Portland Journal* photographer asked Halbrook to hold a basketball as high as he could, and then asked Russell to reach for it. Russell calmly reached up with his long arms and put his hand on top of the ball as his teammates stood by gasping. "Needless to say, that picture never was shown in any of the Corvallis newspapers," Woolpert said. "And our players later said we had beaten Oregon State right there."

Oregon State had improved since its early-season game against USF, which the Dons won easily, 60–34. Halbrook had been academically ineligible for that game, but with his return came a renewed confidence for the Beavers, especially after manhandling UCLA in the Pacific Coast Conference playoffs.

As he often did, Russell went on the court and began the intimidation tactics that many of USF's opponents had watched in awe. Russell, still in his warm-up suit, leaped high over the basket, sometimes with his armpits over the rim. In the past when he did that, according to the team's manager, Bill Mulholland, "most of the [other teams] were mental basket cases." Whether that would work against the Beavers remained to be seen.

Soon after the game began, forward Jerry Mullen went down with a sprained ankle. He was only out four minutes, returning after trainer Vince Briare taped his ankle, but the ankle slowed him down, and it pained him to jump. The Dons needed Mullen, who Woolpert said had turned into a defensive player second only to Russell. With Mullen out the Beavers began collapsing on Russell. Not only did Oregon State have the towering Halbrook, it also had a seven-footer in Phil Shadoin. They ignored Stan Buchanan, who wasn't normally a good shooter, so they could collapse on Russell. Buchanan missed his first two shots, but his teammates told him to keep shooting. "We didn't care if he made the shots or missed them," Jones said. "We needed him to take the shots and force Shadoin away from Bill."

Buchanan drained his next two twenty-footers, and the Beavers abandoned their collapsing defense. "It was an insult," Woolpert said. "Their information was wrong [about Buchanan's shooting]." Buchanan made only two shots that night, but they were enough. As Halbrook and Russell battled for rebounds, the Dons left the court at halftime with a 30–27 lead. This game wasn't turning out to be a walkover.

In the second half USF had an 8-point lead with less than two minutes to play. Then the referees' calls started to go against USF. Oregon State closed to 57–55 with thirteen seconds left after a limping Mullen dropped in one of two free throws. He had almost collapsed on his first free throw. Jones rushed over to him, but Mullen waved him off and calmly sank the second one.

USF called a time-out as the crowd of eleven-thousand two-hundred roared. Then came a bizarre incident that resulted in a foul even though time was still out. K. C. Jones was running back on the court looking over his shoulder when he ran into Oregon State's Bill Toole. Actually it was a technical foul, which meant that the Beavers would not only get a free throw but would also retain possession of the ball. Oregon State's captain, Reggie Halligan, sank the free throw, and the Beavers got the ball out-of-bounds at half court. The other official said it was a bad call, according to Woolpert, but Jones "never said a word. His heart must have been in his shoes."

Oregon State coach Slats Gill called a time-out to set up a play. Later in his career, Gill was asked to name the three best clutch players he had ever coached. One of them was on the floor that night, five-foot-eight Ron Robins. Robins ran to the corner—his favorite spot on the floor—where he received a pass from Toole. Robins fired up a two-handed set shot that bounced off the back of the rim and then off the front and out. "I felt it was good," Robins said. "I had confidence it would go in and knew right away it was a basket. It almost was."

Halbrook grabbed the rebound. As Halbrook brought the ball down, Jones stripped it from him with seven seconds left. Officials called it a jump ball, hardly a situation that boded well for USF with the seven-foot-three Halbrook jumping against six-foot-one Jones. In those days, there was no possession arrow. The two who were tied up with the ball jumped against each other at the Oregon State free-throw circle. But Jones tipped the ball on the way up and got away with it, directing it toward Hal Perry, who doubled over and held the ball until the game was over. Perry swears to this day that a voice told him, "'You stand here. The ball will come to you.' I was a stickler for everybody being in the right spot at the right time, and I knew where I was supposed to be. But this voice told me to stand in the position where the forward should be rather than the guard spot. It was the biggest voice I ever heard, so I did." "Did you see that K.C. jump?" Russell asked after the game. "Man, if I could jump like that." How did Russell do against Halbrook? He scored 29 points; Halbrook scored 18. Russell out-rebounded Halbrook 16–10. Oregon State's Gill said after the game that it was "the best game any team of mine has ever played."

Immediately after the game Mullen boarded a flight home to have his ankle worked on while the team traveled by train. USF team physician James Daly doubted that Mullen would play again in the tournament. "I don't see how he was able to play at all in Corvallis," he said. "Although there is no fracture, the sprain is very bad. The ankle needs a lot of therapy, rest, and a lot of luck. Even so, he has only a 50–50 chance."

Back in San Francisco, Vince Braire took Mullen to get treatment by a trainer at the Olympic Club. This trainer had a reputation for putting athletes back on their feet. Briare, whose knowledge was pretty much limited to taping ankles and patching up minor cuts, was astonished by what he saw. Mullen walked into the club on crutches. The Olympic Club trainer worked on Mullen's ankle with his hands for about forty-five minutes. When he was done, Mullen walked out of the club without crutches.

Following his near-miraculous recovery, Mullen joined the team as it boarded a TWA plane headed for Kansas City, Missouri, to play the Colorado Buffaloes (18-5) in the semifinals. The Buffs would have preferred to play in the NIT—primarily because they wanted to go to New York rather than Kansas City—but as league champions the NCAA required them to play in its tournament.

The Dons climbed the plane ramp with Russell holding aloft a bunch of shamrocks the day before St. Patrick's Day. Mullen was expected to sit out that game but to play the next night either in the championship game or the third-place game. The Dons were surprised to find themselves favored to win it all. The other two teams in the final four were La Salle—which won the tournament in 1954 and was ranked no. 2 behind USF—and Iowa.

Compared to the Oregon State game the rest of the tournament was a breeze for the Dons.

Replacing Mullen in the starting lineup was Bob Wiebusch, who substituted for Mullen when he dislocated his elbow earlier in the year. Wiebusch was a good outside shooter, and like Buchanan, had played for Woolpert in high school. He had Woolpert's confidence. In fact, Woolpert relied heavily on his second team, one many called the best second string in the country. Several of the players could have started for many teams. Woolpert constantly bolstered his reserves by telling them they played against the best team in the nation every day in practice.

Colorado coach Bebe Lee predicted a Buffalo victory. "We are going to win that game against San Francisco . . . a lot of people are going to get a surprise." Lee said Colorado's three strong points were poise in the tough going, defensive play, and rebounding. Colorado hadn't been out-rebounded by any team during the year. The Buffaloes' leading scorer was six-foot-seven Burdie Haldorson, who averaged almost 22 points a game. Colorado had upset Bradley in the Midwest regional to move into the final four. Lee, who played with Hank Luisetti at Stanford, had some scouting help from another former teammate, Bob Burnett, who had coached at Stanford as well. He knew what to expect from USF.

Haldorson remembered that he and his teammates were in awe of Russell. "You were afraid almost. You're thinking, 'I wonder if he can block my hook shot?' Before the game, to be honest with you, Bill was not that imposing, looming figure like he played. I guess I expected to see someone ten feet tall. He looked kind of like me."

Ever the nervous Nellie, Woolpert worried about how the Dons would fare even during the pregame warm-ups. He paced the floor mumbling, "We don't look good warming up. I don't know what it is, but we don't." He called Russell over to tell him to sharpen up. "But coach," Russell replied, "we don't want to show 'em all our stuff before the game starts."

Just before tip-off Tommy Harrold—the Buffs' fastest player and best ball-handler—was warming up when he slipped on a soft drink someone had spilled on the court, severely spraining an ankle. He was forced to sit out the game. "I wouldn't be so brazen as to say with Tommy we could have won the game," Haldorson recalled. But he wondered.

Mullen suited up for the game but sat on the bench. USF found itself behind 16–15 with five minutes to go in the first half. K. C. Jones had picked up his third foul. It looked like trouble for the Dons. Colorado had a more deliberate tempo at coach Lee's direction. "They even played slower than we did," said guard Warren Baxter.

Baxter took over for Jones, and Woolpert inserted Mullen. The Dons had opened a 25–19 lead when Baxter hit a forty-foot shot from almost half court just before the halftime buzzer, only a 2-pointer in those days. Woolpert returned to his original start- ing five in the second half, and the Dons stretched their lead to 44–26 before coasting to a 62–50 win. Although Mullen failed to score he played thirteen minutes, which told Woolpert that his ankle would hold up.

Russell and Jones showed the Colorado players a style of bas- ketball they had never seen before. Russell electrified the crowd when he used a reverse dunk, going up in the air and slamming the ball through the hoop with his back to the basket. It was a shot for the highlight films.

"Did you ever see anything like that?" a San Francisco reporter asked Harry Hanin, a Globetrotters scout.

"No," Hanin said, "and I never saw anything like *him*, either."

Early in the second half, Jones stole a pass, raced down court, and used all of his six-foot-one height to dunk the ball. Haldor- son said the Buffaloes had never seen dunks like Russell's and Jones's. "It was the game played at a different level than what we had ever played against," Haldorson said.

While they were in Kansas City, before the tournament even started, more discrimination marred the Dons' visit when several of the players, including K. C. Jones and Hal Perry, went to a movie. The blacks were expected to sit in the rear of the theater. In defiance their white teammates surrounded them with two on each side and two in front and back to isolate them from others in the theater. Nothing more happened.

USF played La Salle (26-4) for the title the next night, as the Explorers got by Iowa 76–73 behind superstar Tom Gola's 23 points and 13 rebounds. The Dons had played some strong players but none like Gola, the six-foot-six center who had led the Explorers to the NCAA title the previous year and had been called the greatest player of all time. He was the first player in collegiate history with a combined four-thousand career points and rebounds. He scored 2,462 points and pulled down 2,201 rebounds. Some players scored more points and some grabbed more rebounds, but no one got more of both.

After their game, Gola and his teammates gathered in the stands to watch the USF–Colorado game. Gola wasn't impressed with Russell's shooting but said he had "defensive ability that nobody could match." This was La Salle's first look at the Dons. Teams didn't have films to watch in those days, and scouting was limited. La Salle used an employee of the school's public relations office to scout teams. La Salle coach Ken Loeffler would give him ten or twenty dollars and send him off to scout a team.

Word on the street was that La Salle was going to win easily. The afternoon before the game, as Russell and Ross Guidice walked through the lobby of the hotel where both teams were staying, they saw Gola approaching with Loeffler. "Well, we're honored," Russell said to Guidice. "Here comes Mister Gola." Loeffler overhead him. "You'll be seeing a lot of him tonight, fella," he said to Russell. Loeffler's reply shocked Russell. "He took me kind of seriously, didn't he?" Russell said to Guidice. "You know, they might be just a little worried."

Gola said years later that he did not know Russell up to that point. "The West Coast was not a prominent factor in NCAA basketball," he said. "People aren't going to believe me, but Bill Russell was not a big name on the East Coast until they beat us in that tournament. . . . Russell didn't know me, and I didn't know him. In fact, I had never seen Bill Russell until we met in the lobby of the hotel."

The day after the game, a newspaper photo revealed just what Loeffler had in mind for the Dons. The picture showed Loeffler briefing his team, with a blackboard in the background. On the board were tips next to their names on how to handle four Don regulars. Next to Russell's name was simply the word, "Gola." "I think we just can't let that big guy get the ball," Loeffler told the press. "Once he gets his hands on it he shoots. We can stop him only by keeping the ball away from him." As for Russell's thoughts on Gola? "I'm not worrying about Gola, I'm just trying to help my team win. But, man, that Gola would really give the coach an ulcer."

Loeffler should have been a little more worried than cocky. Yes, he had Gola, but he couldn't have known what Woolpert had planned for him. Earlier, he had said that Mullen would guard Gola, but Mullen was still slowed by his sprained ankle. Woolpert had a surprise ready. Not even Woolpert's players knew. He didn't want Russell to guard Gola because the La Salle star was going to bring the ball down court. Jones would guard Gola if he stayed outside, and if he moved inside around the key, Russell would pick him up.

"Coach Woolpert, as always, had done his homework," Jones said. "He knew what made La Salle tick, inside and out. And with that in mind, he turned to me and said, 'You're going to guard Gola.' It was a bit of a surprise . . . but the coach didn't want . . .

Russell to guard Gola because Gola would take Russell away from the basket."

The move came after assistant coach Ross Guidice suggested it to Woolpert. The head coach liked the idea and asked his two former teammates from Loyola—Pete Newell, his rival across the Bay at Cal, and Scott McDonald, who became the Loyola coach—what they thought. They agreed with the plan.

When Woolpert told Jones he was going to guard Gola, Jones said, "That just blew my whole dinner. But it didn't ruin my appetite for basketball." It didn't seem to bother the coaches that Jones, at six-foot-one, was five inches shorter than Gola.

Jones's plan was simple: He wanted to keep Gola outside and not allow him to penetrate to the basket.

How was I going to do this? I had to make my ego match his. I knew as much about defense as he did about offense, and he was a very good offensive player. I figured it would be a wash right there. If your ego doesn't match that offensive player's ego, you have a problem because that's when fear comes in. But I had no fear when we took the court for the game I'll never forget. . . . I found that I could keep Gola from driving around me because I was quicker, and I would harass him when he put the ball on the floor. That meant he would have to shoot from long range or try to drive and pass the ball off. I knew guarding him would be difficult, but I also knew that if he posted up or got by me, Russell would be there. And he did get by me a couple of times. But you're never going to stop a great player one-on-one. The important thing is, I was not intimidated.

Woolpert was nervous before the game, pacing the sidelines. Russell came over, put his arm on Woolpert's shoulder and said, "Sit down, coach. It's not even going to be close."

In the first half Jones limited Gola to 9 points, and the Explorers went scoreless from the floor during the last nine and a half minutes before scoring on a dunk at the buzzer. USF left the court with a 36–24 lead. That drew Woolpert's wrath in the locker room. The coach said Jones had done a great job of guarding Gola, but then he started to get overconfident. Jones went for a steal, and Gola took it the length of the court. Whatever Woolpert said, it worked. "For the rest of the game K.C. restricted his defensive skills to taking care of Gola," Woolpert said.

Thirteen-year-old Billy Packer, who went on to be a longtime Final Four commentator for CBS, was listening to the USF–La Salle game on the radio when he heard about "this guy Russell" who kept blocking Tom Gola's shots. Gola was one of Packer's idols. His father coached at Lehigh and remembered when La Salle scrimmaged against Lehigh. "I remember thinking Tom Gola was an amazing player. . . . I was awed by Gola." While listening to the game, Packer remembers thinking, "That's impossible [blocking Gola's shots]. No one can do that to Gola. Who the hell is this guy Russell?"

USF's dominance continued in the second half, sparked by Jones's steal and dunk. Not only were dunks rare in college basketball, it was even rarer for someone Jones's size to jam the ball. Jones, with Russell's help, held Gola to 7 second-half points, committing only two fouls for the game. Jones held Gola to 8 points below his scoring average as he chipped in 24 points of his own. The Dons won 77–63. Russell finished with 23 points and 25 rebounds. La Salle coach Loeffler was stunned by Russell's play. ◂

When the game ended, USF rooters—about 225 made the fourteen-hundred-mile trip to Kansas City—hoisted Russell on their shoulders in celebration. Later Russell prowled around with a green and gold tinfoil hat and clowned for the crowd. He leaped into the stands to pump his father's hand and hugged his stepmother. He found Woolpert and hugged him while pounding his back. He then sprinted across the court twice to shake Gola's hand. Jones's mother joined the celebration along with Mullen's parents, his brother who was a priest, and his sister and her husband. Mullen's brother proudly bore a badge that said, "Father Mullen—I am the brother of Captain Jerry Mullen."

Woolpert said the key to the game was Jones's defense on Gola, which allowed Russell to hang around the basket. "We were able to win rather handily this way," Woolpert said. "We actually were coasting toward the end of the ball game."

The *San Francisco Examiner*'s Bob Brachman wrote, "It is hard to believe that this completely homegrown gang of kids who started as virtually 'nothing' had come upon everything. But if you look back on their untiring labors, their sacrifices and, above all else, their determination to overcome all obstacles on the road to success, then it should not be such a surprise. No greater team, as such, ever existed."

Regarding Gola and Russell, the *Philadelphia Inquirer* wrote, "Tom Gola, La Salle's three-time All-American, tallied 16 points and rang down the curtain on four seasons of magnificent basketball. But his work was futile and completely overshadowed by Russell."

Russell's 118 points for the tournament broke Gola's record of 111 set the year before, and the USF center was chosen the tournament's MVP, the first African American to earn the honor. But Russell thought the award went to the wrong player. "I always thought K.C. got a bad deal," Russell said. "They gave me the MVP, but it should have gone to K.C."

Gola agreed, saying Jones was the USF player that hurt La Salle the most. "And K.C. was not known for his shooting ability. Russell guarded [backcourt standout] Alonzo Lewis and also sagged off back into the pivot on me. Alonzo just couldn't hit his shots [Lewis made only one field goal]. If he had, it would have been nip-and-tuck all the way. . . . There's always a guy on

1. Phil Woolpert coached the Bill Russell–led Dons to two national championships. He is shown here in the St. Ignatius High School gym where the Dons practiced because they had no gym of their own.

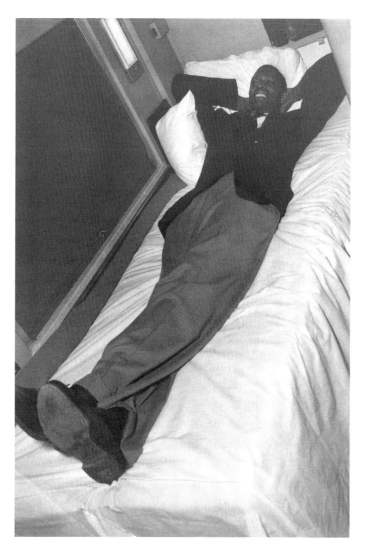

2. Hotels had to provide extra long beds to accommodate the lanky Bill Russell.

3. Bill Russell grabs a rebound in the opening round of the 1955 NCAA tournament against West Texas State.

4. The Dons arrive at the San Francisco International Airport, where six-hundred fans greeted them. Forward Jerry Mullen holds aloft the championship trophy while Bill Russell holds a basketball. K. C. Jones is in front of Russell. Phil Woolpert is the last one leaving the plane at the top of the steps.

5. The 1954–55 USF Dons: (*front, from left*) Hal Perry, Steve Balchios, Rudy Zannini, and Warren Baxter; (*middle row, from left*) Tom Nelson, Stan Buchanan, Bill Russell, Jerry Mullen, Jack King, and Bob Wiebusch; (*back row, from left*) Coach Phil Woolpert, K. C. Jones, Dick Lawless, Bill Mallen, Bill Bush, and manager Ray Healy.

6. The starting lineup for the USF Dons during the 1956 NCAA tournament: (*from left*) Hal Perry, Mike Farmer, Bill Russell, Carl Boldt, and Gene Brown. K. C. Jones was ineligible to play in the tournament because he was a fifth-year senior who had played one game as a junior before missing the rest of the season with appendicitis.

7. Coach Phil Woolpert hollers instructions from the bench as reserve forward Mike Preaseau looks on.

8. K. C. Jones drives to the basket against the St. Mary's Gaels in his last collegiate game, played before the largest crowd ever to watch a basketball game in northern California.

9. Mike Farmer (17) and Bill Russell (6) outjump UCLA's Willie Naulls for a rebound in the finals of the Holiday Festival Tournament in New York City's Madison Square Garden.

10. Bill Russell throws up a hook shot over UCLA's Willie Naulls in the opening game of the 1956 NCAA tournament.

11. Bill Russell admires his stuff shot in the semifinal game against Southern Methodist University in the 1956 NCAA tournament.

12. Bill Russell blocks a shot by Iowa's Sharm Scheuerman in the 1956 NCAA tournament championship game, won by the Dons. Scheuerman went on to coach Iowa from 1959 to 1964.

13. Players carry coach Phil Woolpert off the court after the Dons defeated the Iowa Hawkeyes in the championship game of the 1956 NCAA tournament. Among the players were John Koljian (in the warm-up jacket) and Mike Farmer (*far right*).

14. Team celebration after the Dons won the 1956 NCAA national championship. Among recognizable faces are: Bill Russell (*far right*); Coach Phil Woolpert (*back row, fourth from left with his left arm raised*); Carl Boldt, Mike Farmer, and Gene Brown (*to Woolpert's right*); San Francisco mayor George Christopher (*front row, with arm raised*); K. C. Jones (*kneeling, in front of Russell*); Hal Perry (*kneeling behind Christopher with his right arm on Christopher's shoulder*); Assistant Coach Ross Guidice (*back row, with a rectangular badge on his lapel*); and Warren Baxter (*number 11, behind Jones*).

the team who sacrifices, who plays good defense, who moves the ball, and that was K.C. He was the catalyst for those San Francisco teams."

As for Russell, Gola said, "I have played against bigger men, but never one who jumps with this guy. I've seen most of them including the seven-footer Walter Dukes, but I've never met a guy like this. All you can do is leap and hope." Years later he was asked how the Dons would stack up against today's teams. "Oh, nobody could touch Russell," he said.

Loeffler said after the game, "It was a hopeless feeling, seeing Tom [Gola] going up time and again and not being able to get his hands on the ball. I've never seen a better college team."

Woolpert heaped praise on Jones. "Jones played the greatest basketball game seen by anyone at any time. Jones did things they have never seen in the middle West. His blocks, his leaps to wrest the ball from Gola—you'd say they were impossible, but K.C. did them with the greatest game of his life."

Despite Russell's success, Gola was named Player of the Year after the tournament. "It hurt," Russell said. "It seemed like an injustice," he wrote in *Go Up for the Glory*. Russell had averaged 21.5 points and 20 rebounds a game, a statistic that ranked him second in the nation even though he played no more than 80 percent of any game.

Woolpert, of course, was ecstatic with his team's success. "I said before the season started I wouldn't trade my fourteen players for any other group in the United States. Now I want to say that goes double, triple, and quadruple. They are wonderful, wonderful boys."

Years later, he said, "My greatest reaction to winning . . . the title was numbness. We finally had done it. It was something I never had really figured on or counted on. And yet I knew or felt at the time that it was inevitable because of the team we had at the time. I thought it was a super team. I still do."

Because of Russell's play, there was a buzz about some rule changes before the next season. The legendary Kansas coach Phog Allen was at the USF–La Salle game. Asked what he thought about Russell, he said, "I'm for the twenty-foot basket." That would not happen, but other changes did come about.

# TWELVE
## Russell Brings about Rule Changes

"To this day, I think he's the player of the century."
—Ross Guidice

If the Dons were weary from two games in two days it didn't show. The team and two-hundred backers partied until well after midnight at their Kansas City hotel. The highlight of the night was Hal Perry, the accomplished musician, who pounded away on the drums to jazz music while Warren Baxter jitterbugged with K. C. Jones's mother, Eula. Reportedly nothing stronger than soda pop was served.

The Dons arrived at the San Francisco International Airport at 5:10 p.m. the next day to find that a crowd of six hundred had burst through police lines to swarm the plane, chanting, "We want the Dons." Captain Jerry Mullen was the first off the plane, holding aloft the championship trophy. "This is the night we break training," Mullen shouted over the exultant crowd. Russell followed, holding the game ball high above his head. Fans carried several of the players on their shoulders off the tarmac to a wait-ing bus. From there nine San Francisco motorcycle policemen provided an escort of two-hundred cars to the USF campus about fifteen miles away. The celebration continued on the campus. K. C. Jones ran into one of his teachers and asked, "Does this rate us an A in that test Thursday, father?" The priest replied, "The test shouldn't be any tougher than La Salle."

The next day the team left the USF campus at 10:30 a.m. for ceremonies at city hall and then a parade through the downtown district. As the *San Francisco Chronicle* described it, "Handsome young men perched smiling in the sunshine on the tops of convert-ibles. Pretty girls in light spring dresses sat beside them clutching bouquets of daffodils, the delicate flower of springtime that blooms green and gold, the USF school colors." As ticker tape and confetti rained down, the parade wound its way to the Fairmont Hotel atop Nob Hill where Mayor Elmer E. Robinson feted the Dons with a luncheon and a speech before a crowd of one thousand. Robinson stood on a stool to meet Russell "on even terms."

After countless dignitaries heaped praise on the Dons and called for contributions to the campaign to build a gym for the "Homeless Dons," Woolpert addressed the crowd. "When we went back to Kansas City, we didn't pick on any turkeys," he said. "We beat the best." He introduced each player with special remarks. About Perry he said, "If those people back in Kansas City have trouble getting a comb through their hair, it's because Hal Perry is still in it." Bill Bush, he said, "has a 98.2 grade aver-age. He's the brains of the outfit. We're grateful to him for his contribution to the team . . . and for his intellectual comments on my mistakes." K. C. Jones, he said, "does the best soft-shoe routine you'll ever see. He's the boy who looked Tom Gola in the eye and put him in his place." He praised Russell for his modesty "with all this unaccustomed adulation," calling him a wonderful public relations man for USF.

While the Dons celebrated, praise was pouring in from around the county over Russell's play. A lead paragraph in a March 22, 1955, United Press story atop page one of the *San Francisco Chronicle*'s Sporting Green read, "All-America Bill Russell of USF is so good he may revolutionize the game of basketball." The story went on to quote various coaches paying tribute to Russell's skills.

"You wouldn't believe it unless you'd seen it," said Lou Rossini of Columbia. "Russell does things on offense that could revolutionize the game. A lot of us coaches came away with a new concept of basketball and with mental notes on how to coach our own big men to play as nearly like Russell as they can." He called Russell a master at dunking the ball, saying, "His timing and ability to get into the air are amazing. Not only that, but his hands are so quick the scorers could not be sure whether the original shooter should have got credit for the goal or Russell the 2 points on the rebound," Rossini said.

Eastern coaches clamored for games with USF so fans could see Russell. "It will be a treat for anyone, anywhere, to see the San Francisco team," Rossini said. "There's more to it than Russell, too. The team is superbly coached, and the talent is well balanced."

As the new NCAA champions celebrated, talk began to heat up about the need for rule changes to limit the way Bill Russell operated around the basket. Many of the nation's coaches met during the tournament each year to discuss how the game of basketball was working, and 1955 was no exception. Bill Russell's play was one of the main topics of conversation.

One rule that drew a lot of attention, but for which no action was taken, was the one-and-one free-throw rule that changed beginning in the 1954–55 season. Opinion was divided. The rule gave the player who made the first free throw a second shot. The previous rule was that the player got a second shot only if he missed the first one. Woolpert thought the bonus shot was too much but that one shot alone was inadequate. He favored a compromise plan by Pete Newell, calling for a jump ball after the first free throw was made.

A proposed change to put a shot clock into effect like the NBA used—maybe not twenty-four seconds but thirty or thirty-five—was rejected. Committee members also considered calling technical fouls on teams that deliberately slowed down the game. The opposing team would either get free throws or be allowed to take the ball out-of-bounds. The committee said one conference would try out the proposed change during the following season.

Woolpert opposed technical fouls because they slowed down the game. "The tactic of stalling is a legitimate strategy of the game," he said. "It shouldn't be outlawed any more than the double reverse in football or the intentional pass in baseball. USF is a control team. We feel the fans find us as interesting to watch as a team that runs up 110 points—maybe more interesting. We give them suspense. Basketball isn't all about shooting."

Woolpert had used a seven-minute stall early in his college coaching career and was on the receiving end of a stall by Newell when they coached against each other the next season. The proposed rule change came up once again in 1956. It was a strategy used to combat Russell.

Coaches put two rule changes into effect for the 1955–56 season, one of which became known as the "Russell Rule." It widened the free-throw lane from six feet to twelve feet to keep offensive players from camping under the basket for easy put-backs or tip-ins. Understandably, Woolpert didn't like the new rule, not because it would hinder Russell but because "the continuous rule changes are ruining the game." He accused the NCAA rules committee of trying to pattern the college game after the pros, "and the pros are dying on the vine. . . . We had a better game twenty years ago before they started to monkey around with it."

Woolpert said that a rule change that affects big men has "no logic to it at all. This change won't hurt Russell a bit; in fact it'll make him even better next year because it'll give him more room to operate. They've been jamming up on him this season." Russell had a good laugh over the rule change. He knew that lengthening the foul lane didn't have anything to do with his play. If anything it helped him on defense because he agreed with Woolpert that it spread the offense out more. And he had another good laugh over the name of the new rule: the "Russell Rule." "It couldn't have been better had I written it myself." Russell said the rule change was overdue. "They should have done it a long time ago," he said at the time. "In fact, I think it has helped me a lot. If a big man can move, he'll still be the dominating factor. But if he's slow, the rule will kill him. They didn't get the tall ones with that change. They just killed the fat ones. . . . It doesn't bother me a bit. In fact I figure I might be more effective in the long run." And he was. Woolpert couldn't have agreed more. "He's so much the fastest of the big men that now he'll just leave them further behind," he said.

To further explain what he called absurd rule changes, Woolpert proposed the hypothesis of changing the rules to eliminate height differences between two players. He used as an example the Gola-Jones match-up. "We took our chances with Gola, who's a tremendous player, and Jones did a great job on him. We didn't ask anybody to change the rules . . . La Salle played its game and we played ours, which is the way it ought to be."

Three rule changes that might have been expected didn't happen until after Russell graduated. The most important was offensive goaltending. Russell feasted on errant shots that he steered into the basket while they were in the cylinder. It was a tactic that most coaches deplored. Some say the rule was enacted to stop Wilt Chamberlain when he moved up to varsity play at Kansas for the 1956–57 season.

"They are trying to legislate defense instead of coaching it," Woolpert said. He had two solutions to handling a big man who guided in shots: "The first one is, don't schedule his team. The second is, if you have to schedule them, work up a defense aimed at cutting down his effectiveness."

Pete Newell said, "[USF players] would throw the ball towards the basket, and Bill would guide it in. Or they'd shoot the ball over the basket from the corner, and Bill would catch it and dunk it. That's when people said you couldn't catch the ball in the cone. Catching the ball in the cone had never been a problem before."

Phog Allen, who coached Kansas during Russell's era, noted the incongruity of allowing offensive goaltending but not defensive goaltending. "San Francisco was good, yes. Bill Russell put a funnel and sideboards on the basket. If they let this fellow tap or dunk it in, they ought to let the other fellows bat the ball away." Interestingly, Allen said this just after he had recruited the seven-foot-one Chamberlain to Kansas.

"Russell showed how asinine the rule is regarding goaltending," Allen said. "A defensive player can't touch the ball while it is above the goal, yet Russell and other offensive players can do whatever they want." Allen said he had conducted a survey in 1937 that showed there were only eight players that year between six-foot-eight and six-foot-ten. But in another survey he did in 1955, he found there were 130 players between six-eight and seven-three. "I say let's quit discriminating against the defense," Allen said. "I never attend rules meetings any more because they are so asinine and silly. It makes you lose faith in the coaches' gumption."

*San Francisco Chronicle* sports editor Bill Leiser questioned whether the rule was necessary. "No other athlete ever bothered anybody scoring in that way," he wrote. "If anybody else, anywhere, can master this fabulous play, we'd like to see him do it, and we don't care for whom he plays. Why legislate against a man because he can jump higher than anyone else? Jumping is a part of basketball and a part of shooting, isn't it?"

The second rule that went into effect after Russell graduated was a prohibition against throwing the ball from behind and over the backboard from out-of-bounds. Grabbing the ball after it came over the backboard and slamming it through was one of Russell's favorite plays.

A third rule that allowed one player from the home team and one from the visiting team to take the two spots nearest the basket on free throws was changed to give the opponent of the free-throw shooter both spots. Under the old rule a free-throw shooter could try to miss to the side of the basket where his teammate, Russell for example, could easily tip in the shot. Or even an errant shot could fall right into his teammate's hands. The rule change allowed the opponent of the free-throw shooter to put two bodies under the basket to prevent easy put-backs.

In addition the NCAA rules committee prohibited a player from moving into the free-throw lane until the free-throw shot had hit the rim or backboard. This also was an attempt to keep big men from dominating under the boards.

If the rule changes were designed to slow down the Dons, it wouldn't happen. USF was to begin the next season right where they left off with the addition of two strong forwards to replace the graduating Buchanan and Mullen.

# THIRTEEN
## The Machine Rolls On

"We were like rock stars. Every place we played we packed [them in]."
—Carl Boldt

The Dons returned for the 1955–56 season with high expectations of repeating as national champions. Bill Russell, K. C. Jones and Hal Perry were back, and USF was drawing national attention. Several teams wanted to schedule games against them, and the team would be playing at home to full houses.

The Dons faced the problem of replacing two starting forwards who had graduated. Up from the freshman squad came six-foot-seven Mike Farmer, a rugged player who today would be called a power forward. Farmer hailed from the East Bay oil refinery town of Richmond, where he starred for Richmond High School. He had planned to attend USC, but after watching a USF–Santa Clara game, he said, "I was hooked." Like Russell, Farmer credited freshman coach Ross Guidice with helping him improve his game.

Farmer had played center in high school, but he was too good to play second string behind Russell, so Woolpert switched him to forward. This meant he would have to learn to play facing the basket. He now had to learn to drive and to face-up with a jump or set shot. Woolpert said later in the season, "He has adapted himself as a forward remarkably well. Before this, he was always working around the basket. He's a very aggressive player, shoots well from outside, and continues to improve every game."

Joining him was six-foot-five Carl Boldt, a small forward. A junior college transfer, Boldt was one of three military veterans on the team. Boldt had played ball in the army at Fort Ord in Monterey, California, with Don Lofgran, who starred for USF's 1949 NIT champions. Ross Guidice had seen Boldt play and recommended a scholarship for him. "When I was recruited out of the army, Ollie Matson [the former Dons football star] told me to go to USF because of Russell. Ollie said I'd be playing for the greatest winner of all time," Boldt said.

Boldt had played at Glendale College in Southern California from 1951 to 1953, ranking eleventh in scoring with 1,024 points in sixty-three games, before going into the army. He made the army All-Star team and then joined USF for the 1955–56 season.

Boldt recognized that his job was not to move onto the championship team and "start trying to take over. There's a job to be done here, and I want to do it," he said. Woolpert described Boldt as "an excellent outside shooter, a good hustler, can go either to his right or left, although he favors right, is a top hustler and ball handler, and has improved tremendously on defense. His trademark [is] a quick release set shot from fifteen or twenty feet from the basket."

Perry said years later that the Dons started an "all-minority" team because in addition to the three black players, Farmer was a Cherokee Indian and Boldt, who was white, lived in a Los Angeles foster home with a black family for nine months. But Boldt said that Perry "was the only non-minority on the team because [his] background and experience were totally white."

Another newcomer to the varsity, guard Gene Brown, a six-foot-three African American, was an All-City player two years in a row at George Washington High School in San Francisco's Richmond District. Assistant coach Ross Guidice had seen Brown play and invited him to a workout. USF was the only school to recruit Brown.

Two years before, in his first year, Brown was the leading scorer for the USF freshmen, but he ran into academic troubles. The next year, Woolpert told Brown that he needed to go to junior college and get his grades up. Brown sat out the next basketball season, the championship year, to improve his studies and then returned to USF with three years of eligibility remaining.

With Brown the Dons had five African American players on the roster, including Warren Baxter, a holdover from the championship team. Baxter was the only black player recruited by any major college, lending credence to the blacks' belief that they were discriminated against because of skin color.

Brown would become a key player in the 1956 NCAA tournament, replacing K. C. Jones, who had been declared ineligible. The CBA had granted Jones another year of eligibility—his fifth at USF—because he missed all but one game all of the 1953–54 season with the appendicitis attack, but the NCAA refused to allow him to play in the tournament.

Brown more than adequately took Jones's place. At least two players thought that Brown, a more athletic player than Boldt, should have started during the season. They had the feeling that Woolpert was leery of starting four blacks or even playing four blacks at one time, although that happened occasionally on the road.

Moving up from the freshman squad in addition to Farmer and Brown was Hal Payne from Oakland. Payne was an unlikely team member. He didn't play basketball at Castlemont High School in Oakland because he was too short, so he served instead as the ball boy. After high school Payne joined the navy where he grew to five-foot-eleven and made the all-navy team as a guard. He had scholarship offers from Stanford and Cal but joined the Dons after watching Russell, Jones, and other players practice during a recruiting visit. Payne was twenty-three when he enrolled at USF. Vince Boyle, twenty-four, of San Francisco was the old man of the team. Boyle had played for USF's freshman team in 1950 and then went into the navy for four years, where he gained valuable experience playing basketball. He returned to USF as a walk-on.

Transfers included Mike Preaseau from Redding, who moved up from Menlo College. Preaseau was one of the rare players Woolpert actively recruited. He had planned to attend Stanford, but after Woolpert visited with his parents, who were devote Catholics, he chose USF. He also had scholarship offers from Cal and USC. A teammate at Menlo, John Koljian, transferred to USF with Preaseau. Koljian, from Springfield, Massachusetts, was the only out-of-stater on the team. He, too, had planned to attend Stanford, but Indians' coach Howie Dallmar urged him to get a year's experience at Menlo first. Koljian was one of the few players in the country who still used the then-out-of-favor two-handed set shot.

The Dons found a way to get away from basketball by enjoying time exploring the city, especially the five African American players who were enjoying their celebrity. As might be expected, the white players hung around together, especially those who made lifetime friendships while attending St. Ignatius High School. On campus the black and white players mixed with other students. Off campus the blacks and whites went their separate ways. Russell often went home on weekends. But on the road, black and white players often roomed together—K. C. Jones and Carl Boldt, for example.

Russell loved to go to the coffee houses in San Francisco's North Beach. Although he didn't consider himself a beatnik, he found himself drawn to their culture. He would go to nightclubs like the hungry i to hear Mort Sahl, Pete Seeger, Josh White, and the Limelighters. "My nights in such places had stretched through the middle of the 1950s, at a time when the white society seemed dormant. . . . Those coffee houses opened up a new way of thinking for me, because I saw that at least some white people got the blues, were irreverent, and weren't tight-assed. Most of the white folks at USF walked like moving fence posts, while the beatniks looked more like sloping question marks." Sometimes the African American players would go down to the predominately black Fillmore District to get barbecued ribs, sweet potato pie, and red soda.

The Dons approached their much-tougher schedule that year one game at a time, putting aside thoughts of winning another championship, maintaining their winning streak, or even having a perfect season. "Every game was like a war," Jones said, "every loose ball a battle; and we were trying to stop a man from shooting; you get the ball, you run—there's no time for thinking about the end of the year."

Boldt, Brown, and Farmer made USF a better shooting team than the '55 champions as well as "a more poised and smart team, more efficient," Woolpert said. Guard Warren Baxter told the school newspaper, *The Foghorn*, that the 1956 team was stronger, "but last year the team was a closer knit outfit because most of the players were together longer."

The team didn't have set plays—not even for Russell—but the players tried to "balance the floor," Boldt said—meaning that they tried to spread evenly around the court. Most of the time, they passed the ball until they found a teammate with an open shot.

In those days players could get off set shots, something never seen in today's game.

Three games into the 1955–56 season, the Dons traveled to play in the Chicago Invitational Tournament against Marquette, which had a twenty-two-game winning streak dating back to the previous season. It was the closest game of the season as the Dons squeaked past the Warriors by only 7 points.

"It was a tough basketball game," Woolpert said. "We didn't appear to be playing our normal game. . . . I didn't know until after the end of the season that a member of our traveling party, . . . unknown to me, had taken the entire basketball team on a tour of a Chicago museum. They were gone four and a half hours, up and down stairs and everything that goes with touring an outstanding museum. It was understandable why they were a little below par in their game."

The Marquette coach might have been wise to listen to the advice given in a scouting report about the Dons. It said, "After seeing this team my advice to you is simple: Cancel the game."

Then the Dons dismantled DePaul 82–59. Russell blocked 15 shots and was selected MVP. "They could name the score against any college team in the country," said one coach. DePaul coach Ray Meyer said Russell was as good as the Minneapolis Lakers' George Mikan but that he preferred Mikan's traditional way of playing. "He backed his defensive man under the basket and always had such good position," he said.

The Dons also stopped off at Wichita, Kansas, to play the University of Wichita before a crowd of 10,500 in the school's new field house. The Dons won 75–65, but the fans' booing each time Russell and Jones went to the foul line marred the game. "I assume the home crowd was booing the officials for making the call," said Woolpert, who noted that the crowd also cheered when Russell and Jones left the floor.

Wichita coach Ralph Miller apologized after the game. He told the Wichita press that it was a "bad situation" and that school officials should have had better control of the crowd "if they want teams to continue playing here."

USF players must have wondered what they faced next when they headed to New Orleans to match up with Loyola of the South two days before Christmas.

# FOURTEEN
Into the Deep South


"Self-respect and dignity do not have to be sacrificed in
order to see a sporting event."
—From the *Louisiana Weekly* about a December 4, 1954,
game against the integrated La Salle basketball team

The Supreme Court's landmark *Brown v. Board of Education* decision in May 1954 mandated school desegregation, although
most schools interpreted the decision as not affecting athletic
endeavors.

Loyola University of the South in New Orleans, a Jesuit school,
was different. It was one of the first schools in the South to accept
black students when it allowed religious women of color to enroll
in 1952, followed by black laymen and women. Desegregation
came almost without protest, with only a handful of students
leaving the school. "We have lost a few contributions to our college funds, but that is a small price to pay for a clear conscience,"
said the school's president, Andrew Smith.

Then, beginning in 1954, Loyola went out of its way to schedule at least three games against teams with black players, one of them the national champion USF Dons. The Reverend Ralph Tichenor, USF's athletic moderator, said, "You know, one of the big reasons we booked a date in New Orleans with Loyola was that school officials there said we could help along their integration program." The Loyola athletic director, the Reverend James J. Molloy, said, "[Neither Tichenor nor I] expect any difficulty in any way for the game."

Woolpert saw it as a chance to make a statement. He said the game with Loyola would show that "whites and Negroes can play together" in the segregation-conscious South. "We thought it might help relations. Loyola is the first team in that area to open up mixed petition. I guess it was something of a small crusade on our part."

Perhaps only Catholic schools could have gotten away with playing an integrated basketball game in the South. This decision also came at a time when several northern schools' only protest came when they refused to play southern schools that would not play racially integrated teams.

The first of the three games Loyola played was December 4 against the 1954 NCAA champion, La Salle—another Catholic school—and marked the first interracial game in the South. La Salle had one black starter, six-foot-two sophomore Alonzo Lewis, who starred alongside All-American Tom Gola.

The Loyola–La Salle game went off without incident. All of the six-thousand five-hundred theater-type seats in Loyola's new field house were sold on a first-come, first-served basis. This meant that there were no special sections for black spectators. "Comfort facilities" were integrated as well.

On December 4, 1954, the black newspaper the *Louisiana Weekly* noted, "Negro sports fans of this community and surrounding areas will for the first time be treated as normal, ordinary human beings. For the first time in the lives of many they will not have to face the humiliating experience of being segregated, 'going around the back,' and 'up the alley' to sit up in buzzard's roost to see a sporting event."

On December 20, 1955, Loyola played host to the second integrated basketball game in the South. Players from Bradley University in Peoria, Illinois, traveled to New Orleans to take on Loyola in a game that was not without incident, and it gave the Dons some cause for concern. They were scheduled to play Loyola three days later.

A black Bradley player, Shellie McMillon, fouled out of the game and gave the fans the middle-finger salute. The crowd, which had cheered him during the pregame introductions, jeered him by singing "Bye, Bye, Blackbird," and the band struck up "Dixie," the marching song of the Confederate army. But Molloy said nothing racial was to be made about the song, as it was Loyola's "secondary fight song," which was played regularly at games. "It was merely coincidental that the Loyola band played 'Dixie' when the spectators were standing and at the same time the Bradley cager fouled out."

Loyola coach Jim McCafferty said he thought McMillon, a six-foot-five sophomore, "lost his head" and became "disgusted" with himself for his fouls. He said he doubted the incident would affect future games in which Loyola played against African Americans. In a side note McMillon led Bradley to an NIT championship in 1957. Press accounts said that a second Bradley player, Curley Johnson, behaved like "a gentleman" but was booed when he left the game because of McMillon's behavior.

When Woolpert heard about the incident, he called his assistant, Ross Guidice, who was scouting the game. Guidice saw no cause for alarm. "Come on down," Guidice said. "There's no problem." Woolpert said McMillon had only himself to blame. "I don't think my boys will act like that," he said. Guidice told

Woolpert he didn't think the reaction toward McMillon was racially inspired. "Our boys are pretty much of the opinion that the Bradley boy stepped out of line," he said.

Molloy issued a 450-word statement that said the occurrence with McMillon was "not in any way a 'racial' incident. . . . It is not unusual for a boy in a moment of anger or disappointment to forget his sportsmanship." Bill Keefe, sports editor of the *New Orleans Times-Picayune*, wrote that McMillon showed poor sportsmanship. And the consensus is that he was not booed any more than a white player guilty of his offenses would have been booed, making it evident that the fact he is a Negro had nothing to do with the criticism directed at him."

Woolpert said he would pull his team off the floor if a racial incident occurred. "I don't know exactly what happened down there," he told the *Associated Press*. "Maybe it was actually a small thing. But I'm going to find out. And when I do I'm going to put the decision up to the players. If they vote not to play, that's it." Guard Gene Brown, who had regained his eligibility, said, "There was some talk that we might not play, but at a team meeting, we put it all behind us." He said the togetherness of the team "got us through those troubled times."

The Dons and their five black players would be in New Orleans just three weeks after the national attention accorded Rosa Park's arrest for refusing to give up her seat on a bus in Montgomery, Alabama. Tensions were running high in the South following the one-day Montgomery bus boycott on December 4, 1955, often called the beginning of the civil rights movement.

When the Dons arrived in New Orleans one of the first things they saw were restroom signs in the airport for "white" and "colored." "That shook some guys up," Jones said. Woolpert told the black players that they should never go anywhere by themselves, that they shouldn't make eye contact with white people, and that they should "walk on thin ice." The situation in New Orleans was in keeping with the "racial etiquette" of the Jim Crow era in the southern and border states.

When they went to the hotel, a hotel employee told them, "Get those Negroes out of here." Woolpert was livid and asked the black players to wait outside while he made arrangements for them to stay at Xavier University, a Catholic school for blacks, while the white players stayed in the hotel.

The blacks were forced to use segregated restrooms, restaurants, and public transportation. On one occasion when the team tried to eat breakfast together in a restaurant, Woolpert told the waitress they wanted to eat as a team. The waitress relented, offering to allow the whites to sit on one side of the table and the blacks on another with a partition down the middle to separate them. Woolpert decided against that and ordered box lunches to eat as they took a bus to the airport.

Guard Warren Baxter, who grew up in New Orleans, tried to placate them. "These were kids from the Bay Area who had no idea of the magnitude [of racism in the South]," said the team's manager Bill Mulholland. "Everyone wanted to get the hell out of there," said Tom Nelson. Guard Gene Brown said the black players were uneasy about the racial situation in the South. The lynching of a fourteen-year-old black boy, Emmett Till, four months earlier was on their minds. "We just tried to block out all those things and just play ball," Brown said. "We thought [the treatment of blacks] was wrong, but we just accepted it," forward Steve Balchios said. "That was one situation where the coach wouldn't have to give us a motivating speech," Russell said. Unbeknownst to the coaching staff and teammates, Carl Boldt and forward Bill Mallen chose to stay in a black hotel in New Orleans to show support for their teammates. No one knew until the next day.

The night before the game the team attended a banquet at Booker T. Washington High School honoring Baxter, who had played on the state championship team in his junior year. His high school coach, Charles Perkins, called him "one of the all-time Booker T. Washington greats. . . . [He] is undoubtedly one of the best dribblers in college basketball. He's gifted with a great pair of hands and a natural touch."

Each player took the floor to say something at the banquet. Russell wrote down some notes before he spoke and then got up to say, "Ladies and gentleman, the greatest place to be from in America is New Orleans." And then he gave a speech designed to defuse any racial tension the gathering may have felt.

A write-up in the black newspaper the *Louisiana Weekly* praised the USF black players but made no mention of race until the eighteenth paragraph of a twenty-two-paragraph story. In those final paragraphs the *Weekly* mentioned race a total of three times, referring to "sepia players," "Negroes," and "a tan forward."

In the locker room before the game, Woolpert told his players to play a hard clean game to avoid an incident like the one during the Bradley game. "He told us to keep our cool," Brown said.

As the game started, the integrated crowd of five-thousand five-hundred—about a quarter of them black—almost dutifully cheered the black players. Friends and family of Bill Russell and Warren Baxter attended the game. Russells drove in from Monroe, Louisiana, and Baxter had family in New Orleans. The tension before the game was thick.

At tip-off the referee made an attempt to mimic black speech patterns. The referee said, "Y'all know what we're doing when this ball is up in the air." The Dons took it out on the other team as the Loyola players tried to intimidate the USF players with racial taunts.

With about seven minutes gone in the game, Russell and two Loyola players went for a rebound. Russell got the ball and the two Loyola players crashed to the ground. Russell looked at them, put the ball down, and helped the players to their feet. The crowd roared with approval. After fifteen minutes the Dons led

24–8 and stretched it to 31–12 at halftime. When Russell, Jones, and Warren Baxter left with the game safely in hand with eight minutes to go at 48–23, they received a "thundering ovation." The reserves mopped up, and the final score was 61–43. "They're great," McCafferty said, "that's all there is to it."

Russell was gracious after the game. "It was a wonderful crowd, a wonderful crowd," Russell said. Woolpert said his players weren't tense because of the Bradley incident three days earlier. "Three of the boys found it difficult to adjust to southern restrictions," he said. "But Loyola played a clean game. And the crowd was as nice as could be."

An article in the *New Orleans Times-Picayune* the day after the game made no mention that any of the USF players were African Americans, but curiously the only USF players mentioned were four of the five black players. Perhaps one of the reasons the integrated game failed to attract much attention was that basketball was not nearly as popular as football in the South.

In 1956 Louisiana enacted a law banning both interracial athletic events in the state and black and white spectators from sitting together at events. The law came about because Louisiana didn't want black players accompanying their football teams to the Sugar Bowl. It is unclear how much impact the USF–Loyola game had on enactment of the law, but it almost certainly didn't go unnoticed. Not long after the law passed, three northern schools protested by withdrawing from the Sugar Bowl Basketball Tournament, even though they had no black players. Loyola and Centenary College, a Methodist school also in Louisiana, bowed to the new law and canceled games against northern schools.

The San Francisco Dons had made their statement, and they were ready to leave the South. It had been an eye-opening experience, not only for the black players but for the white ones as well. Up next was a trip to New York for the Holiday Festival Tournament where they got to show their game in Madison Square Garden.

# FIFTEEN
## Holiday Travel and the Stall

"The duel was going to be between Russell and me. I knew it, and he knew it, too."
—Tom Heinsohn

The tail end of the toughest road trip the team faced came at the Holiday Festival Tournament in Madison Square Garden in New York City. In none of Russell's books did he mention his experiences in Louisiana. But the visit to New York rated mention in his autobiography *Go Up for Glory*.

"It was my first visit to New York," he wrote. "I was not impressed. I wasn't accustomed to the cold and the snow and I was on the spot again. Everyone wanted to see how I'd make out in the big leagues." He made out just fine.

The Dons' first game was a rematch with La Salle, although Tom Gola had graduated and coach Loeffler had left for Texas A&M. The game started poorly for Russell. He missed his first three in-close shots and the crowd jeered him. But then he got in his rhythm. "The looks of doubt and derision changed into looks of incredulity and awe," wrote *Sports Illustrated*'s Roy Terrell. "All the words they had read had not really prepared the crowd for Bill Russell."

The Explorers gave the Dons a terrific battle, leading 45–43 four minutes into the second half. Then USF tightened its defense, and Russell took over on offense. The Dons pulled away 79–62 as Russell wound up with 12 blocked shots, 26 points, and 22 rebounds.

In the semifinal game, USF played Holy Cross and its star, Tom Heinsohn, who later became a teammate of Russell's and Jones's with the Celtics. Russell could tell during warm-ups that the Holy Cross players were "totally distressed." At the jump ball to start the game, Russell noticed that Heinsohn was not intimidated. He would yell at his teammates, "Don't be afraid of Russell. Don't be afraid of him."

During the second quarter, as the two teams were walking to the foul line, Heinsohn dug an elbow deep into Russell's stomach. It hurt Russell, but he didn't let on. He waited for his time. A few minutes later, Russell fired a ball to Jones in the corner. He knew that everyone would be looking at the ball. That's when Russell struck. He jammed an elbow into Heinsohn's stomach, and Heinsohn collapsed to the floor. He had no trouble with Heinsohn after that.

Later in the game Jones backed into a corner to try to make a long set shot. Russell leaped into the air, caught it, and stuffed it through the basket. Heinsohn was astonished. "No one I ever played against had done anything like that before," he said.

It was one of many times Russell redirected errant shots into the hoop. "It started by accident," Russell said. "I was under the basket, getting pushed around as usual, when I saw a shot coming which was off the mark. So I helped it go into the bucket. Since it worked, I decided we might as well use it more regularly." After Russell graduated, this goaltending maneuver became illegal.

Early in the game Russell decided to give Heinsohn a message. The Holy Cross player went up for a hook shot, and Russell knocked it three rows into the stands rather than direct it down court as he usually did. Heinsohn was astonished and frustrated. He went over to the team bench and kicked it so hard he put this foot through it. "What I saw was an incredibly talented and athletic big man, but more than that a player bringing a new dimension to the game that had never been seen before," Heinsohn said. "He could absolutely control a game defensively. I knew right there he was something special."

The Crusaders led the Dons 23–14 at one point, but the Dons closed to 32–29 at halftime. Then Heinsohn picked up his third foul and went to the bench. With him out the Dons started to pull ahead. Heinsohn came back assigned to go head-to-head with Russell. "I gave him one of my best fakes," he said. "Faking was a big part of my game. When I faked guys, that was it; goodbye, see you later. I'd be gone. So now I faked Russell—left him standing five feet away—and I headed for the basket when, whack, he batted the ball right out of my hands. I was thinking, 'Where the hell did he come from?' Then he did it again, and again, and now I was shooting hook shots and the sonofabitch was blocking those. He did a total number on me; just took my game away. I didn't score a single point in the whole second half."

USF won 67–51. Russell finished with 24 points and 22 rebounds while Heinsohn, considered to be the best player on the East Coast, was held to 12 points, all on outside shots. In the crowd that night was Celtics coach Red Auerbach, who had heard of Russell but came to scout Heinsohn. Despite Heinsohn's poor night, Auerbach didn't lose interest in him. But Russell impressed him immensely. Auerbach decided then and there to find a way to get him on the Celtics squad. K. C. Jones, too, but he was a lesser-known quantity, and Auerbach would have a little trouble drafting him.

Three future hall of famers played in that game—Russell, Jones, and Heinsohn, all of whom wound up playing for the Boston Celtics. The future stars drew a horde of professional scouts to the game, including Eddie Gottlieb, owner of the Philadelphia Warriors. About Russell he said, "You'd have to take him [in the draft] if you could get him. Otherwise, he'd be sure to cause you trouble." How right he was.

In the finals USF faced its old nemesis, UCLA. The Bruins no longer put fear in the Dons as they had during the first game the year before. The two teams were staying in the same hotel in New York City. Crowded conditions forced them to eat their pregame meal in the same dining room. The Bruins were solemn, paying attention to business, while the Dons carried on, joking and needling each other, even having a few choice words for Coach Woolpert, who was celebrating his wedding anniversary.

Then the two teams took the court, and the Dons routed UCLA 70–53 as Jones held Taft to 13 points. Russell chipped in 17 points and 18 rebounds. North Carolina's coach Frank McGuire and St. John's Joe Lapchick praised the Dons. McGuire said he had never seen anyone play like Russell, and Lapchick called USF the best college basketball team he had ever seen. "They played a defense I never saw before," Lapchick said.

"Russell's defensive play kills you," UCLA coach John Wooden said after the game. "Because of Russell's work on the boards, USF can change its style of defense. They (USF) would be a good team without Russell, but with him they're simply great."

"The best way I can say it is [Russell] dominated in a nice way," forward Mike Farmer recalled. "Probably the other end of that spectrum would be a guy like Shaquille O'Neal, who dominates differently. Russell was very fluid, very cerebral. It was like a chess match out there." Today's basketball fans are used to a more physical game with a lot of banging on offense and defense. In Russell's time it was more a game of finesse that rivaled ballet in its symmetry.

Traveling with the team was Bill Ferroggiaro, the editor-in-chief of USF's student newspaper, *The Foghorn*. Used to more well-behaved West Coast spectators, he was appalled at the rowdiness of the New York City fans. "During the time that USF would be shooting foul shots, fans behind the goal and close to the floor would rise from their seats and jeer, scream and wave handkerchiefs to distract the boys from San Francisco. Not once did the astute officials discourage this practice." Today that's common practice and would be considered relatively tame.

When the team returned home, Russell and Woolpert spoke about the trip to New York before the northern California sports writers and sports broadcasters at their weekly meeting. Russell joked about how he was treated in the New York newspapers. "Those New Yorkers wrote some very nice things about me," he said. "Let's see if I can remember some of them. 'Turkey neck, so skinny his bones rattle, arms hang all the way to the floor.' Really makes a fellow feel good." And he had praise for UCLA's Naulls. "[He] is really strong. He and I both went for a ball under the bucket. I held on with 'the Whale' for a few seconds and then I let go. If I hadn't, he would have shot me through the basket. That man can have the 2 points."

Even though Russell was a senior, he still had his run-ins with Woolpert. At one practice, Russell was shooting free throws much like a set shot instead of underhand as Woolpert preferred. The coach told Russell to shoot underhand and walked away. Russell continued to shoot push shots. Woolpert again walked over to Russell and threw him out of practice. Vince Boyle, who saw the incident, thought to himself, "Oh, oh, there goes the season." But Woolpert and Russell patched up their differences, and Russell was back the next day.

If they hadn't reached an agreement, Woolpert said, he would have kicked Russell off the team. "It wasn't so much that I wanted him to do it our way, but basketball is played by five players," he said. "We couldn't afford to let Bill disobey the coaching instructions, which his teammates had faith in. If we had let Bill do the thing his way it could have led to trouble. The teams that win are the teams that play as a unit. We had unity at USF."

Russell wasn't the only one to run into trouble with Woolpert. After the Holiday Festival Tournament, forward Bill Mallen was kicked off the team because he kept complaining that he thought he should be starting ahead of Boldt or Farmer. He had played well in New York, scoring 10 points against Holy Cross and 4 versus UCLA. News accounts of his departure said that he was leaving to concentrate on his law studies. He returned to the team for the 1956–57 season.

A week later the Dons opened league play against Pepperdine, whose coach Duck Dowell commented, "Some coaches have been known to say 'we respect them, but we don't fear them.' Well, you can say we definitely fear them." The Dons won the two meetings with Pepperdine 62–51 and 68–40.

The Dons were closing in on the winning-streak record of thirty-nine games held jointly by Long Island University and Seton Hall. But to get to the record they had to play the California Golden Bears, coached by Pete Newell, Woolpert's predecessor and former teammate—the same Newell who helped Woolpert devise a strategy for stopping Gola in the previous season's championship game. This time around they matched wits against each other. "Our practices were always open, but Pete closed the gym for the week we were preparing for the USF game, and we set up different defenses depending on where K. C. Jones went during the game," forward Larry Friend recalled.

◈ This became a game to remember because of its bizarre action, or rather its lack of action. A sellout for weeks, scalpers sold dollar-fifty tickets for as much as thirty dollars. Since the game wasn't scheduled on network television, Charles Harney, who later built Candlestick Park, put up $3,000 to have it shown on the new educational station, KQED.

Newell was looking for a way to slow down the USF juggernaut. Woolpert knew his former teammate all too well. He told his players in the locker room before the game, "[Cal] will try to get ahead and slow up the game," Woolpert said. "They'll try to make you play it their way. Don't let them do it." He was right.

Cal went into two stalls totaling more than ten minutes, in which one player stood with the ball tucked under his arm at midcourt. A stall was nothing new to Newell, and Woolpert, who had been his assistant, was aware of it because Newell had used the stall against USC for nine minutes when he coached USF. The strategy was to draw Bill Russell out from underneath the basket. But Woolpert told Russell to stay put.

The game turned into one of the most controversial in northern California history and perhaps the history of college basketball. The *San Francisco Chronicle* put a headline over the story that read, "The Day the Game Stood Still," a play on words from the title of the 1951 movie *The Day the Earth Stood Still.*

Newell wanted to end the Dons' winning streak in Cal's gym. The stalling strategy almost worked. "If you played 'em straight, they'd have you by 22 points after about ten minutes," Newell said. Cal opened a 16–7 lead on USF by employing a strategy to have six-foot-seven center Duane Asplund, a good shooter, draw Russell into the corners where they could screen him from getting rebounds or blocking shots under the basket. But the tactic flagged as USF began closing the gap. The Dons managed to hold a 20–18 lead at halftime, which they stretched to 24–19 with three minutes and forty-five seconds gone in the second half.

Then Asplund fouled out. Newell had to devise a new strategy. Cal was down only 5 points, so if the Bears could score a basket the margin would be 3. Then Cal needed to stop USF defensively on the next trip down the court so the Bears could have a chance to cut USF's lead to one, making it anyone's game.

Newell had six-foot-eight Joe Hagler hold the ball almost at midcourt for ninety seconds. Then Hagler saw guard Bernie Simpson open, passed him the ball, and Simpson sunk a twenty-footer. So far so good. But a foul on USF's Jones allowed him to make both free throws using the underhand method, and the margin opened again to five at 26–21.

Once again Newell had Hagler hold the ball. About fourteen minutes remained in the game. Newell's new strategy was to hold the ball until six minutes before the final buzzer if Russell wouldn't leave his spot under the hoop. "So there we were," Newell said. "Russell wouldn't come out to get Hagler. Naturally, I didn't blame him. He played it smart. But we couldn't operate with the big guy under the bucket. Under those circumstances we had absolutely no chance to win."

Russell said years later he couldn't think of any reason for going out to guard Hagler. "[He] was the only guy in northern California who was a worse shooter than I was," Russell said. "There wasn't a whole lot to worry about. They were behind. They're the ones who had to make a move. It made the game interesting, definitely. It would have been just another forgettable game if that hadn't happened."

With six minutes left in the game, Newell said, "anything can happen." Hagler held the ball under his arm about ten feet from the west stands just across the half-court line and thirty feet from the basket for eight minutes. Referees kept an eye on him to make sure he didn't move his pivot foot. "I collected ten minutes of nationally televised time," Hagler said with a chuckle. "They said I was shaking like a leaf from the nerves, but it was really that damn drafty gym."

"People were sitting on the floor. It wasn't one of the more enjoyable games to watch," Woolpert said. "I would have played it exactly the same way if I had been in Pete's spot."

Jones said, "All I can recall is that he just stood there with the ball, and we relaxed under the basket. I don't know that I've ever seen anything like it. . . . It was like at a greyhound race when the mechanical rabbit breaks down. The dogs just stop and look at each other. Well, that's what we did." Mike Farmer chimed in, "We expected teams to slow it down against us, but never anything like this." Newell added, "The funniest part was Hagler himself. He says to me later, 'Pete, I forgot which foot was my pivot foot. And I had to pee.'"

Cal's Earl Robinson, also a black player, stood next to Jones, talking to him about what they were going to do after the game. Two Cal players, Bob Blake and Larry Friend, discussed old times with Carl Boldt, with whom they had attended junior college. They even got into a game of "Rock, Paper, and Scissors." Hal Perry did a little shadow boxing. "It was like fighting Rocky Marciano," Friend said. "Would you want to fight three or fifteen rounds? In fifteen rounds, he's probably going to tag you, but in three you might get lucky."

The Dons' Warren Baxter sat on the bench watching the non-action. "I was ticked," he said, "because I knew I wasn't going to get in that game." Nonetheless, he called the stall "a damn good strategy."

When the clock got down to six minutes Newell put six-four Bob Washington, a good shooter, in the game for Hagler. Washington took a long shot and missed. USF got the ball, and Brown was fouled. He made both free throws, making the score 28–21. The game was essentially over.

"My kids had been under terrific pressure from the Dons. I knew they were tired. I thought we might be able to rest up, save our energy for the big push and then try to win it in the final six minutes," Newell said. "Actually, I thought we came fairly close. We got six good shots in that final stretch. Not enough of them went in, but it was our best chance. . . . Any statement that we were merely trying to hold the score down by the 'freeze' is ridiculous. What difference does it make if you lose by nine or nineteen? The important thing is to try to win."

With a final score of 33–24 USF had its record-setting fortieth victory. Woolpert said about the record, "Shucks, it felt no different than any other time. It's always a thrill for me to watch this ball club."

The next day, the newspapers called Hagler "Old Smallpox" because no one would get near him. Newell defended his actions in the barrage of criticism that came his way. "We were in the middle of our season, and if Russell had blocked our shots, we'd be so intimidated that two weeks after, when Bill was five-hundred miles away, my guys would still be afraid to shoot for fear of him." Newell remembered the game when Russell had dominated Bob McKeen in 1953. "McKeen still had not gotten over that game. I didn't want the same thing to happen again."

The Dons accepted the tactic without complaint, noting that it helped their top-ranked defense keep the score down. Woolpert praised Newell's strategy. "It was smart basketball, and I warned our kids in advance that they might run into something like that. I'll tell you this—USF has been in some tough ones. But we've never had to sweat it out quite this much. Believe me, we could have lost."

But the television viewers sure complained. The *San Francisco Chronicle* received more than fifty phone calls about the game, calling Cal un-American, unsportsmanlike, and cowardly. The NCAA asked for reports on the game and the next year passed a rule that every ten seconds a player had to penetrate toward the basket to prevent such stalls.

UCLA coach John Wooden hoped there would be more stalls

because it would hasten the introduction of a twenty-four-second shot clock, which he favored.

The pressure of maintaining the winning streak wore on the coach and the team. Woolpert, tense most of the time, lost his appetite. His wife claimed he was hard to live with. Said Russell, "I never, ever experienced pressure like I did during the streak."

Players often got on each other's nerves. Boldt once needled Russell and Jones about their fame because of all the publicity they received. Boldt quipped that if the team plane crashed, the headlines would read "Bill Russell Killed" and that the back pages would list those who were "also dead." Russell lost his cool. "Lay off, Carl," he said with a glower. "Just remember, with me under the basket, your shots can be guided out as well as in." Woolpert called a team meeting and said, "Any more of this, and whoever is guilty gets bounced off the team."

Years later Russell said about the streak, "We never concerned ourselves—at least I never concerned myself—about any game but the next one and the game we're playing tonight."

Said assistant coach Ross Guidice, "Everyone was aware we had a record in sight, but nobody seemed to want to admit it." As the season neared an end Woolpert said he would be playing his starters more because he worried they weren't getting enough playing time as a result of all the blowout wins. He wanted to get them prepared for the tournament. One of the teams not expected to give them trouble was hapless Pepperdine.

Waves' coach Duck Dowell noted that the Dons would work out at the Long Beach City College gym the day before the game, and "then they will hold another workout at nine o'clock Friday night. That's when they play the Pepperdine Waves, now 2-22." Either Dowell was trying to make the Dons overconfident or he was saying that the game would be no harder than a practice for USF.

Woolpert specifically wanted to give Gene Brown more work at the end of the season to prepare him to step in for Jones during the NCAA tournament because he had been ruled ineligible as a result of playing that one game during his junior year before missing the rest of the season with an appendix attack.

Woolpert was uncertain what Jones's loss would mean to the Dons' chances of winning their second title. "At best it's only a hypothesis, but obviously you can't lose a man of K.C.'s ability and not feel a loss," he said. Perry said Brown had all the tools to be a great player. "Like every other sophomore, he has to build up his confidence by making good on his first shot in every game," he said.

Woolpert said the Dons might have to "retrench" on defense, "shorten up our pressing tactics with [Brown] in the lineup. That'll reduce the possibility of error." Brown was a better shooter than Jones, but Jones was the better defender. Woolpert also had guards Bill Bush and Warren Baxter available. "We can shift Brown to a forward if one of the big guys does a lot of fouling and use Bush as a guard without much weakening effect," Woolpert said.

Russell had some kind words to say about Jones as he wrapped up his career. "Without K.C.," he said, "I would be nothing. I rate him an All-American and a half. He made it for himself, on his own ability, and he's the main reason I was picked [as an All-American]."

K. C. Jones's last game was against cross-Bay rival St. Mary's before a crowd of 15,732 at the Cow Palace, then the largest crowd to ever watch a basketball game in the Bay Area. This also was the last regular season and "home" game for Russell and Perry. With the Dons comfortably ahead in the second half—a game highlighted by a nifty behind-the-back pass by Russell to Jones for an easy basket—Woolpert substituted for Jones. The fans evidently thought Jones was through for the night. Woolpert said he had planned to take Jones out for some rest, put him back in the game, then take him out with a minute to go to give the fans a chance to acknowledge him. But the ovation was so strong, "I never did get K.C. back into the game." The ovation lasted three minutes. The St. Mary's players applauded as well. One-by-one the USF players came over to shake Jones's hand. "It was the biggest thrill I've ever received in basketball," Woolpert said. "I could feel the chills down my back."

As USF's streak continued, Woolpert was asked how long he thought it might last. "I don't know," he replied. "I'm surprised it has lasted this long. Months back I had thought somebody would sneak up on us and catch us on an off night or with our guard down. They haven't. . . . The competition is bound to get better. . . . This is a great bunch. They have all had big moments in games. It isn't always Bill Russell, you know, although he, of course, is the big man on the floor. His work makes you appreciate the defensive art of the game, but the way the rules makers are handling the game today I don't know but what they want the defensive phase of the game all but eliminated."

At the end of the regular season, the National Association of Basketball Coaches named Russell and Jones first-team All-Americans, with Russell Player of the Year. St. Louis University coach Ed Hickey, who was chairman of the selection committee for the Olympic team, said of Russell, "There isn't a player in the world who can jump high enough to take the ball away from Russell under the basket." North Carolina coach Frank McGuire chimed in: "I've never seen anybody like him. When he sticks those long arms up in the air, you just can't get a shot off within twelve or fifteen feet of the basket. USC coach Forrest Twogood recalled, "We had a fast break going, and our kid laid the ball up. Suddenly that Russell—coming from nowhere—swooped down like a big bat and pinned the ball in the rim before it could drop in. No man, I say no man, who ever stepped on a court could do that."

Jones was praised for his accurate shots from backcourt and for his sharp passes as the team's playmaker in the Dons' deliberate ball-control attack. Defensively, Jones drew kudos from Woolpert: "He played everybody nose-to-nose and stopped them all." The coaches cited Jones's 12 of 14 clutch free throws in the stall game against Cal as proof of his value to the Dons.

After the success of his junior year, Russell had begun to think about a professional career. "I remember that the game lost some of its magical qualities for me once I thought seriously about playing for a living," Russell confessed in his second autobiography, *Second Wind*. "As a result, all through my senior year at USF I played with the idea of turning professional, and things began to change. Whenever I walked on the court I began to calculate how this particular game might affect my future. Thoughts of money and prestige crept into my head."

The Dons headed for their second NCAA tournament with high hopes, but questions lingered about how they might do without the steadying influence of K. C. Jones. "No man," Russell said, "will miss K.C. during the tournament as much as I will. You take a slingshot. I'm the fork and K.C. is the rubber band. He makes the operation go." Said Woolpert, "We'll miss Jones, but we have a fine replacement in Eugene Brown. He'd be a star on any other team." Said Russell, "It's not a giant step down to Brown. [He and Jones] are different types. Jones is always looking for the key pass—he's a playmaker. Brown looks for the good shots. So we'll lose some and gain some. I know Brown will do a terrific job for us."

Woolpert was also playing coy about his plans for the tournament. "The boys have been planning on [playing without Jones], and they all know what we're going to do," he said. "Maybe it's just as well not to show our plans now. The teams we're going to play later are all scouting us and waiting to find out."

As the tournament approached, not everyone agreed that USF was the best team in the country. Ned Irish, who was described as the man most responsible for taking college basketball out of the obscurity of college gyms and placing it in the national limelight, said the Dayton Flyers could beat the Dons. Irish had seen USF play its three games in the Holiday Festival Tournament. He said Dayton's seven-footer, Bob Uhl, could handle Russell, and the rest of Dayton's team was stronger. He also criticized USF's "weak" schedule.

Irish's analysis didn't bother Woolpert. He said there was little way of knowing without seeing the two teams actually play each other. But he pulled out a letter from referee Jim Enright, who officiated USF's games at the Chicago Invitational, that said USF could "whip every other team in the nation six days a week and twice on Sundays." Woolpert agreed that the CBA was not as strong that year as in the past, "but our overall schedule, I think, is just about as representative as any in the country."

Speculation arose in the press that the Dons might pass up the NCAA to play in the NIT because that would allow Jones to play. It also would match them up against Dayton, which had already accepted a bid to the NIT. But the Dons were set on playing in the NCAA. Newspapers also speculated that if USF lost in the first round of the NCAA tournament then the Dons could still get into the NIT. That wasn't going to happen, either.

As it turned out, Russell and Uhl were selected to play in the annual East–West game. Woolpert said about the matchup, "I would bet Russell against anybody. I've never seen Uhl or Dayton, even in the movies. But Russell always has reacted well to playing against big men. I know he's looking forward to the game." It was no contest. Russell scored 19 points while Uhl managed 7 as the West routed the East 103–72. K. C. Jones chipped in 15 points.

Before the NCAA tournament began, *United Press* again named Woolpert Coach of the Year in a poll of 319 sportswriters and radio broadcasters. The voters pointed out that while the Dons did not play a particularly strong schedule, USF was "on the spot" from the beginning of the season after winning the national championship the year before, and still the Dons had maintained their record-winning streak.

In addition they pointed out the fact that Woolpert had lost all four of his forwards from the 1955–56 team and had replaced them with better players—Carl Boldt and Mike Farmer. The sportswriters and broadcasters also stressed that he had kept the team's egos in check, a difficult task on any successful team. He did all of this with mostly homegrown talent.

Woolpert also had some backhanded praise for Russell by praising the star center's father, Charlie. "Charles Russell," Woolpert said, "is a wonderful man. He has passed his virtues on to his son Bill. For that, we at USF are fortunate."

Russell's father replied, "I would be proud of my boys [Charles Jr. and Bill] if they never played a game. I had to leave 'em alone a lot. But they never got into trouble. They were always at the playgrounds instead of running the streets."

# SIXTEEN

## Two in a Row

"Intimidation was our major weapon, and we didn't mind using it."
—K. C. Jones

USF was confident entering the NCAA tournament, which, for the first time, would have a representative from four regions—the Far West, the West, Midwest, and East. The Dons wanted to become the first undefeated team in NCAA tournament history. "Going into our second national championship, we just didn't think anyone could stop us," K. C. Jones said. "We really did feel invincible, and we approached every game that way—go out and destroy the opposition."

Two of the nation's top teams, no. 3 Dayton and no. 6 Louisville—both independents—chose not to enter the NCAA tournament, instead opting for the NIT. They were the only two teams in the top ten to pass up the NCAA games. It was a tribute to the Dons that the two teams declined to challenge them.

Jones traveled with the team to the regionals in Corvallis, Oregon, where he lent moral support while sitting on the bench in street clothes next to Woolpert and Guidice, almost as a third coach. "He's been playing with these fellows and probably can spot some things I might miss. Besides, he's been almost what amounted to a playing coach all along. He's been the playmaker, you know."

Asked by a reporter whether they would miss Jones, Russell replied, "We'll merely be changing spokes, but the wheel will keep right on rolling." Gene Brown took Jones's spot in the starting lineup. Brown, who had Michael Jordan–type moves, was a better shooter than Jones but paled in comparison on defense, although he was more than adequate. "Brown might conceivably tie up," Woolpert said, "but we don't expect him to." Woolpert called Brown "quick as a cat. He's an excellent dribbler, has a great jump shot, and has been playing a contained defensive game. Naturally he needs more experience and confidence. You don't find guys any quicker than Eugene. He doesn't recover as fast as K.C., but then I've never see a man who did."

Duquesne coach Dudley Moore called Brown "the best substitute in the country." While lauding Jones, Russell said it was no great step down when Brown joined the starting lineup. "K.C. has been the playmaker, but Brown will find more opportunities to shoot. We'll keep on rolling along." Forward Mike Farmer said Brown didn't get the publicity he deserved. "He was big—six-three—but he could play the point and shoot and was a great defender. Just an outstanding player." Jones joined in, "Gene had some stuff in his game that nobody had for about another five years. . . . He was awesome." Brown took the challenge in stride, saying he felt proud to follow Jones. He recalled watching Jones play when Brown was a freshman in high school, when Jones was his idol. He hardly missed one of Jones's games.

To open the tournament, the Dons played UCLA, the last team

to beat them in the third game of the 1954–55 season. In 1956 Wooden was in the seventh year of building his dynasty at UCLA and he had his best team yet, including Willie Naulls and Morris Taft, two gifted athletes who carried the Bruins to their sixth Pacific Coast Conference title in eight years. Naulls was one of only three Bruins to average a double-double in his three-year college career. And now the Bruins were in the NCAA tournament, their first appearance under Wooden.

Whenever two great basketball players met on the court, talk often turned to who was the better player. And it cropped up over Naulls's and Russell's meeting. Woolpert said he'd hate to make a choice, while Wooden said Naulls was a better all-around player. "I don't believe in making comparisons," Woolpert said. "Naulls is as good a player as we've seen all year long and definitely an All-American, just like Russell. Willie has tremendous all-around ability." But, he said, he had never seen a man dominate a game as Russell had. "Bill is great at both ends of the court. He is so great defensively that his value to the team is beyond belief." He said that if a pro team landed both Naulls and Russell "what a team it [would] be." And that's what happened as Naulls and Russell played together for the Boston Celtics from 1963–66, winning three NBA titles.

When UCLA took the floor against the Dons, it was the fourth time Wooden had seen Russell play against his Bruins. "We are much improved since our [last] meeting in Madison Square Garden last December. Our team is in a good frame of mind and good condition for this playoff game." Wooden was asked how the Bruins could handle Russell. "[He] may be contained on offense. He does the containing defensively."

*Sports Illustrated* speculated that the best game of the tournament might not be played in the finals, semifinals or even at one of the four quarterfinals. The magazine claimed it would be the first-round game between UCLA and USF.

Woolpert's former teammate at Loyola, Scott McDonald, who was now coaching an American Amateur Union (AAU) team, said UCLA had little chance against the Dons, calling them the best college team he'd ever seen. "It is pretty well agreed that the only way to beat them is to draw Russell out from under the basket on defense. The only trouble is that he won't go for the bait unless a team happens to pile up a quick 10-point lead and starts playing keep-away. Russell can guard the deep corner man with a dirty look. He gets the shooter so jittery he can stay back under the basket and scare him to death by scowling at him."

USC coach Forrest Twogood disagreed. "I don't intend to put any uncalled-for heat on UCLA, but I actually think the Bruins can beat USF. I didn't think so before they played us last weekend, but I sure do now." He said Willie Naulls and Morris Taft would be too much for San Francisco to handle.

UCLA coach John Wooden thought the Bruins had a good chance against the Dons because of better bench play and the fact that Taft had been ill when USF beat them in the New York tournament. He didn't feel that Jones's loss would slow down the Dons. But, he said, "you take Bill Russell out and the team is 50 percent weaker. Take out anybody else, and they won't miss them. Russell dominates a game more than any man I've seen in basketball."

The Dons started slow. They missed their first 8 shots but managed to turn things around to take a 24–12 lead after fifteen minutes. USF led at halftime 39–21, then stretched it to 51–31. But USF hit a cold streak, and UCLA battled back to 57–48. The Dons finished by holding off the Bruins 72–61.

At one point in the game, John Wooden couldn't believe what he saw. Wooden had seen some spectacular plays, but the best was yet to come. It was early in the game when the six-foot-six-inch, 225-pound Naulls, who went on to have a ten-year career in the NBA, came steaming down the court, driving to the basket. He encountered Russell, ten pounds lighter but four inches taller waiting for him. Naulls faked Bill Russell one way and Russell went for the fake. Naulls slipped by Russell, driving for the hoop, going to the rim with the ball in both hands. As Naulls was getting ready to dunk the ball, Russell's big hand got between the basket and the ball, blocking the shot. It was a tremendous show of strength to force the ball away from the downward trajectory of Naulls's stuff. Wooden leaped off the bench demanding that the referee call "goaltending." But the referee ruled that because the ball never left Naulls's hands it was a clean block. "I think it really shook up the team and probably was the turning point of the game," Wooden said.

Brown lit up UCLA with 23 points on 9 of 16 from the floor, most of them from fifteen to twenty-five feet away, and Russell had 21 for USF. "All Brown needed was to hit that first shot, and he was set," Woolpert said, "We always knew he would be able to do it, but you have to prove it in competition."

The Dons limited Naulls to 6 field goals. Naulls was 6 of 18 from the floor, while Taft made only 6 of 23, although each player scored 16 points. As a team UCLA shot 28 percent on 18 of 66 shots.

The loss meant that Wooden would have to wait until 1963 to get his first national championship.

USF's next opponent was Utah, which beat Seattle University 81–72. The Utes kept up their high-scoring shooting against the Dons with 77 points, but the Dons still won by 15 with Russell netting 27 points. Russell had picked up three fouls with four minutes left in the half and played gingerly the rest of the way. At one point, USF simultaneously played four players in their first collegiate year, and even *they* held their own with the Utes.

The Dons led 44–41 at halftime, and Utah pulled to within 1 at 56–55 in the second half. Russell had picked up his fourth foul, but Woolpert left him in the game. San Francisco then went on a

15–2 run in three and a half minutes to put the game away, sparked by Russell's two behind-his-back stuffs and even a twenty-foot set shot. Those shots were almost as common as the jump shot, which was slowly taking over the game. Russell had grabbed 45 rebounds in two games. Brown continued to show that he was a strong replacement for Jones, posting 18 points.

Brown picked up some advice from Jones in the locker room at halftime. Utah's Curtis Jensen, who scored 16 points in the first half, had been beating Brown on drives. Jones told Brown to watch the baseline and to force Jensen to drive toward Hal Perry so that they could pinch in and cut him off before he could drive to the hoop. Faced with this new strategy Jensen was held to 5 points in the second half.

Forward Mike Preaseau scored 14 points for the Dons, a rare high total for him. Woolpert had preached to Preaseau that his job was to play hard defense and that he was not to shoot unless he had touched the ball at least three times on each USF possession.

Utah coach Jack Gardner praised the Dons after the game. "This probably is the greatest college basketball team ever assembled," he said.

"This is a good one for us to get over," Woolpert said. "We hadn't met a fast break like this all season, and we were playing too close to the boards in the first half. Russell really went to work in the second half." He said that Brown's being named to the all-tournament team gave the guard a confidence boost.

Woolpert said Utah sneaked up on the Dons. "We built all our plans to beat UCLA," he said. "We figured on meeting the same team we had seen in the same tournament last year, and after we saw them whip Seattle University on Friday night we had no qualms. But they gave us a scare."

K. C. Jones attributed the Dons' success to "freelancing," allowing players to use their own judgment in play calling. During the previous season, he said, the team had worked on set plays. "This man goes here. You pass off there. . . . Everything was down on paper, and we played by the diagrams. . . . When we started practice this season, it was different. Coach Woolpert told us we were champs, and we had the experience. . . . He told us to freelance from the patterns we'd already learned."

Jones and Perry worked with each other by instinct. When Brown moved into the starting lineup, he was ready. "We knew Gene would have to step in when the nationals began," Jones said. Woolpert had been working with Brown all season preparing him for the tournament.

In the final four at Evanston, Illinois, USF faced a strong Southern Methodist University (SMU) team with future NBA player Jim Krebs, Joel Krog, and Larry Showalter on a nineteen-game winning streak, the winner of 25 of their last 27 games. The Mustangs had won their regional by handily beating Oklahoma City 84–63.

Woolpert knew little about the Mustangs, but he wasn't worried. "I don't even know the color of their uniforms," he said. "I'm going to pick up a program when I get back [to Evanston], and that'll be the first I know of their personnel. . . . They have to beat us, not us them. They have to outscore us and outplay us. And I don't want to sound cocky when I say that isn't easy. They could have us scouted to their heart's content, but what they have seen and what actually happens during the game is far different." Ironic that this positive attitude came from the same coach who became a nervous wreck during every game.

"We haven't made any special preparations for SMU," Woolpert said. "We seldom prepare in advance for any team. After the game starts, though, and they tip their hand as to what they plan to do, we adjust." Even as confident as he sounded, Woolpert said it was absurd to make USF a hands-down favorite to win the title. "The thing that everybody overlooks is the luck factor," he said.

"We could run into something in the first quarter, somebody gets racked up real good, and we'd be hurting, and bad. Just suppose, for instance, Bill Russell got hurt in the early going. We have every intention of winning, but we've been lucky about injuries so far, and we'll need to keep on being lucky."

Several of the players had blisters from wearing new shoes when they played Utah. "They don't amount to much," Woolpert said. Russell had a sprained finger on his right hand, but it wasn't expected to slow him down.

Southern Methodist coach Doc Hayes said after the Oklahoma City game that he was too tired to think much about USF, but he managed to comment, "I hope we can give San Francisco a good game. People who haven't seen them play don't realize what a tremendous task we face." Three days later Hayes said that although he wasn't predicting an upset, "My boys always feel they have a chance to win."

When they took the floor, the Dons stormed to a 41–19 lead over SMU and never looked back, winning 86–68. The Dons opened with a 32–10 run. SMU got the score back to 46–40 with sixteen minutes left. But the Dons steadily increased their margin and took control at 71–60 with less than five minutes left.

"We didn't play too good a game," Russell said. "Or at least I didn't. Farmer and Perry and the others did. But we won, and that's what we came down for." USF got a big boost from an unexpected source—Farmer, who scored 26 on 11 of 18 shots. Perry, who was chosen captain for the tournament, chipped in 14, while Russell finished with a "paltry" 17 and pulled down 23 rebounds.

"SMU caught fire," Woolpert said, "and we had to come back [with] an all-out effort. But it proves what I've always said. The other team has to beat us." Santa Clara coach Bob Feerick, an observer at the game but one who knew the Dons well, summed it up this way: "This is the only team in history which can look bad and still win by 18 points."

SMU coach Hayes couldn't believe what he saw. "I don't think there's a college team that can beat them. It was Farmer who broke our back. Our scout said he couldn't shoot from outside too well. We found out. Their aggressive defense was a factor, too. We couldn't hold their pace. We expected them to be great, and they were." Hayes's prediction against Iowa? "San Francisco can beat Iowa [in the finals]. San Francisco can beat any basketball team I know of. San Francisco can beat the Russians."

Hoping to become the third team in NCAA history to win consecutive titles, the Dons faced Iowa in the championship game. The Iowa Hawkeyes had a seventeen-game winning streak. They had beaten Temple in the semifinals. Iowa's Bill Logan had outscored Hal Lear, 38–32. The night before the game the Iowa team went to a movie. Then the Dons walked into the same movie and sat a few rows in front of them. "Russell stood up," said the Hawkeyes' Bill Schoof, "and took off his trench coat and blocked the screen. At that point, I think all of us knew we were in for a hell of a game. He was just huge, and he played huge."

Again Woolpert huddled with his former teammate and mentor, Pete Newell, to discuss strategy for the Iowa game. A reporter asked Newell what he'd do if he were in his shoes. "I don't know," Newell said, "but I'd sure be uncomfortable. Phil wears a size smaller than I do." When Newell's Cal team played for the national championship in 1959, Woolpert was on hand. After Cal won the game, Woolpert called his wife to tell her, "Pete didn't know it, but I coached his team through every second, just as if it were my own. I'm exhausted."

On the bus ride to the arena, Woolpert as usual was his uptight self, but his relaxed players sang ribald songs and unmercifully teased one another. They even goofed around in the locker room. Woolpert liked a loose team but wondered if they weren't too loose, perhaps not taking the Hawkeyes seriously enough.

A picture in *Life* magazine showed some team members playing penny-ante poker. One of the players, Hal Payne, who came from a strong religious upbringing, remarked that he sure hoped his mother didn't see that picture. Another *Life* picture showed Russell, Jones, and other players cracking jokes in their hotel room, while a third picture showed forward Carl Boldt stretched out on a bench sound asleep before the game. Someone asked him how Boldt could sleep before a big game, and he replied, "I don't think we are going to lose." As usual, Bill Russell was nervous and throwing up in a toilet while Boldt slept.

The Dons took the floor at the Northwestern gymnasium to see signs on poles waved by rooters that said "2 in a row, let's go;" "Woolpert for President;" "The West Knows How;" and "All the way in NCAA." Flag-like bunting hung from the walls, giving the gym a political convention look.

Iowa pulled out to a 15–4 lead behind Carl "Sugar" Cain, K. C. Jones's future brother-in-law. Cain was killing the Dons by scoring off a back-door play while Boldt guarded him. Iowa put the six-foot-seven Logan at the free-throw line, drawing Russell away from the basket. When Logan got the ball, he lobbed it to Cain who laid it in. Boldt just wasn't quick enough to stay with Cain, although he was a more than adequate defensive player. Woolpert called a time-out.

Jones, in his civilian clothes, forced his way into the huddle when the Dons were down 15–4. "You guys have the fat head," he said. "You're choking, really swallowing the olive. You lose this one, and that winning streak you're gloating about won't mean a thing. Gene, watch that fake of Cain's. Don't go with it. Now, let's see if all of you have any guts."

Woolpert made a defensive adjustment, putting Gene Brown on Cain instead of Boldt. That turned the game around. While Boldt took a breather on the bench, Mike Preaseau took the guard Brown had been covering. Once the game turned in the Dons' favor, Boldt returned and wound up scoring 16 points.

Russell was asked after the game if he was nervous when Iowa pulled ahead by 11 points. "Nervous? No, I wasn't nervous. I was just flat scared," he said. Perry stepped up his defense, hounding his man with his customary handclapping as he chased the offensive player.

"We switched our game plan early because of a change in the starting lineup, the tremendous shooting of Iowa, and a defensive breakdown on the part of our team," Woolpert recalled. Perry and Farmer said that it was unusual for Woolpert to offer his players suggestions. "He wanted us to think it through, figure it out and do it [most of the time]," Perry said. Farmer said Woolpert was "an idea guy, very philosophical. He did things that were necessary, but he also left us alone, let us do our own things. We had more mature guys than most teams. He didn't have to push us. A lot of the motivation we had came from the [winning] streak."

Woolpert said he wasn't worried early in the game. "I wasn't too concerned when Iowa got that 15–4 jump on us. We trailed by 11 points against Holy Cross and California this season. And I knew we would break through."

The Dons went on a 20–8 run, with Russell blocking 3 straight shots, and passed Iowa at 24–23 with a little more than six minutes left in the half. They opened up a lead of 38–33 at halftime. USF increased its lead in the second half, but then Iowa pressed to cut the lead to 7 points with four minutes remaining. A worried Woolpert saw the Dons pull their game together and walk away with an 83–71 victory. Russell blocked 12 shots, scored 26 points and had 27 rebounds. *Time* magazine, with some overblown superlatives, described Russell as a "joyous giraffe, dancing in the air." He held Logan to 12 points, forcing him to take tentative shots from the corner. Cain, who had scored 10 of Iowa's first 15 points, only scored 7 more during the rest of the game under Brown's tenacious guarding. The Dons' winning streak stood at fifty-five.

Said Logan, "You jump as high as you can and you're still only high enough to tap Russell on the shoulder." Iowa coach Bucky O'Connor said Russell was the difference. "But I'm satisfied. You don't find many teams that can win by 12 points and still be as scared as they were. We played them on even terms, and we kept in there right until the end. It's tough to have the ball batted back at you after you shoot."

After beating Iowa Woolpert said about USF, "This team is the finest I've ever seen. I can say that in all honesty now. It has done everything asked of it. The difference—without a doubt—was Russell." Russell must have been pleased that he finally received from Woolpert the recognition that he so long had craved.

During the trophy presentation, Perry urged Jones to leave the bench and join the team on the floor. Certainly Jones was as much a part of the team's success as any player, including Russell. "I wanted to show my respect for the man," Perry said. A team picture taken with the trophy after the game showed Woolpert in typical fashion. He was always eager to praise his team and play down his own role. In the picture all the players are animated with raised fists, shouts, or huge smiles. In the background, barely visible, stands Woolpert with not a trace of a smile. He knew that day belonged to his team. "This must be the finest undergraduate team since Naismith first hung the peach basket," the *San Francisco Chronicle* opined.

Incredibly the MVP award went to Lear despite Russell's dominating performance. Lear had scored a record 160 points in five games, 48 in the third-place game against SMU. All Russell would say is, "It's all part of the game. I refuse to say more because it might incriminate me." Woolpert thought the award should have gone to Russell. "They must have forgotten that Russell played at both ends of the court and tied up both backboards," he said. "Lear probably wouldn't have looked as good as Carl Cain of Iowa if he had been forced to play against Russell."

Peter Bjarkman wrote in *Hoopla—A Century of College Basketball* that "the college game had undergone a most radical change during [Russell's] tenure. Team basketball would now never be quite the same, and the search for the perfect winning ingredient would from this time forward always seem to reduce itself to a search for the perfect shot-blocking and board-clearing big man." Meanwhile, Louisville defeated Dayton 93–80 for the NIT title. Bjarkman noted that "it did so in relative obscurity. And this state of decreasing prestige for the original Madison Square Garden year-end event would remain the case from this point on."

An indication of the NCAA tournament's rise in popularity can be seen by the record attendance of 132,513 who watched the twenty-nine games. That broke the record of 115,712 set in 1952. Some 10,653 attended the USF–Iowa game.

Russell finished the year as the first player to average more than 20 points (20.7) and 20 rebounds (20.3) a game in a season. Statistics on blocked shots weren't kept until about five years later, but Russell estimated that he blocked at least 15 shots a game. "I had advantages because most of the players had never seen [his shot-blocking abilities]," Russell said. His scoring average would have been higher were it not for the fact that he was a poor free-throw shooter. His field goal percentage was higher than that of his free throws—51 percent as compared to almost 50. Russell may have had the most awkward free-throw stance of any college player. He stood with his left leg forward and right leg behind him and then tossed the ball underhand toward the rim.

In the Dons' 29 straight wins during the season, they outscored their opponents by nearly 20 points a game. They averaged 72 points a game while giving up 50. And they finished no. 1 in the country in defense.

Russell recalled, "We were a great team, but once we got this terrible 'unbeatable' monster idea loose, all we had to do a lot of times was show up at the gym and we had the game won."

The day after the championship game, Russell was leaving the hotel in Evanston, Illinois, when he came across a young newspaper boy selling the *Evanston Morning Star*. According to Carl Boldt, who overheard the boy ask Russell, *"Morning Star?"* the USF center patted the kid on the head and jokingly said, "Morning, son."

When the Dons' flight arrived home an hour late, they found two-thousand fans waiting for them at the San Francisco International Airport. But Woolpert, Jones, and Russell didn't disembark, disappointing the crowd, because they had gone from Illinois to the Shrine East–West game in Kansas City, Missouri. The team was welcomed home with an eight-piece band and banners waving in a bone-chilling wind. The banners proclaimed "Woolpert for President;" "Well Done, Dons;" and "Welcome Champs."

When Hal Perry left the plane decked in a green blazer and a checkered vest, the fans lifted him on their shoulders as he hoisted the championship trophy high in the air. A caravan of one-hundred cars led by eight motorcycle policemen drove the Dons the fifteen miles back to the campus.

Winning the championship a second time tempered the celebration somewhat, but still the Dons were treated to a "Citywide Salute to the Champs" nine days later. The event took place at the Sheraton-Palace Hotel for $12.50 a head, with a portion of that money going to help finish the new USF gym.

The two championship seasons helped USF raise the $700,000 necessary to build the gym. Groundbreaking took place on the eight-thousand-seat stadium in December 1956.

## SEVENTEEN
### A New Sport for Russell

"Russell showed up in an outfit calculated to draw attention and demoralize all opponents."
—Track teammate Ed Griffin

Russell had a busy spring in 1956. In addition to leading the Dons to their second national championship, he joined the track team where he excelled in the high jump. He wanted to participate in track for one simple reason; he loved to run and jump.

He had to get permission from his track teammates to skip workouts because he was too tired from the grind of the basketball season. He also needed time to rest to catch up on his class work, and he had just returned from the Olympic tryouts. A high jumper who also played on the USF freshman team, Ed Griffin, came to Russell's defense. "Look," he told his teammates, "I played basketball against him all season. He is in terrific shape. He is an unbelievable jumper. He can outrun anybody. Even if he doesn't come to practice, with him we're going to be better than we are. Besides, a chance to be on the same team with Bill Russell? He was just named National Player of the Year. We've got nothing to lose. Let's do it." The team agreed. Also on that team were basketball reserves Jack King and Mike Preaseau, who also was a high jumper.

Russell had been on the track team as a sophomore, but he hadn't developed physically to the point he was much of a threat in the high jump. At his first meet at San Francisco State College, a group of sportswriters were standing around chatting and taking notes when they spotted Russell and K. C. Jones walking through a gate. They all sprinted over to interview Russell, who was wearing a kind of Ben Hogan golf cap in school colors. He wore sunglasses, a long wool scarf, and a green varsity letter jacket with "USF" and "NCAA Basketball Champions" stitched on it. He was also wearing green sweat pants and basketball shoes. His manner of dress was designed to play mind games with his opponents.

Unbeknownst to his teammates the track coach, Bill Magner, let Russell participate in the broad jump, an event whose name was changed to the "long jump" years later. Russell took off his outer garments—all except his scarf—and walked to the broad jump runway. Griffin remembered the look on his face. "I had seen that look before," he said. "It was his business face." Today, it would be called his "game face."

Russell took only nine long strides—Griffin counted them—and launched himself into the air. He jumped from a foot behind the board, flew through the air with his scarf trailing, and still landed in the pit with a jump of twenty-two feet, six and one-half inches—enough to win the event. "He had no form in particular," Griffin said. "He just flung himself into the air and stretched out those legs on his landing."

Russell put his outer garments on and strolled over to the high jump pit. The jumping started at five-foot-six. Russell cleared it easily without removing his outer clothes. As Griffin put it, "It was a vintage Russell mind game."

Russell enjoyed track because he liked psyching out his opponent. "Track really is psychic," he said. "There wasn't a guy I jumped against I couldn't beat if I had a chance to talk to him beforehand. I talked to Charlie Dumas, and we tied. After that he went on to break world records. I recall one meet with thirty-four jumpers. They wanted to start the bar at five-eight. I said, 'Let's start it at six-four—let's get rid of the garbage.' I wore a silk scarf, basketball shoes and black glasses. I had no trouble."

The next jumper was a five-foot-seven-inch jumper from San Francisco State who also cleared the bar with ease. The jumper looked familiar to Griffin, who quickly discerned that it was Johnny Mathis, a sometime singer at San Francisco night clubs who would go on to receive national fame.

Years later Mathis recalled that he had seen Russell jump higher than the world record in practice. "I remember thinking, 'Here's the world's greatest high jumper, and he's fooling around with basketball.'" Mathis has a picture of Russell jumping over the bar while he stood under it. "We were like Mutt and Jeff," he said. Mathis himself once jumped within two inches of the world record. He was asked to try out for the 1956 Olympic team but signed a contract to sing for Columbia Records instead.

By the fourth round of his first meet only Russell, Mathis, Preaseau, and a Cal Poly jumper remained in the competition. By this time Russell had removed his outer garments and was shooting for six feet. All four cleared the bar. On the next jump at six-two only Russell remained. He kept jumping, finally missing at six-eight. And his performance came on the first meet of the season with no practice.

Sportswriters went nuts over Russell's performance. Darrell Wilson of the *San Francisco Chronicle* wrote that Russell might well become the high jumper of the century. "After the meet experts concluded that Russell stands only some practice sessions away from becoming the first jumper in history to clear seven feet."

Soon thereafter the university's president called him into his office and pointed at a newspaper article about his feat. "Mr. Russell," he said, "that's good. I want you to jump a few inches higher and get a world record. It will be good for the university." Russell left thinking the president was weird for speaking to him about the high jump record like he was "order[ing] up a world record from Sears."

The next meet on a slippery, rain-soaked track against a cold, strong wind Russell won another high jump event with a leap of six-eight. Now Russell was in demand for the big meets, not the team meets, with the top jumpers in the country. At the All-Comers Meet in San Jose, Russell finished second with a jump of six-six against three of the world's best jumpers. Russell's performances had earned him top billing in the local newspapers, complete with pictures.

Soon hate letters began to arrive because Russell was black. Racism was rearing its ugly head again, a fact that only steeled Russell's resolve. Russell traveled to the Fresno Relays where he tied Charlie Dumas, the best jumper in the world, with a six-nine and one-quarter-inch jump. Dumas wanted to call it a tie, but Russell insisted they try for seven feet. Dumas missed badly on all three jumps, while Russell just barely ticked the bar off on each of three tries. Dumas would later become the first jumper to clear seven feet on June 29, 1956.

Russell thought he might try out for the Olympic track team. With little training he ran the 440-yard run in 49.5 seconds—the world record was about 46 seconds—and considered trying the 400-meter hurdles. "I'd have an advantage over the other boys," Russell said. "They have to jump over the hurdles. All I have to do is walk over them." One sports writer said Russell looked like "an antelope heading for the chow line" when he ran the hurdles.

Russell kept winning at the high jump but decided not to pass up a chance to travel with the basketball team on a forty-five game goodwill exhibition tour through Latin America beginning June 15. The Dons took along UCLA's Willie Naulls as a special guest. Fourteen players made the trip; the only one left behind was Hal Perry, who turned pro and was playing for the College All-Stars against the Harlem Globetrotters on a nationwide tour.

That summer Russell was invited to the White House to a physical fitness meeting with President Eisenhower, representing college basketball. Russell didn't have the money to go, but USF put it up. He, his father, stepmother, and girlfriend, Rose Swisher, drove across the country for the meeting. He joined boxer Gene Tunney; baseball's Ford Frick, Willie Mays, and Hank Greenberg; and basketball's Bob Cousy.

Eisenhower came into the room and shook everyone's hand before telling the group, "You all look a lot bigger on television— all but Mr. Russell."

Russell remembered somebody reading a long report on fitness that said, among other things, that the youth of America couldn't even do ten pushups. "That's nothing," Russell said to himself, "I can't, either." Russell said it was untrue that Eisenhower asked him to remain an amateur so he could play in the 1956 Olympics. He said that even if the president had asked, he would have told him he didn't know what he was going to do. Thoughts of becoming a pro basketball player preoccupied him.

# EIGHTEEN
## The Aftermath

"Find a way to get this guy, because he can play against anybody in the NBA and come out a winner."
—Don Barksdale to Boston Celtics coach Red Auerbach

Phil Woolpert had hoped the Dons as a team would represent the United States in the 1956 Olympic games, but it was not to be. Olympic rules had been changed to prohibit the NCAA championship team from competing in the qualifying tournament. Rather, fourteen seniors were to be picked from various colleges to play against the AAU champion. Players would be selected from the two teams.

The selection process angered Woolpert. "This gives the colleges very little chance," he said. "I'd match USF as a unit against any amateur outfit in the country, but putting fourteen strangers under a new coach for a couple of weeks and then sending them against an AAU team is something of a penalty."

Woolpert's former college teammate Pete Newell said that the Dons could probably beat any AAU team. "It doesn't make any sense to me that only two members of the current USF team should get a chance to make the Olympic squad," he said. "If the NCAA picks an All-Star squad for its team in the playoffs, why doesn't the AAU do the same thing? You can bet the AAU won't go for a plan like that."

Santa Clara coach Bob Feerick noted that the "top colleges always are just as good as the top AAU clubs." But the college All-Stars lost. Only Russell and Jones from the USF team were invited, and officials selected both of them for the Olympic team. Woolpert was so angry over the rule change that he turned down an offer to coach the Olympic team.

The 1956 U.S. Olympic team, with Russell and Jones leading the way in Melbourne, Australia, walked all over its opponents while averaging nearly 100 points a game in eight games. Their closest game was a 35-point victory over the Soviet Union. Russell was the leading scorer, averaging 14 points over eight games. He picked up only five fouls in those eight games. Four players averaged double figures, including Jones with almost 11 points a game.

The world had never seen anything like Russell. In a game against Bulgaria, Russell put in one of his "steer" shots. "No goal," an astonished referee from Singapore ruled. Only some fast-talking from U.S. coach Gerald Tucker got the goal allowed as perfectly legal.

In the mid-1990s, K. C. Jones was strolling down a street in Seoul, South Korea, when a man who had played against the 1956 Olympic team recognized him. "He recalled the game against the United States and said he never played another game after he played us," Jones said. Jones asked him why not. "Because every shot I took, Bill Russell blocked." Jones replied, "You shouldn't really feel bad about that, because that's what he did in the United States, same as the Olympics."

Russell said that when he received his gold medal, his thoughts returned to his freshman year in college when "I was told I could go to the Olympics. I thought then, 'People like me don't go to the Olympics. There are millions of basketball players out there.' Being there was an honor." Even so, Russell fumed about the segregated housing for black athletes.

Woolpert also helped Russell with his efforts to turn pro. Along with the Olympics and marriage to his longtime girlfriend, Rose Swisher, Russell's thoughts turned to playing professional basketball. Before he left for the Olympics he entertained an offer to sign with the Harlem Globetrotters, although he and Jones preferred to play in the NBA. "But you've got to think about the money," Jones said. "I've been Russell's roommate for three years. He's a natural born funnyman. As well as I know him, I've got to laugh a hundred times a day. Best part of it he knows he's funny and enjoys it. If one of those clown teams offers him a passel of jack, I wouldn't be surprised" to see him take it.

Globetrotters' owner Abe Saperstein threw around figures as high as $50,000 in the newspapers, claiming he was going to offer that much to Russell to sign with the Globetrotters, an unheard-of sum in those days. "I'm shocked," Russell said. "That would increase my yearly earnings by $50,000. I'm interested, but I'm not committing myself."

Russell also knew that the Celtics wanted him. Saperstein telephoned Russell. "I want to talk to you in your hotel and tell you what we'll do for you. And I want you to have your coach with you so you'll know everything is on the up and up." When they sat down Russell discovered the offer was only $17,000. But then Saperstein proceeded to incense Russell by disrespecting him. He had brought an assistant with him to the meeting, while Woolpert and assistant coach Ross Guidice joined Russell. Russell sat with Saperstein's assistant on his left and Woolpert on his right, and Saperstein across the table. Saperstein ignored Russell, talking directly to Woolpert about the advantages of being a Globetrotter. In the meantime, the assistant was joking with Guidice and Russell. "Right or wrong, I took it to mean, 'As one Great White Father to Another Great White Father, this is what we'll do for this poor dumb Negro boy who unfortunately doesn't understand the language too well.' No, maybe I was wrong, but before he had finished talking, I was thinking, 'All right, you want to talk to Woolpert, you just get Woolpert to sign a contract with you.'"

The Globetrotters raised their offer to $30,000 when he returned from the Olympics, but by then it was too late. Russell said he never seriously considered playing for the Globetrotters because it was more vaudeville than sport. "I wouldn't have accepted three times the amount," he said. "To begin with, the Globetrotters live up to their name. They travel all over the world, and keep at it something like forty-eight weeks of the year. It would be impossible to establish any sort of home life. In the second place, their specialty is clowning, and I had no intention of being billed as a funny guy in a basketball uniform."

Russell also said that Saperstein hurt the effort of black players to move into the professional ranks. He said Saperstein "liked to portray himself as the benefactor of all Negroes in sport. He also believed he had earned a monopoly on the services of every black athlete in the country. [He] worked against the aspirations of an entire race just to keep his little franchise." Russell believed black players could use Saperstein to help them negotiate with the professional teams. "When the Globetrotters bid for you, it helps you get a better deal with the pros." Russell signed with the Celtics for $22,500 only after Auerbach had checked him out with coaches and former players he trusted.

Woolpert told Auerbach that Russell would have no trouble adjusting to the Celtics' fast break because Russell had been a trackman at USF. Pete Newell assured him that Russell was no liability as a shooter. Don Barksdale, who had played for Auerbach, said that bigger players could not push Russell around, despite his thin frame. "He can't hit the broad side of a barn," Barksdale told Auerbach, "but he can get you 18 rebounds a game, his passing ability for a big man is better than any college player I've ever seen, and he can block shots with such finesse that he can swat the ball directly to a teammate."

Barksdale also worked on Russell to sign with the Celtics. "I asked Bill and his father to name me somebody on the Harlem Globetrotters outside of the center [Meadowlark Lemon] and the guy who has the ball," Barksdale said. "They couldn't do it. I was telling them that in the NBA, at least the box scores would get out. People know you all across the country, and you're in town more than once. But the Trotters are in town once a year, and you're gone."

Bill Reinhart, Auerbach's coach at George Washington University, started watching Russell as a sophomore. "Russell can absolutely destroy an opponent's game plan. He runs faster than any big man I've ever seen, and he has an exceptional sense of how to out-rebound even a player three inches taller than himself. Above all, he's smart and he's clever." Auerbach was convinced. When Russell played his first game, he drew a sold-out crowd to Boston Garden. In his first full swing around the league, a total of 78,000 fans watched him play.

Because of the Olympics and his honeymoon, Russell missed the first twenty-four games of the season. Even so, he led the team in field goal percentage and rebounds as the Celtics won their first NBA title. In the space of thirteen months, he had won an NCAA title, an Olympic gold medal, and an NBA title. Russell said those three championships were the highlights of his career.

In Russell's first full season, he confirmed Auerbach's faith in him by becoming the first player in NBA history to average more than 20 rebounds a game for an entire season, something he accomplished ten times in his thirteen seasons.

Speculation had arisen that Woolpert might be leaving USF, but he quickly put an end to it. He said he liked living in California. "While leaving USF is not in my thinking at this time, it doesn't mean I'm turning a deaf ear on everything," he said. "Naturally, I'd listen to an offer if it came along. It would have to be a fabulous one, however. Frankly, I'm not the kind of man who needs a lot to be happy. I like San Francisco and USF very much." He said he and his wife, Mary, were looking for a new home in Sausalito, California, across the Golden Gate Bridge in Marin County, a fifteen-minute drive from the campus.

Surely Woolpert would have considered another coaching job if it meant a salary increase. USF paid him $10,500 during his first championship year, and the school threw in a $1,000 bonus. In 1956 he made $11,000 and received a new car.

Woolpert stayed put, and the Dons continued their winning ways. The following year the Dons turned in another impressive performance, finishing third in the NCAA tournament, losing to Kansas and Wilt Chamberlain 80–56 in the semifinals. "We thought we could win it again," guard Gene Brown recalled. "Then we ran into Wilt. He was just impossible to stop. Nobody in the country could stop him." USF's record for the season was 22-7. Bill Russell's older brother, Charlie, who had been in the army, played on the team but was a little-used reserve.

During the season the Dons stretched their record for consecutive wins to sixty. In their sixth game of the season, Illinois beat them 62–33 on December 17, 1956, two years to the day the streak started. "When we lost it, we really lost it," forward Mike Farmer said. "We got beat so bad that after a while we were just numb. It was very cold in that gym. Illinois had heaters on their bench, but we didn't have any. It was freezing in there, terrible. [But] I think it would have been harder to accept if we'd lost at home."

During the sixty-game streak, the Dons held opponents below

60 points forty-seven times. In twenty-four games, opponents scored less than 50 points a game. The Dons lost a game before Illinois beat them, but it didn't count because it was an exhibition game.

Woolpert said more than twenty years later that he was "damned proud of the string. Not so much because it was so long as because there is not one game that I feel guilty about. We never, as far as I know, took advantage unfairly of another team."

Woolpert said the team felt pressure because of the streak. "We couldn't ever really forget it, although we tried like hell. But it wasn't as bad as some people might think. You know, teams really do play games one at a time, as the old cliché has it. And, of course, I was aware all along that we were benefited by a really fortuitous set of circumstances. That combination of kids—with their pride and their conviction that they could not be beaten— is a rare, maybe even unique thing." Always the believer in a strong defense, Woolpert was also proud that his teams had led the nation in defense for four straight years.

All-American forward Mike Farmer said the 1956–57 squad was his favorite team because it played so well without Jones and Russell. "It was probably the most fun I had in college, seeing us come back and do what we did," Farmer said. "The '56–'57 team, was really a joy to be on. The guys really put everything into it. To see where we ended up was so gratifying." Said teammate Mike Preaseau, also a junior forward on that team, "It was a big plum for us because nobody gave us a snowball's chance in hell to get back there without Russell and Jones, and we did."

The next year San Francisco had an even better record at 25-2 but lost to Seattle in the second round of the NCAA regionals at the Cow Palace when Elgin Baylor hit a last-second shot. It denied the Dons a fourth straight final four. The loss came despite the fact that the Dons had beaten Seattle twice during the regular season.

After the 1958–59 season, in which the Dons went 6-20, Woolpert at the age of forty-four took a leave of absence "due to the rigors of coaching" and after sustaining a serious back injury in a fall while on a basketball tour of the Far East. "Ultimately, that did it," Woolpert said. "I was a nervous, jangled wreck." He started the practice season, but he was in so much pain that the day before the first game he announced he was taking the leave of absence.

It was the tension, Woolpert said, "pure and simple. Here we are, three days before the season even begins, and I can't sleep. I talked to the people at USF and to my doctor. . . . The doctor said I should get away from the whole thing for a year." Woolpert called basketball an intense sport "that is a continuously active thing with a tremendously quick tempo." Woolpert used to rant and rave on the bench during games, letting off steam to relieve the tension. Then the West Coast Athletic Association in 1954 put in a rule that coaches should behave themselves on the bench. "In most ways it was a good rule," he said.

Woolpert said he was going to look into a new field, perhaps in the social services. "But outside of coaching, I have no specific training." He said his wife was resigned to his decision, although she was "in a state of shock. She couldn't believe I really meant I would stop coaching."

Guidice took over for Woolpert during his leave of absence. Six months later, Woolpert announced he was quitting for good. His nine-year record was 153-78. In the four-year span from 1954 to 1958 he won 104 games and lost 10.

Woolpert had become increasingly disenchanted with the emphasis on winning and the continuing stress. "In retrospect, I should have done what I wanted to do—resign at the end of that second national championship in 1956," he said, "but, hell, I've got my dread of insecurity and my intrinsic need for recognition as much as the next fellow. And I suppose I was foolishly, childishly motivated by the fear that people would say, 'There's a guy who can't stand the pressure.' So I stayed."

Woolpert always was modest about his coaching skills.

> In all candor, I considered myself an average coach, a coach who during that time was blessed with great players—as must be any coach who is successful, in my opinion. My biggest asset at the time was my ability to teach defense and fundamentals. I reflect back to my coach in college, Jimmy Needles, . . . and he certainly grounded me in good, solid basketball. I was never a chess player, as far as coaching was concerned. During a game, I was aware of situations but did not have the facile ability to make quick adjustments as some coaches are able to do. I attempted to overcome this by trying to imagine situations which might arise and having our players so well-grounded in fundamental basketball that we could adjust to any situation. And we did that reasonably well.

After leaving USF Woolpert coached the San Francisco Saints of the American Basketball Association during the 1961–62 season, but he was fired after fifteen games. The Saints had won six games. The firing shocked Woolpert, who said he had no idea his job was in jeopardy. The Saints' president George McKeon said the team was not playing as a unit. He said that despite having the best personnel in the league, the team scored the fewest points, took the lowest number of shots and gathered in the fewest rebounds.

Woolpert never had much use for the professional game. He thought the players just liked to run and gun, and they didn't play defense. Bringing his slow offense and tenacious defensive style to the game just didn't fit with the pro style. "They hippodrome the game to the point of absurdity. The college game was a beautiful game."

In 1962 the University of San Diego hired him as basketball

coach and athletic director, where his teams went 90 and 90. He resigned as basketball coach after seven years, citing stress and a loss of interest in the game. He stayed on as athletic director two more years and then quit. "I'm just plain tired," Woolpert said. "My interest in the game has very definitely waned from a personal approach. I didn't want to inflict my dragging interest and enthusiasm on this bunch of kids with great potential. Coaching is the product of the macho mentality. When we were kids, winning was everything. It always has been. There is something wrong when winning becomes the motivating factor. We come to believe the only measure of accomplishment is victory. There has to be something more rational."

About his loss of interest in basketball, he said, "I've been this way for some time, but I kept pushing my feelings into the background thinking they might go away. Well, they haven't. I've become more and more irascible with my family, and my role as a father and counselor to my [five] kids has to come first."

He retired to Sequim, Washington, on the northern tip of the Olympic Peninsula, where he drove a school bus for about ten years. A heavy smoker, Woolpert died of lung cancer at home on May 5, 1987, at the age of seventy-one. When he died, K. C. Jones called him a "very caring person. He was a great coach and a very high-quality person. I learned a great deal from him, and I use some of his philosophy [as coach of the Celtics]." Said Hal Perry, "The thing I loved about him more than anything else was he was concerned about everybody on the team. Part of me is gone."

Woolpert's death also saddened Russell. "The friendship that I had with Phil had very little to do with basketball," he said. "I wrote him a letter recently and told him that what I most admired about him was his humanity. He was always fair and he taught his players to be fair. Phil was my coach and my friend. The greatest gift that one person can give another is friendship. And Phil has given me that in abundance. And forever."

Like Jimmy Needles before him, Woolpert also groomed future coaches. When Woolpert died, Jones was coaching the Celtics, Russell the Sacramento Kings and Bernie Bickerstaff, who played for Woolpert at San Diego, the Seattle SuperSonics. All three were black. Russell became the first black coach in professional basketball in 1967 when he was player-coach of the Celtics.

Bickerstaff said about his time with Woolpert at San Diego, "I had a chip on my shoulder. I thought I was vindicated in it, because of some racist-type things that I had experienced in my life. But all I was really looking for was fairness. That was the key. That's what I got with Phil. At that stage of my life, I could have been turned away. I needed direction badly at that time. And Phil gave it to me. He was before his time in terms of dealing with all people and caring about all people. He's always been ahead of his time in terms of doing what's right."

# NINETEEN
## Epilogue

"It's just a shame that we haven't been close to Bill, or closer to Bill."
—Former USF president John Lo Schiavo

It has been said that you can determine how successful a coach has been by looking at what his former players have accomplished five or ten years later. By any stretch of the imagination, Woolpert was an overwhelming success. Here's a rundown of what happened to his assistant coach, aides, and former players:

### Ross Guidice

Guidice stayed with Woolpert for nine years. He continued to teach high school during those years while serving as Woolpert's assistant. In addition, in 1954 he opened a San Francisco furniture store with a partner. When Woolpert resigned, Guidice reluctantly agreed to take over as USF's head coach. "I know most coaches dream of someday becoming top man, but I was satisfied [as an assistant]. I have a furniture store on the side that takes time, and I really wasn't looking for a job."

Guidice stepped down in 1960 after a season of 8 wins and 16 losses. "I never wanted to be a head coach," Guidice said. "Five years before I took over . . . I knew I didn't want to be a head coach. But I took the job because I considered it my duty as an assistant coach." Guidice then devoted all his time to his furniture business. He retired in 1995 and lives in San Rafael, California.

## Bill Russell

As a member of the Celtics, Russell played on eleven NBA championship teams—two when he was also coach—in thirteen seasons. He was the NBA's MVP for five years, a member of the All-NBA first team for three years and the All-NBA second team for eight years, a twelve-time NBA All-Star game participant, *Sports Illustrated*'s Sportsman of the Year in 1968, and the *Sporting News* Athlete of the Decade in 1970. In 2008 ESPN named Russell the fourth best player in college basketball history, behind Kareem Abdul-Jabbar, Oscar Robertson, and Bill Walton.

Russell holds the NBA's single-game record for most rebounds in a half with 32. He also grabbed a career-high 51 rebounds, making him only one of two NBA players to pull down more than 50 rebounds in a game. He has been declared the greatest player in the history of the NBA by the Professional Basketball Writers Association of America and named to the NBA's fiftieth anniversary all-time team. He holds Celtic team records that may never be broken. The Celtics retired Russell's no. 6 jersey. He was elected to the Naismith Memorial Basketball Hall of Fame in 1975. In 2006 he was one of the first five people inducted into the National Collegiate Basketball Hall of Fame, including John Wooden and Oscar Robertson.

Russell set other marks as well; one of the most important

was his being named head coach of the Celtics, the first African American head coach in U.S. major league team sports history. He coached the Seattle SuperSonics from 1973–77 and the Sacramento Kings from 1987–89 but fell short of any championships, probably because he didn't have a guy named Russell playing for him.

During his years with the Celtics as well as after his retirement he was active in the civil rights movement. He worked as a TV commentator and wrote three books, *Go Up for Glory*, *Second Wind: The Memoirs of an Opinionated Man*, and *Russell Rules*.

Russell has distanced himself from USF over the years because of a number of slights on their part, including the university's failure to pay his tuition when he returned to finish his degree. "I went back to dear old USF to complete my scholarship," he wrote in his first autobiography. "I planned on waiving the scholarship and paying for the semester as a gesture of goodwill. The gesture was unnecessary. No one offered me the remainder of the scholarship. Dear old USF charged me full retail for my tuition. The scholarship, it turned out, was only good while I was playing basketball." He felt disrespected by the school after helping it raise the basketball team to a national level. Since those years, he has received numerous honorary degrees, including ones from Georgetown and Princeton.

Lo Schiavo said both sides are to blame for Russell's estrangement from the university. "We, for not letting him take those courses that summer when he wanted to finish his degree work," he said. Lo Schiavo added that the decision to charge Russell tuition was made by a former university treasurer—"a cranky old Jesuit priest."

Lo Schiavo tried to get Russell back in the fold in 1985 by offering to grant him his degree if he would give a few talks to classes and write a paper about his NBA experiences, but Russell refused. Lo Schiavo also tried to get Russell to return for the school's 150th-anniversary celebration, but he never heard from him. "You know, I've washed my hands of it. We tried, and it just seems like Bill is not interested—and I don't see why we should go bowing and scraping anymore."

But his former coach, Ross Guidice, hasn't given up. Guidice, who remains close to Russell, said, "I'm going to start working on him about this because he means so much to USF, and I hope USF means a lot to him. I'm sure it does."

Lo Schiavo said that Russell and Woolpert got over their differences years later, after Russell learned what it was like to coach. Russell noted thirty years after he left USF that while he criticized Woolpert for the way he was handled, he never criticized him as a person. "I was thinking as an individual. Phil had to be thinking in terms of layers. He and Ross [Guidice] taught me how to play basketball. Until I came to USF, I had never even run a play. Ross taught me now to move one foot in front of the other, and Phil taught me discipline. I could never have made it with the Celtics without that."

About twenty years after Russell left USF, he and his family and Woolpert's family took a round-trip, eight-day drive in a van from Los Angeles to Vancouver, but they never talked about Russell's criticism of Woolpert, although it was obvious that they had patched up their differences.

Russell lives on Mercer Island, near Seattle. He plays golf and makes a number of public appearances.

### K. C. Jones

K. C. Jones had many options after he graduated. The Los Angeles Rams selected him as a receiver in the thirtieth round of the NFL draft after the 1954–55 season, but he decided against playing for the Rams at that time. The Celtics drafted him in the second round in 1956. Instead, he wound up playing with the dominant Olympic team and then went into the army until 1958. He played basketball on the Fort Leonard Wood team and was named an AAU All-American in the 1957–58 season.

In the summer of 1958 Jones, just out of military service, tried out for the Los Angeles Rams under coach Sid Gillman. Despite never having played football in college, Jones showed enough grit and athleticism to interest Rams general manager Pete Rozelle. He nearly made the team, too, but for a preseason collision with blocking lineman Roosevelt Brown of the New York Giants as Jones was trying to stop a sweep around the end attempted by Frank Gifford. Brown laid a vicious hit on Jones that injured a muscle in his neck. The injury was aggravated every time Jones tried to play. As a result Jones became a Boston Celtic that fall. Backup center Gene Conley was cut by Red Auerbach, and K.C. stayed. Jones became a key player for Auerbach. He played from 1958 to 1967 and won eight NBA championships. The Celtics have retired his number, 25.

After Jones's pro career ended he coached a number of college and professional teams, including Brandeis and Harvard universities, the Lakers, the Bullets, the Celtics, the SuperSonics, and the Pistons. His best seasons were 1984 and 1986 when he led the Celtics to two titles. His record at Boston was 308 wins and 102 losses. He was elected to the Naismith Memorial Basketball Hall of Fame in 1989. Today he works as a special assistant for the University of Hartford. He's also a color analyst for Hartford's men's basketball games, and he assists the university with fundraising and community endeavors.

In 2003 the park where he played as a child in the Bayview district of San Francisco was renamed in his honor. At the dedication Jones said, "This is where I grew up. This is where I got my start. It's home." He now lives in Hartford, Connecticut.

## Hal Perry

Perry played for a brief time with the Harlem Globetrotters, but Trotters' owner Abe Saperstein said Perry was too smart for that kind of life. Saperstein told him he should go to law school, and when Perry agreed Saperstein paid his way to the Lincoln Law School in San Francisco. He practiced civil rights law for many years in the Oakland area. He is now retired and lives in El Cerrito, California.

Perry fondly remembers his college years. "It was the most extraordinary, the most extraordinary experience a group of young students could have," he said in 1998. "A spiritual thing, like going to the mountaintop to receive the laurel. And to have two of them. Incredible."

### Mike Farmer

Farmer played in the NBA from 1958 to 1966. He was the second player taken in the 1958 NBA draft. He played with the St. Louis Hawks, the New York Knicks, and the Cincinnati Royals. After his playing days he became a scout and later the coach of the Baltimore Bullets. He took a hand at announcing basketball games on radio and TV, owned a pizza parlor, raised cattle, and became a partner in an executive search company. Finally Farmer decided he needed to get the degree from San Francisco that he had abandoned, thirty-two units shy, in 1958.

He returned to USF after the school offered to give scholarships to athletes who had left school without graduating. "I enjoyed it thoroughly," Farmer said. "I have great rapport with students." He finally graduated when he was fifty years old. He is an adjunct professor in exercise and sports sciences at USF and lives in Santa Rosa, California. He is one of five USF basketball players to have his number retired.

### Gene Brown

After he left USF Brown spent three years as a recreation director in San Francisco and then in 1963 became a San Francisco police officer for six years. He left that job to work in the community relations section of the U.S. Justice Department. In 1978 he served as San Francisco's first African American sheriff. He later worked for the Small Business Administration, then as a recreation director at the San Francisco Youth Guidance Center. He is retired and lives in Pittsburg, California.

## Carl Boldt

The Detroit Pistons drafted Carl Boldt, but he wound up playing for the semipro Buchan Bakers in Seattle, Washington. He later worked as a scout and assistant coach for the ABA's Los Angeles Stars in the '70s as well as for other ABA teams. He was also head basketball coach at St. Francis High in Southern California where he produced ten Division I players, including NBA player Mike Newlin.

For seventeen years Boldt has sold Café Chic, a Costa Rican brand of coffee that is known throughout the United States, Europe, and Japan. In addition Boldt has addressed more than 125,000 youngsters in Southern California about the dangers of using illegal drugs. He resides in Arcadia, California.

## Steve Balchios

Balchios is a retired middle school teacher, coach, and still-avid tennis player who lives in San Bruno, California.

## Warren Baxter

Baxter retired after forty-four and a half years with the San Francisco recreation department. He splits his time between San Francisco and Palestine, Texas.

## Vince Boyle

Boyle attended USF in 1950 for one year before he was drafted, serving in the navy during the Korean War. A six-foot-five center, Boyle returned to USF as a walk-on during the championship years but played very little. "I had the best view in the house," he said.

After graduating as an English major Boyle taught, coached, and was a counselor at Sir Francis Drake High School in San Anselmo, California. He is now retired and lives in San Rafael, California.

## Vince Briare
Briare was the team's trainer while he earned his teaching credential. He fell into the job after he suffered a career-ending knee injury while playing football at USF. The school asked him to become the trainer during Woolpert's first year as head coach. Briare later taught history and was a guidance counselor at Santa Clara High School before retiring after thirty-seven years.

## Stan Buchanan
Buchanan coached for two years at St. Vincent's in Vallejo, California, before becoming head coach at St. Ignatius High School, his alma mater. He led the team to a city championship while also coaching the freshman at USF. When Guidice stepped down as head coach in 1960, Buchanan applied for the job but didn't get it. He later taught and coached at Redwood High School in Larkspur, California, retiring as head of the English department. The tennis courts at the high school are named in his honor.

## Bill Bush
Bush graduated with honors from USF's law school in 1963 and clerked for a year with a judge in the California Court of Appeals. He is now a retired civil litigation attorney and lives in San Francisco.

## Jack King
King had the distinction of being the only player to play on all three teams that made it to the final four in the NCAA tournament. After the 1956–57 season he was named the most inspirational athlete at USF that school year. He went to law school at USF where

he roomed with former teammate Tom Nelson, who today is his best friend. He is now a semi-retired civil litigation attorney who lives in Petaluma, California.

## Gordon Kirby
After graduation, Kirby served two years in the army. He retired after twenty-nine years as director of industrial relations with the California Trucking Association. He now lives in Livermore, California.

## John Koljian
Koljian played on the 1956 national championship team and the final four team in 1957. He dropped out of school his senior year to take care of his ailing mother and never returned to finish his degree. He is now a retired title insurance executive who lives in Walnut Creek, California.

## Dick Lawless
After graduation, Lawless played a year of professional baseball before going into the army for two years. He then returned to Oakland, where he worked in financial services before retiring to Lake Wildwood, a community about ten miles west of Grass Valley in California's Mother Lode country.

## Bill Mallen
Mallen attended law school at USF, served in the San Francisco district attorney's office, and in 1982 was appointed a Municipal Court judge in San Francisco. He died in 1992 of a heart attack at the age of 55.

## Bill Mulholland
Mulholland became the student manager of the USF basketball team after he tried out for the freshman team but knew "within

twenty-four hours I wasn't good enough." Woolpert asked him to be the manager. He also served as junior class president during the 1955–56 school year. After graduation, Mulholland taught and coached at public and private schools, ending his career as assistant superintendent of the Chico Unified School District in Chico, California, where he still lives today.

### Jerry Mullen

After graduation, Mullen was drafted by the New York Knicker-bockers but chose to play AAU ball for six years for Vickers Petro-leum in Wichita, Kansas. He then returned to California where he was a sale representative for Cummings Engines in Eureka. He later worked as a branch manager for an international manage-ment and personnel consulting firm in Carmichael, California. He died in 1979 at the age of 45.

### Tom Nelson

Nelson is a semi-retired insurance lawyer and a civil litigator, who lives in Los Altos, California.

### Hal Payne

Payne played during his freshman and sophomore years and then left school to get married. He is a retired railroad conductor who lives in Rio Rancho, New Mexico today.

### Mike Preaseau

Preaseau is the retired owner of a gourmet cookware store. He lives in Portland, Oregon.

### Bob Wiebusch

Wiebusch left school without graduating and worked as a mer-chant seaman, owned a bar, and was a liquor salesman before settling down as a deckhand on the Golden Gate Transit ferry until he retired in 1988. He lives in Sonoma, California.

## Rudy Zannini

Zannini went into the army after graduating in 1955 and then became an assistant basketball coach at Riordan High School in San Francisco under former USF teammate Rich Mohr. He later became head basketball coach at Riordan, coaching for fifteen years before assuming administrative duties at the school. He is retired and lives in Napa, California.

As for the USF basketball program, its teams have met with modest success since those spectacular seasons. In mid-1985 USF abolished the program because of misconduct by alumni and players that its president said threatened the "integrity and credibility" of the university. Alumni were accused of breaking NCAA rules by helping to finance players. That NCAA violation was the third since 1976 to scandalize the basketball program. "An alumnus for whose actions the NCAA holds the university responsible has paid money on numerous occasions to an enrolled student athlete who did not work for it," Lo Schiavo said. He said whether the program would be reinstated "will depend on whether those responsible for this university are convinced that the factors that destroyed the program are not going to beset us again, and that a sound, constructive program can be developed and maintained to contribute positively to the life of USF rather than to afflict it."

The school expected outrage from its basketball faithful but was instead praised for its courage and morality in making such a difficult decision. Lo Schiavo admitted that without a big-time sport, he "sensed a void on campus."

K. C. Jones was shocked. "I might not have been in college at all if it hadn't been for them. Same with Bill Russell. Took a guy with nothing and gave him a reason to stick his chest out."

Three years later the program was restored, but it has never again reached the dizzying heights of the mid-1950s. Despite the estrangement between Russell and USF, Russell agreed to help the university's basketball program at a welcome-back dinner. He "gave just a terrific talk," Lo Schiavo said. "He talked about the school and he quoted some of his professors, shared some of the things he learned in class, especially philosophy class. He certainly didn't sound like someone who didn't enjoy USF. He sounded like someone who fondly remembered his years at USF."

When the Dons won their championships they received plaques. Players didn't receive rings in those days. But fifty years later the school gave them rings to commemorate their achievements. "Now . . . you've got to go out and show it off to some of your buddies," said Dick Lawless. "And then they ask 'You're who?' or 'You played with them?'"

# NOTES

Preface

ix  *We changed the game*  Anderson, "In Their Own Style," 98.

ix  **Woolpert's wife minced**  Johnson, "Triumph in Obscurity," 71.

x  **The inclusion of black players**  Newell, *Pete Newell's Defensive Basketball*, 116.

x  **In one of the least recognized**  Isaacs, *All the Moves*, 196–97.

xi  **When you played Russell**  *Seattle Times*, March 30, 1986.

xi  **The Dons' two championship seasons**  *San Francisco Chronicle*, April 3, 2005.

xi  **Said *Sports Illustrated***  Deford, "Defensive wizard revolutionized the college game," March 14, 2005.

xii  **At first**  Fitzpatrick, *And The Walls Came Tumbling Down*, 58.

xiii  **Perry later said**  *St. Louis Post-Dispatch*, February 6, 2005.

xiii  **Wolpert's son, Paul**  *St. Louis Post-Dispatch*, February 6, 2005.

xiii  **Bill Russell said**  *Seattle Times*, May 7, 1987.

xiv  **A lot of coaches**  *Seattle Times*, May 7, 1987.

xiv  **Said forward Mike Farmer**  Mike Farmer interview, October 10, 2006.

xiv    **Not to take anything**    Anderson, "In Their Own Style," 98.

xiv    *Sports Illustrated* **writer**    Deford, "The Ring Leader," 96+(1).

xiv    **Carl Boldt**    *San Francisco Examiner*, March 27, 1996.

xiv    **Said one coach**    Lee, "Bill Russell, K. C. Jones, Unstoppable San Francisco," 38.

xiv    **Guard Hal Perry said**    *Oakland Tribune*, Dec. 15, 1999.

xiv    **Blocking shots became**    Tax, "The Man Who Must Be Different," 29–30.

xv    **Pete Newell coached**    Tax, "The Man Who Must Be Different," 29–30.

xv    **Tom Heinsohn**    George, *Elevating the Game*, 150.

xvi    **We weren't planning**    www.hickoks.com/biograph/russellbill .shtml, downloaded August 12, 2006.

xvi    **In 1967 the dunk**    Fitzpatrick, *And The Walls Came Tumbling Down*, 239.

xvi    **In the view of**    Bjarkman, *Hoopla*, 105.


Introduction

xxii    **We weren't trash-talkers**    *San Francisco Chronicle*, August 28, 2006.

xxiii    **Boston Celtics coach**    Packer and Lazenby, *College Basketball's 25 Greatest Teams*, Introduction.

xxiii    **Packer is expert**    Packer and Lazenby, *College Basketball's 25 Greatest Teams*, 43.

xxiv    **Eddie Einhorn**    Einhorn and Rapoport, *How March Became Madness*, viii.


1.    Russell's Coming of Age

1    **I saw that head of his**    *Contra Costa Times*, October 1, 1999.

1    **This was unheard of**    Smith, *A Coach's Life*, 27.

1    **He told Harp**    Einhorn and Rapoport, *How March Became Madness*, 143.

2    **I was so skinny**    Russell, *Go Up for Glory*, 28.

2    **Another said Russell**    Fahey, *Great Black Americans*, 322.

2    **One day he heard**    Russell, *Go Up for Glory*, 26.

2    **A widely reproduced picture shows**    Shapiro, *Bill Russell*, 32.

2    **My father always told me**    *New York Times*, September 19, 2007.

3    **His athletic fortunes**    Linn, "Bill Russell's Private World," 64.

3    **Russell would say**    Russell, "We are grown men playing a child's game," 87.

3    **This is a compassionate man**    http://www.insidebayarea.com/portlet/article/html/fragments/print_article.sp?article=3398995, downloaded Sept. 23, 2006.

3    **After his experience**    Russell, *Go Up for Glory*, 27.

3    **On the first day of practice**    *Sports Illustrated*, August 20, 2007, http://sportsillustrated.cnn.com/2007/writers/ian.thomsen/08/20/Russell/2.html, downloaded September 13, 2007.

4    **Russell didn't even make**    Russell, *Second Wind*, 61.

4    **One of his classmates**    Quoted from *Sports Illustrated* in *Investor's Business Daily*, May 31, 2001.

4    **Powles put Russell**    O'Liam, "They Make Rules to Stop Russell," 22+(1).

4    **Allowing me to share**    Russell, "We are grown men playing a child's game," 43.

4    **But George**    *San Francisco Chronicle*, January 16, 2006.

4    **Powles said he kept**    Klein, *Pro Basketball's Big Men*, 17–18.

4    **One of Russell's problems**    Klein, *Pro Basketball's Big Men*, 17–18.

4    **Russell had difficulty**    Russell, *Go Up for Glory*, 28.

5    **In time Russell**    Russell, *Go Up for Glory*, 27–28.

5    **Powles gave Russell**    Russell, "We are grown men playing a child's game," 87.

5    **Russell also practiced**    *Oakland Tribune*, December 13, 1999.

5    **Powles once told Russell**    Russell, "I Was a 6′9″ Babe in the Woods," 25.

5    **He also told the boys**    Linn, "Bill Russell's Private World," 64.

5    **You are a Negro team**    Russell, *Go Up for Glory*, 29.

6    **There were times**    Linn, "Bill Russell's Private World," 64.

6    **Powles repeatedly admonished**    *Milwaukee Journal Sentinel* (Wisconsin) April 16, 2000.

6   [Powles] may not have known   Terrell, "The Big Surprise of 1955," 17 (2).

6   Now as a starter   Russell, *Russell Rules*, 119.

7   USF freshman forward   *The Union*, Nevada County, California, November 22, 2005.

7   Hal DeJulio   *Contra Costa Times*, October 1, 1999.

8   Is he as good   Taylor, *The Rivalry*, 51.

8   Powles told DeJulio   Newell, *Pete Newell's Defensive Basketball*, 63.


2.   A Road Trip to Discovery

9   The very idea   Russell, *Second Wind*, 70.

9   I was happier than   Russell, *Second Wind*, 62.

10   His new touring team traveled   Russell, *Second Wind*, 64.

10   This was difficult   Fitzgerald, *Champions Remembered*, 60.

10   At McClymonds   Russell, *Second Wind*, 64.

10   Swegle was willing   Russell, *Russell Rules*, 21.

10   Russell said that   Russell, *Second Wind*, 66–67.

11   Russell would practice   Russell, *Second Wind*, 68.

12   Early in his burgeoning career   National Public Radio interview, "Former NBA Star: 'Iconoclast,' Bill Russell." November 17, 2005.

12   Russell discovered   Russell, *Second Wind*, 72.

12   It scared me   *New York Times*, December 28, 1955.

12   Even so, blocking shots   Nelson, *Bill Russell: A Biography*, 20.

13   Russell also realized   Russell, *Second Wind*, 68.

13   He had found   Russell, *Second Wind*, 68.

13   What I really liked   Russell, *Second Wind*, 68.

13   When Russell returned   Russell, *Second Wind*, 75–76.


3.   On Catholic Schools and Race

15   For many American colleges   Deford, A Heavenly Game?, 58.

16   The team members   Diverseeducation.com/artman,publish/printer_5985.shtml, downloaded May 8, 2007.

17   In 2005 Gonzaga   *USA Today*, February 29, 2005.

17 **That's the way** Deford, A Heavenly Game?, 58.

18 **And because private schools** Deford, A Heavenly Game?, 58.

18 **Questions arose** Jones, *Rebound*, 50.

19 **We were right** *San Francisco Chronicle*, April 3, 2005.

19 **The decision touched off** Quoted in Fitzpatrick, *And The Walls Came Tumbling Down*, 45.

20 **It certainly didn't help** Spivey, "The Black Athlete in Big-Time Intercollegiate Sports, 1941–1968," 123.

20 **The student newspaper** *The Foghorn*, September 19, 1952.

21 **K. C. Jones remembered** Jones, *Rebound*, 52.


4. Another Surprise Recruit

23 **There's something that** Packer and Lazenby, *College Basketball's 25 Greatest Teams*, 47.

23 **His coach** Jones, *Rebound*, 45.

24 **While Jones excelled** Jones, *Rebound*, 46.

24 **A white history teacher** Jones, *Rebound*, 46.

25 **There was some** Thomas, *They Cleared the Lane*, 228.

25 **Like Russell** Jones, *Rebound*, 46.

25 **When Woolpert gave** *St. Louis Post-Dispatch*, February 6, 2005.

26 **The summer between** Jones, *Rebound*, 49.

26 **If you're black** Jones, *Rebound*, 49.

26 **Woolpert, he said** Jones, *Rebound*, 50.

26 **Jones figured** Jones, *Rebound*, 50.

27 **But Jones also** *Rebound*, 51.

27 **In Jones's sophomore year** Jones, *Rebound*, 51.


5. A School He'd Never Heard Of

29 **I was determined** Linn, "Bill Russell's Private World," 65.

29 **It is not surprising** *San Francisco Chronicle*, November 22, 1985.

29 **To Russell, the City** Russell, *Second Wind*, 79–80.

29 **Russell saw USF** Linn, "Bill Russell's Private World," 65.

30 **DeJulio said that when he met** *Contra Costa Times*, October 1, 1999.

30  **Russell was surprised**  Klein, *Pro Basketball's Big Men*, 18.

30  **If Woolpert offered**  Lee, "Bill Russell, K. C. Jones, Unstoppable San Francisco," 38.

30  **When he found the campus**  Russell, *Second Wind*, 76.

31  **Woolpert clearly remembered**  Johnson, "Triumph in Obscurity," 74.

31  **He was as fiercely competitive**  Johnson, "Triumph in Obscurity," 74.

31  **Years later, Russell said**  *San Francisco Chronicle*, November 22, 1985.

31  **A future teammate**  *St. Louis Post-Dispatch*, February 6, 2005.

31  **Another onlooker**  Hal Perry telephone interview, April 9, 2007.

31  **The Dons' starting center**  *Hayward Daily Review*, February 20, 1976.

32  **Russell said Woolpert**  Linn, "Bill Russell's Private World," 65.

32  **He didn't know it**  Linn, "Bill Russell's Private World," 65.

32  **After his tryout**  Russell, *Second Wind*, 78.

32  **You could count**  Quoted in Goudsouzian, "The House That Russell Built," 7.

33  **The way Russell**  Wooden, *Wooden on Leadership*, 66.

33  **When Russell arrived**  Taylor, *The Rivalry*, 58.

33  **It was like this**  *San Francisco Chronicle*, March 16, 1955.

33  **Bob Feerick**  Taylor, *The Rivalry*, 56.


6.  Roommates and Friends Forever

35  **[Russell] and I became**  Jones, *Rebound*, 52.

35  **K. C. Jones was sitting**  Jones, *Rebound*, 51.

35  **For a whole month**  Russell, *Go Up for Glory*, 32.

36  **When the ice had been broken**  Jones, *Rebound*, 52.

36  **[Russell] had a gift**  *Contra Costa Times*, June 12, 2006.

36  **Jones became like**  Russell, *Go Up for Glory*, 33.

36  **When Russell arrived**  www.jewishworldreviewe.com.cols/matthews042800.asp, downloaded Aug. 22, 2006.

36  **Russell took advantage**  *San Francisco Chronicle*, November 22, 1985.

37   **Once in a philosophy**   *Go Up for Glory*, 47.

37   **Still Russell kept**   *Go Up for Glory*, 50.

37   **K. C. Jones enjoyed school**   Jones, *Rebound*, 54.

37   **Carl Boldt, a forward**   Carl Boldt telephone interview, March 17, 2007.

37   **When Guidice once asked Russell**   "USF Dons: How They Changed the Game," http://www.athletesunitedforpeace.org/am-usf.html, downloaded July 8, 2007.

38   **Russell said Guidice always**   Russell, *Second Wind*, 81–82.

39   **Guidice never accepted credit**   Newell, *Pete Newell's Defensive Basketball*, 64.

39   **Russell never forgot**   Russell, *Second Wind*, 82.

39   **He couldn't get in enough**   Russell, *Russell Rules*, 116.

39   **They would think**   Russell, *Second Wind*, 84.

39   **The barest mention**   Russell, *Second Wind*, 83.

40   **If I were playing**   Russell, *Second Wind*, 83.

40   **Ever since my freshman year**   Russell, *Russell Rules*, 179.

41   **By blocking shots**   Russell, *Russell Rules*, 179.

41   **His ability to block shots**   Jenkins, *A Good Man*, 64.

41   **It didn't hurt**   O'Liam, "They Make Rules to Stop Russell," 92.

41   **Jones said it was difficult**   Jones, *Rebound*, 52.

42   **For example in practice**   Tax, "The Man Who Must Be Different," 29.

42   **As defense-minded players**   Jones, *Rebound*, 53.

42   **In 1981 Russell said**   *Seattle Times*, March 30, 1981.

42   **Jones couldn't wait**   Jones, *Rebound*, 53.

42   **They almost didn't get the chance**   Russell, *Russell Rules*, 150–51.

43   **It was the right decision**   *San Francisco Chronicle*, November 22, 1985.

43   **It wasn't always easy for Bill**   *San Francisco Chronicle*, November 22, 1956.

43   **Because he felt out of place**   *New York Times*, November 26, 1981.

7. Time to Produce

45 **If you can't shoot** "Dons on Defense," www.time.com/time/printout/0,8816,807029,00.html, downloaded January 17, 2007.

45 **Russell had frustrated** *Hayward Daily Review*, Feb. 20, 1976.

46 **After three losing seasons** Lee, "Bill Russell, K. C. Jones, Unstoppable San Francisco," 39.

47 **Moving up** *Oakland Tribune*, Dec. 15, 1999.

49 **Perry—the only black** *San Francisco Chronicle*, April 3, 2005.

49 **Undaunted, he countered** Gergen, "San Francisco comes of age,—1955," http://www.sportingnews.com/archives/ncaa/1955.html, downloaded July 6, 2007.

49 **On the ride home** *St. Louis Post-Dispatch*, February 6, 2005.

49 **Perry never regretted** *San Francisco Chronicle*, March 12, 1998.

49 **Nor did Woolpert** *San Francisco Chronicle,* March 9, 1956.

50 **Woolpert had always** USF *media guide for 1955–56 season.*

50 **He was also fond** NCAA *March Madness*, 36.

50 **He taught the Dons** Lee, "Bill Russell, K. C. Jones, Unstoppable San Francisco," 38.

50 **Woolpert was without a doubt** Packer and Lazenby, *College Basketball's 25 Greatest Teams*, 43.

51 **Although Woolpert was** Lee, "Bill Russell, K. C. Jones, Unstoppable San Francisco," 38.

51 **One of his players** Urban, *Life's Greatest Lessons*, 49–50.

51 **Woolpert was also a stickler** *The Associated Press*, February 26, 1956.

52 **Woolpert believed** *San Francisco Chronicle*, April 3, 2005.

52 **Woolpert wanted** Russell, *Go Up for Glory*, 34.

52 **Sometimes, just for fun** Russell, *Russell Rules*, 22.

53 **He was brought up** Russell, *Russell Rules*, 23.

53 **I admit** *New York Times*, November 26, 1981.

53 **About Russell** *United Press International*, May 21, 1981.

53 **I studied the rules** Quoted from *Sports Illustrated* in *Investor's Business Daily*, May 31, 2001.

53 **Russell and Woolpert** Johnson, "Triumph in Obscurity," 74.

53  **Although he recognized**   Rappoport, *The Classic*, 101.

53  **Russell had other problems**   Russell, *Go Up for Glory*, 41.

53  **Two years after**   Johnson, "Triumph in Obscurity," 74.

54  **Woolpert also kept after**   *Newspaper Enterprise Association*, May 12, 1966.

54  **Fellow sophomore**   *Long Beach Independent-Telegram*, July 1, 1968.

54  **One thing happened**   Russell, *Go Up for Glory*, 31.

54  **Although he could**   Russell, *Second Wind*, 85–86.

55  **I concentrated on**   *San Francisco Chronicle*, February 28, 1955.

55  **Russell and Jones**   Russell, *Second Wind*, 85–86.

56  **Perry told Russell**   Gergen, *The Final Four*, 89.

56  **Perry said he "saw something**   *Oakland Tribune*, Dec. 15, 1999.

56  **Russell would come tearing**   *San Francisco Chronicle*, April 3, 2005.

56  **Sometimes Russell**   "USF Dons: How They Changed the Game," http://www.athletesunitedforpeace.org/am-usf.html, downloaded July 8, 2007.

56  **Russell learned a psychological side**   Packer, *College Basketball's 25 Greatest Teams*, 48.

56  **What I try to do**   Russell, "We are grown men playing a child's game," 76.

57  **As Russell's reputation grew**   Russell, "We are grown men playing a child's game," 76.

57  **It all started with**   Newell, *Pete Newell's Defensive Basketball*, 248.

57  **Newell, who was a mentor**   Newell, *Pete Newell's Defensive Basketball*, 116.

57  **He later remarked**   Newell, *Pete Newell's Defensive Basketball*, 106.

57  **He called Russell**   Newell, *Pete Newell's Defensive Basketball*, 109.

58  **Jones, he said**   "USF Dons: How They Changed the Game," http://www.athletesunitedforpeace.org/am-usf.html, downloaded July 8, 2007.

58   **And if those weren't**   Newell, *Pete Newell's Defensive Basketball*, 112.

58   **Woolpert also used**   Jenkins, *A Good Man*, 14.

58   **Woolpert pinned**   Russell, *Russell Rules*, 41–42.

59   **Like Woolpert**   Jones, *Rebound*, 53.


8.   A Disappointing Season

61   **We were worse**   *San Francisco Chronicle*, March 23, 1995.

61   **Some observers have said**   *Alameda Times-Star*, March 15, 2004.

62   **The game was played**   *Alameda Times-Star*, March 15, 2004.

62   **Said the San Francisco Chronicle**   *San Francisco Chronicle*, Dec. 2, 1953.

62   **Woolpert was asked**   *San Francisco Chronicle*, Dec. 17, 1953.

63   **As play began**   *Oakland Tribune*, Dec. 15, 1999.

63   **Russell recalled**   *Contra Costa Times*, June 12, 2006.

63   **So I try that**   sportsillustrated.cnn.com/2007/writers/ian
.thomsen/08/20/Russell/2.html, downloaded September 13,
2007.

64   **Russell "covered the backboard**   *San Francisco Chronicle*,
December 1, 1953.

64   **His defensive play**   *Alameda Times-Star*, March 15, 2004.

64   **Two years later**   *New York Times*, Dec. 28, 1955.

64   **Cal's Bob Albo**   *New York Times*, Dec. 28, 1955.

65   **Five days after the game**   *San Francisco Chronicle*, December
6, 1953.

65   **The pain became worse**   *San Francisco Chronicle*, December
8, 1953.

65   **We almost got to him**   Lee, "Bill Russell, K. C. Jones, Unstoppable San Francisco," 39.

65   **While Jones was in a coma**   Jones, *Rebound*, 53–54.

66   **Woolpert was also touched**   *San Francisco Chronicle*, December 17, 1953.

66   **With Jones out**   Russell, *Russell Rules*, 41.

66   **One player chastised**   Nelson, *Bill Russell, A Biography*, 29.

66   **It was not a very**   Stan Buchanan telephone interview, May 15, 2007.

66   **Russell never openly**   Whalen, *Dynasty's End*, 42.

66   **Perry wasn't quite so diplomatic**   Goudsouzian, "The House That Russell Built," 9.

66   **Cliques tended to split**   Gordon Kirby telephone interview, May 7, 2007.

67   **A turning point**   Russell, *Second Wind*, 120.

67   **But Russell had gone**   Russell, *Russell Rules*, 42.

67   **After the blistering**   Whalen, *Dynasty's End*, 42.

67   **[Woolpert] walked away**   Russell, *Russell Rules*, 43.

68   **Without those injuries**   Dick Lawless telephone interview, April 3, 2007.

68   **Russell, decidedly**   Packer and Lazenby, *College Basketball's 25 Greatest Teams*, 47.

68   **We had wall-to-wall jerks**   Russell, *Second Wind*, 121.

69   **Woolpert—livid**   Whalen, *Dynasty's End*, 43.

9.   An Unlikely Coach

71   **He could make coffee nervous**   An often quoted remark by Mike Farmer.

71   **Phil Woolpert may have been**   Johnson, "Triumph in Obscurity," 70.

72   **At six-two**   Johnson, "Triumph in Obscurity," 71–72.

72   **During his years of coaching**   *Hal Payne telephone interview,* May 10, 2007.

72   **At Loyola under**   Jenkins, *A Good Man*, 12.

72   **Two years later he was drafted**   Johnson, "Triumph in Obscurity," 72.

72   **Newell practically had to beg**   "USF Dons: How They Changed the Game," http://www.athletesunitedforpeace.org/am-usf.html, downloaded July 8, 2007.

72   **Not only did Newell**   *Los Angeles Times*, May 31, 1992.

73   **Athletic programs were simpler**   E-mail, The Reverend Michael Kotlanger, Feb. 25, 2008.

74   **Woolpert coached USF's**   Johnson, "Triumph in Obscurity," 71.

74    **Needles had to do some**    Johnson, "Triumph in Obscurity," 74.

75    **Woolpert's motivating technique**    Mike Farmer interview, Oct. 9, 2006.

75    **Woolpert also saw to it**    Zannini telephone interview, March 14, 2007.

75    **We held our own**    King telephone interview, May 15, 2007.

75    **He tried to avoid**    Anderson, "In Their Own Style," 98.

76    **[Woolpert] was very innovative**    *Contra Costa Times*, April 4, 2005.

76    **Woolpert, Russell said**    Anderson, "In their Own Style," 98.

76    **There never was any question**    Mike Preaseau telephone interview, April 18, 2007.

76    **While Woolpert helped**    Johnson, "Triumph in Obscurity," 74.

77    **Woolpert often wondered**    Urban, *Life's Greatest Lessons*, 49–50.

77    **The cerebral, bespectacled coach**    Johnson, "Triumph in Obscurity," 70.

78    **Woolpert could talk**    Johnson, "Triumph in Obscurity," 70.

78    **Phil was his own**    Krause and Pim, *Basketball Defense Sourcebook*, 246.

78    **He was much harder**    Russell, *Go Up for Glory*, 41.

79    **I can't believe**    Russell, *Go Up for Glory*, 43.

79    **In another instance**    Russell, *Go Up for Glory*, 42.

79    **At least one other player**    Carl Boldt telephone interview, March 16, 2007.

80    **Said guard Hal Payne**    Hal Payne telephone interview, May 10, 2007.

80    **Vince Boyle agreed**    Vince Boyle telephone interview, April 17, 2007.

80    **Guidice would not be drawn**    Ross Guidice telephone interview, March 20, 2007.

80    **After Russell became a coach**    *San Francisco Chronicle*, November 22, 1985.

80   **The years have tended**   NCAA, *March Madness*, 39.

10.   A Surprising Move

83   **Like the big left hand**   *San Francisco Chronicle*, March 23,
     1995.

83   **At the start of the 1954–55 season**   NCAA, *March Madness*, 38.

83   **It bothered Woolpert**   Deford, "The Ring Leader," 96.

83   **Russell responded**   *Contra Costa Times*, June 12, 2006.

83   **Junior guard Hal Perry**   *St. Louis Post-Dispatch*, February 6,
     2005.

84   **If Perry was struggling**   Packer and Lazenby, *College Basket-
     ball's 25 Greatest Teams*, 48.

84   **Jones noted**   Packer and Lazenby, *College Basketball's 25 Great-
     est Teams*, 47.

85   **Forward Dick Lawless**   Dick Lawless telephone interview,
     April 3, 2007.

85   **Woolpert said about his starting lineup**   *A Centennial Album:
     The 1955 Don*, Associated Students of the University of San
     Francisco, and 1955 USF yearbook.

86   **The team has a world**   *San Mateo Times*, February 14, 1955.

86   **Stan is a court opportunist**   *1955 USF yearbook*.

87   **He had been widely sought**   *San Francisco Foghorn*, March 6,
     1956.

87   **According to forward Vince Boyle**   Vince Boyle telephone
     interview, April 17, 2007.

87   **This team got along**   Russell, *Go Up for Glory*, 43.

87   **Jones said the men**   Jones, *Rebound*, 56–57.

88   **In that game, Russell and Jones cooked up**   Russell, *Go Up
     for Glory*, 40.

88   **Loyola coach Bill Donovan**   *Los Angeles Times*, December 15,
     1954.

88   **Then came the game**   *Hartford Courant*, February 1, 2003.

89   **Russell took the blame**   Wolff, *100 Years of Hoops*, 151.

89   **There was a transformation**   *Hartford Courant*, February 1,
     2003.

89  **That the Dons stayed close**   Packer and Lazenby, *College Basketball's 25 Greatest Teams*, 47.

89  **Jerry Mullen**   *Humboldt Times Standard*, January 26, 1973.

89  **Having seen Perry's play**   Rappoport, *The Classic*, 102.

89  **Woolpert said the move**   Hal Perry telephone interview, June 19, 2007.

89  **Forward Jack King**   Jack King telephone interview, May 18, 2007.

89  **He wasn't supposed to play**   *San Francisco Chronicle*, May 17, 1987.

89  **Russell was overjoyed**   Russell, *Go Up for Glory*, 42–43.

90  **Fourteen years later**   *Long Beach Press-Telegram*, July 1, 1968.

90  **Guidice said he and Woolpert**   Ross Guidice telephone interview, April 15, 2007.

90  **Toward the end**   *San Francisco Foghorn*, March 6, 1956.

90  **Said forward Dick Lawless**   *The Union*, November 22, 2005.

90  **Jones agreed**   Celtic Nation Interview. www.celtic-nation .com/interviews/kc_jones/kc_jones_page3.html, downloaded August 22, 2006.

91  **Two stories are told**   cowpalace.com/cowhist.html, downloaded January 27, 2007.

91  UCLA **coach John Wooden**   *San Francisco News*, January 10, 1955.

92  **We played a lot**   *Humboldt Times-Standard*, January 26, 1973.

92  **Ten days after** USF   *San Francisco Chronicle*, December 29, 1954.

92  **Baxter was never told why**   Warren Baxter telephone interview, April 17, 2007.

92  **When the players and coaches arrived**   *San Francisco Examiner*, March 27, 1996.

93  **That was when we bonded**   Bob Wiebusch telephone interview, May 21, 2007.

93  **Woolpert kept Perry**   *New York Times*, November 26, 1981.

93  **When the Dons took**   Jones, *Rebound*, 55.

93  **Jones became upset**   *San Francisco Examiner*, March 27, 1996.

93 **Russell told Woolpert** Jones, *Rebound*, 55.

93 **Regarding that incident** Rappoport, *The Classic*, 102.

93 **When he was inducted** *The Associated Press*, November 18, 2006.

94 **Against George Washington** *San Mateo Times*, January 13, 1973.

94 **A *Daily Oklahoman* sports writer** *Daily Oklahoman*, December 21, 1954.

94 **His brother told Miller** *Seattle Times*, March 30, 1986.

94 **Although Woolpert was happy** Rappoport, *The Classic*, 102.

94 **After the win over Oklahoma City** Jones, *Rebound*, 56.

94 **The Dons also received** *San Francisco Foghorn*, March 25, 1955.

95 **After routing George Washington** *San Francisco Chronicle*, March 23, 1995.

95 **"Tonight," Perry said** Gergen, San Francisco Comes of Age—1955, http://www.sportingnews.com/archives/ncaa/1955.html, downloaded July 6, 2007.

95 **It's realistic to remember** *St. Louis Post-Dispatch*, February 6, 2005.

95 **After the tournament** *United Press*, January 4, 1955.

95 **During the course** Lee, "Bill Russell, K. C. Jones, Unstoppable San Francisco," 85.

95 **The country wasn't really ready** Packer and Lazenby, *College Basketball's 25 Greatest Teams*, 48.

96 **In USF's 10–1 record** Lee, "Bill Russell, K. C. Jones, Unstoppable San Francisco," 85.

96 **Perry's job** *Oakland Tribune*, February 6, 1977.

96 **Said Jones, "Our confidence"** *San Francisco Examiner*, August 8, 1999.

96 **The Dons still were primarily** Klein, *The Rivalry*, 57.

97 **Back home the Dons waltzed** *San Francisco Call-Bulletin*, February 14, 16, 1955.

97 **Russell had nothing** *San Francisco Call-Bulletin*, February 14, 1955.

97    **Woolpert complimented Mullen**    *San Francisco Call-Bulletin*, February 16, 1955.

97    **Guidice told Woolpert**    *San Francisco Chronicle*, March 23, 1995.

97    **Stanford coach Howie Dallmar**    O'Liam, "They Make Rules to Stop Russell," 91.

97    **Dallmar said teams need**    *Palo Alto Times*, January 31, 1955.

98    **During the Stanford game**    Russell, *Second Wind*, 85–86.

98    **The next night, against Cal**    usfdons.cstv.com/trads/Russell_years.html, downloaded January 27, 2007.

98    **The Dons, who were now on**    *San Francisco Chronicle*, February 7, 1955.

99    **Their appetites are such**    Dons on Defense, www.time.com/time/printout/0,8816,807029,00.html, downloaded January 17, 2007.

99    **Woolpert also answered critics**    *The Associated Press*, February 8, 1955.

99    **Jones said that after graduation**    *San Mateo Times*, February 14, 1955.

99    **USF's style of play**    *New York Times*, November 26, 1981.

99    **In mid-February Hank Luisetti**    *San Francisco Chronicle*, February 12, 1955.

99    **Luisetti said the Dons brought back**    *San Francisco Examiner*, January 31, 1955.

100    **A week later retired**    *San Francisco Chronicle*, February 18, 1955.

100    **USF raced through**    *Sacramento Bee*, March 19, 2006.

100    **Fifty years later**    http://santaclarabroncos.cstv.com/sports/m-baskbl/spec-rel/012507aaa.html downloaded February 6, 2008.

101    **The choice of Sears**    Russell, *Go Up for Glory*, 41–42.

101    **Russell was further incensed**    *Los Angeles Times*, January 9, 1999.

101    **Russell told Woolpert**    Johnson, "Triumph in Obscurity," 74.

101    **Russell said he was offended**    *The Manchester Union Leader*, June 15, 2002.

101    Years later Russell adopted    Vancil, NBA at 50, 79.

102    A backer named J. T. O'Connor    *San Francisco Chronicle,*
       March 4, 1955.

102    K. C. Jones said years later    *Washington Post,* August 1, 1982.


11.    The Trail to the Title

103    K. C. Jones was the best    http://www.athletesunitedforpeace
       .org/am-usf.html, downloaded July 8, 2007.

104    As the *San Francisco Chronicle* noted    *San Francisco Chroni-
       cle,* March 24, 1955.

104    Before the decision    *San Francisco Chronicle,* February 15,
       1955.

106    I was quite upset    Rappoport, *The Classic,* 102.

106    Jones said, "It was rough    Celtic Nation Interview. www
       .celtic-nation.com/interviews/kc_jones/kc_jones_page4.html,
       downloaded Aug. 22, 2006.

106    The report also described    *San Francisco Chronicle,* March 11,
       1955.

106    Russell had a habit    *Richmond Independent,* February 2, 1955.

106    Guard Hal Perry    Hal Perry telephone interview, June 19,
       2007.

106    If ever there was a game    *San Francisco Chronicle,* March 17,
       1956.

107    With Russell out    *San Francisco Chronicle,* March 17, 1955.

107    Perry said they shouldn't    Telephone interview, June 19,
       2007.

107    The coaches found    Rappoport, *The Classic,* 102.

108    Forward Gordon Kirby    Telephone interview, May 7, 2007.

108    Al Brightman    *San Francisco Chronicle,* March 16, 1955.

108    UCLA coach John Wooden wondered    *San Francisco Chronicle,*
       March 14, 1955.

108    The Dons received a morale boost    Rappoport, *The Classic,*
       103.

108    As he often did    *San Francisco Chronicle,* March 23, 1995.

109    The Dons needed Mullen    Rappoport, *The Classic,* 101.

109    Buchanan missed his first two    Celtic Nation Interview. www

.celtic-nation.com/interviews/kc_jones/kc_jones_page5.html, downloaded Aug. 22, 2006.

109   **Buchanan drained**    Rappoport, *The Classic*, 100.

110   **The other official said**    *San Francisco Chronicle*, March 14, 1955.

110   **Robins fired up**    Oregon State Alumni Association, *Beaver Clips*, October 17, 2003.

110   **Perry swears to this day**    *San Francisco Examiner*, March 27, 1996.

110   **Did you see**    Lee, "Bill Russell, K. C. Jones, Unstoppable San Francisco," 92.

111   **Oregon State's Gill**    Anderson, "In their Own Style," 98.

111   **USF team physician**    Lee, "Bill Russell, K. C. Jones, Unstoppable San Francisco," 86.

111   **Back in San Francisco**    Vince Briare telephone interview, May 12, 2007.

112   **Colorado coach Bebe Lee**    *San Francisco Chronicle*, March 16, 1955.

112   **Haldorson remembered**    *Oakland Tribune*, December 17, 2004.

112   **Ever the nervous Nellie**    *Long Beach Press-Telegram*, March 3, 1956.

113   **Just before tip-off**    *Colorado Springs Gazette*, March 30, 2007.

113   **They even played slower**    Warren Baxter telephone interview, April 9, 2007.

113   **Did you ever**    Taylor, *The Rivalry*, 61.

113   **Early in the second half**    *Colorado Springs Gazette*, March 30, 2007.

114   **After their game, Gola**    Packer, *Golden Moments*, 62.

114   **The afternoon before the game**    Lee, *Bill Russell, K. C. Jones, Unstoppable San Francisco*, 86.

115   **Gola said years later**    Packer and Lazenby, *College Basketball's 25 Greatest Teams*, 40.

115   **The picture showed**    Lee, "Bill Russell, K. C. Jones, Unstoppable San Francisco," 92.

115   **I think we just can't**    Terrell, "The Big Surprise of 1955," 19.

115 **Coach Woolpert, as always** O'Donnell, *Basketball Digest*, December 2000.

116 **When Woolpert told Jones** O'Donnell, *Basketball Digest*, December 2000.

116 **Jones's plan was simple** O'Donnell, *Basketball Digest, December 2000*.

116 **I knew guarding him** Packer, *Golden moments of the final four*, 49.

116 **Woolpert was nervous** *San Francisco Chronicle*, March 23, 1995.

117 **Whatever Woolpert said** Rappoport, *The Classic*, 98.

117 **Thirteen-year-old Billy Packer** Feinstein, *Last Dance*, 114.

118 **Woolpert said the key** Rappoport, *The Classic*, 104.

118 **The *San Francisco Examiner*'s** Quoted in Schneider, 1953–56 NCAA Championship Seasons: The Bill Russell Years, usfdons.cstv.com/trads,Russell_years.html, downloaded August 12, 2006.

118 **Regarding Gola and Russell** Schneider, usfdons.cstv.com/trads/Russell_years.html, downloaded August 12, 2006.

118 **But Russell thought** *Idaho Mountain Express*, June 27, 2001.

118 **Gola agreed, saying** Packer, *Golden moments of the Final Four*, 49.

119 **As for Russell, Gola** *San Francisco Chronicle*, March 20, 1955.

119 **Years later he was asked** Packer, *Golden Moments*, 63.

119 **Loeffler said after the game** Lee, "Bill Russell, K. C. Jones, Unstoppable San Francisco," 86.

119 **Woolpert heaped praise** Schneider, Usfdons.cstv.com/trads/Russell_years.html, downloaded August 12, 2006.

119 **Despite Russell's success** Russell, *Go Up for the Glory*, 44.

119 **Woolpert, of course, was ecstatic** *San Francisco Chronicle*, March 20, 1955.

119 **Years later, he said** Rappoport, *The Classic*, 101.

120 **Asked what he thought** Rappoport, *The Classic*, 101.

12. Russell Brings about Rule Changes

121 **If the Dons were weary** *San Francisco Chronicle*, March 21, 1955.

121　**The Dons arrived**　*San Francisco Chronicle*, March 22, 1955.

122　**The next day the team**　San Jose *Mercury News*, March 31, 2005.

122　**After countless dignitaries**　*San Francisco Chronicle*, March 23, 1955.

123　**While the Dons celebrated**　*United Press*, March 22, 1955.

124　**Woolpert opposed technical fouls**　*San Francisco Chronicle*, March 20, 1955.

124　**Coaches put two rule changes**　*San Francisco Chronicle*, March 25, 1955.

125　**And he had another good laugh**　Russell, *Go Up for the Glory*, 44.

125　**Russell said the rule change**　*New York Times*, December 2, 1955.

125　**Woolpert couldn't have agreed more**　www.hickoksports .com/biograph/russellbill.shtml, downloaded August 12, 2006.

126　**They are trying to legislate defense**　*The Associated Press*, March 29, 1956.

126　**Pete Newell said: "[USF players] would throw**　*Oakland Tribune*, December 13, 1999.

126　**Phog Allen, who coached**　*San Francisco Chronicle*, March 22, 1955.

126　**San Francisco Chronicle sports editor**　*San Francisco Chronicle*, March 29, 1956.

13.　The Machine Rolls On

129　**We were like rock stars**　Anderson, "In Their Own Style," 98.

129　**Up from the freshman squad**　Mike Farmer interview, Oct. 9, 2006.

130　**Farmer had played center**　*San Francisco Chronicle*, March 13, 1956.

130　**When I was recruited**　Packer, *Golden moments of the final four*, 50.

130　**Boldt recognized that his job**　*San Francisco Chronicle*, March 12, 1956.

130 **But Boldt said that Perry**   Carl Boldt telephone interview, March 15, 2007.

131 **The CBA had granted**   *Hayward* (California) *Daily Review*, January 17, 1956.

133 **Russell loved to go**   Russell, *Second Wind*, 230.

133 **Every game was like a war**   Isaacs, *All the Moves*, 195–96.

133 **Guard Warren Baxter**   *San Francisco Foghorn*, March 6, 1956.

133 **The team didn't have set plays**   Carl Boldt telephone interview, March 17, 2007.

134 **Three games into**   Rappoport, *The Classic*, 105.

134 **The Marquette coach might have been wise**   *San Mateo Times*, December 21, 1955.

134 **They could name**   Goudsouzian, "The House That Russell Built," 17.

134 **DePaul coach Ray Meyer**   Goudsouzian, "The House That Russell Built," 17.

134 **The Dons also stopped off**   *San Francisco Chronicle*, December 21, 1955.

14.  Into the Deep South

137 **Desegregation came**   Anderson, *Black, White, and Catholic*, 130.

138 **The Reverend Ralph Tichenor**   *The Associated Press*, December 23, 1955.

138 **Woolpert saw it**   *The Associated Press*, November 22, 1955.

138 **We thought it might**   *San Francisco Chronicle*, December 21, 1955.

139 **It was merely coincidental**   *Louisiana Weekly*, December 31, 1955.

139 **Loyola coach Jim McCafferty**   *The Associated Press*, December 21, 1955.

139 **When Woolpert heard**   Ross Guidice telephone interview, May 8, 2007.

139 **Woolpert said McMillon**   *The Associated Press*, December 22, 1955.

139 **Guidice told Woolpert** *San Francisco Chronicle*, December 22, 1955.

140 **Molloy issued a 450-word statement** *The Associated Press*, December 21, 1955.

140 **Woolpert said he would pull** *The Associated Press*, December 21, 1955.

140 **Guard Gene Brown** *San Francisco Examiner*, March 27, 1996.

140 **When the Dons arrived** *San Francisco Chronicle*, April 3, 2005.

140 **The situation in New Orleans** www.jimcrownhistory.org .resouces/lessonplans//hs_es_etiquette.htm, downloaded, July 10, 2007.

141 **When they went to the hotel** Bill Mulholland telephone interview, May 6, 2007.

141 **We just tried to block out** Gene Brown telephone interview, May 5, 2007.

141 **We thought [the treatment of blacks]** Steve Balchios telephone interview, May 10, 2007.

141 **Unbeknownst to the coaching staff** Carl Boldt telephone interview, March 14, 2007.

141 **His high school coach** *Louisiana Weekly*, December 24, 1955.

142 **Each player took the floor** Goudsouzian, "The House That Russell Built," 18.

142 **A write-up** *Louisiana Weekly*, December 24, 1955.

142 **He told us to keep our cool** Gene Brown telephone interview, May 5, 2007.

143 **They're great** *The Associated Press*, December 24, 1955.

143 **Russell was gracious** *The Associated Press*, December 24, 1955.

143 **An article in the *New Orleans*** *New Orleans Times-Picayune*, December 24, 1955.

15. Holiday Travel and the Stall

145 **The duel was going** Heinsohn, *Give 'em the Hook*, 27.

145 **It was my first visit** Russell, *Go Up for Glory*, 48.

145  **He missed his first three**   Terrell, "The Tournaments and the Man Who," 38.

146  **Russell could tell during warm-ups**   Russell, *Russell Rules*, 78.

146  **Later in the game**   Heinsohn, *Give 'em the Hook*, 27–28.

146  **It was one of many times**   *New York Times*, December 28, 1955.

147  **What I saw was**   *Boston Herald*, May 26, 1999.

147  **The Crusaders led**   Heinsohn, *Give 'em the Hook*, 28.

147  usf **won 67–51**   Fitzgerald, *Champions Remembered*, 62.

148  **Three future hall of famers**   *Time*, Picked for the Pros, 64.

148  **The two teams were staying**   Gergen, *The Final Four*, 89.

148  **MaGuire said he had never seen**   Gergen, *The Final Four*, 89.

148  **Russell's defensive play**   *Los Angeles Times*, January 4, 1956.

148  **The best way I can say**   *Contra Costa Times*, April 4, 2005.

149  **Traveling with the team**   *San Francisco Foghorn*, January 13, 1956.

149  **When the team returned home**   *San Francisco Chronicle*, January 4, 1956.

149  **Vince Boyle, who saw**   Vince Boyle telephone interview, April 17, 2007.

150  **If they hadn't reached an agreement**   *Newspaper Enterprise Association*, May 12, 1966.

150  **A week later the Dons**   *Los Angeles Times*, January 4, 1956.

150  **This time around they matched wits**   Cal's official athletic site: calbears.cstv.com/trads/cal-m-baskbl-harmon.html, downloaded March 18, 2007.

151  **This became a game to remember**   *San Francisco Chronicle*, December 3, 1991.

151  **Newell was looking**   *The Associated Press*, January 30, 1956.

151  **The *San Francisco Chronicle* put**   *San Francisco Chronicle*, December 3, 1991.

151  **Newell wanted to end**   Newell, *Pete Newell's Defensive Basketball*, 83.

151  **If you played 'em straight**   Newell, *Pete Newell's Defensive Basketball*, 83.

152  **Newell's new strategy**   *San Francisco Chronicle*, December 3, 1991.

152  **[He] was the only guy**   Jenkins, *A Good Man*, 85–86.

152  **With six minutes left in the game**   *San Francisco Chronicle*, December 3, 1991.

152  **I collected ten minutes**   Cal's official athletic site: calbears .cstv.com/trads/cal-m-baskbl-harmon.html, downloaded March 18, 2007.

153  **People were sitting**   Rappoport, *The Classic*, 106.

153  **I would have played**   *San Francisco Chronicle*, January 30, 1956.

153  **Jones said, "All I can**   *San Francisco Chronicle*, December 3, 1991.

153  **Newell added, "The funniest**   Jenkins, *A Good Man*, 86.

153  **Cal's Earl Robinson**   *San Francisco Chronicle*, December 3, 1991.

153  **It was like fighting**   Cal's official athletic site: calbears.cstv .com/trads/cal-m-baskbl-harmon.html, downloaded March 18, 2007.

153  **The Dons' Warren Baxter**   Warren Baxter telephone interview, April 9, 2007.

153  **My kids had been under**   *San Francisco Chronicle*, January 30, 1956.

154  **Woolpert said about the record**   *United Press*, January 29, 1956.

154  **Newell defended his actions**   *Examiner*, March 27, 1996.

154  **Newell remembered**   *San Francisco Chronicle*, December 3, 1991.

154  **The Dons accepted the tactic**   *United Press*, January 29, 1956.

154  **I'll tell you this**   *Hayward Daily Review*, January 30, 1956.

155  **The pressure of maintaining**   Lee, "Bill Russell, K. C. Jones, Unstoppable San Francisco," 86.

155  **Said Russell, "I never, ever**   quoted in Goudsouzian, "The House That Russell Built," 19.

155 **Players often got on each other's** Goudsouzian, "The House That Russell Built," 20.

155 **Years later Russell said** *New York Times*, January 29, 2008.

155 **Said assistant coach Ross Guidice** Lee, "Bill Russell, K. C. Jones, Unstoppable San Francisco," 86.

155 **Waves' coach Duck Dowell** *Long Beach Press-Telegram*, February 28, 1956.

156 **Woolpert was uncertain** *San Francisco Chronicle*, March 14, 1956.

156 **Woolpert said the Dons might** *Long Beach Press-Telegram*, March 1, 1956.

156 **Russell had some kind words** *San Francisco Chronicle*, March 9, 1956.

157 **But the ovation was so strong** Lee, "Bill Russell, K. C. Jones, Unstoppable San Francisco," 86.

157 **I could feel the chills** Gergen, *The Final Four*, 89.

157 **As USF's streak continued** *Long Beach Press-Telegram*, March 3, 1956.

157 **At the end of the regular season** Fay, 1956 All-American Team, 35–37.

158 **After the success of his junior year** Russell, *Second Wind*. 87.

158 **The Dons headed** Packer, *Golden moments of the final four*, 51.

158 **Said Woolpert, "We'll miss** Terrell, "Even the loss," 45.

158 **Said Russell, "It's not"** *San Francisco Chronicle*, March 14, 1956.

158 **Woolpert was also playing coy** *San Francisco Chronicle*, February 24, 1956.

159 **As it turned out** *Oakland Tribune*, February 28, 1956.

160 **Before the NCAA tournament began** *San Francisco Chronicle*, March 9, 1956.

160 **Woolpert also had some backhanded praise** *San Francisco Chronicle*, March 9, 1956.

16. Two in a Row

161 **Intimidation was our major weapon** *New York Times*, March 13, 1991.

161 **Going into our second national championship** *New York Times*, March 13, 1991.

162 **Jones traveled with the team** *Long Beach Independent*, March 12, 1956.

162 **Asked by a reporter** http://usfdons.cstv.com/sports/ m-baskbl/spec-rel/031406aab.html, downloaded August 12, 2006.

162 **Gene Brown took Jones's spot** *United Press*, March 12, 1956.

162 **Woolpert called Brown** *San Francisco Chronicle*, March 14, 1956.

162 **Duquesne coach Dudley Moore** Gergen, *The Final Four*, 90.

162 **K.C. has been the playmaker** *The Associated Press*, March 6, 1955.

162 **Forward Mike Farmer said** *San Francisco Examiner*, March 27, 1996.

163 **Woolpert said he'd hate** *United Press*, March 5, 1956.

163 **When UCLA took the floor** The Associated Press, March 6, 1956.

163 **The magazine claimed** Terrell, "It's Dayton and the Dons," 21.

164 **Woolpert's former teammate** *Los Angeles Times*, March 16, 1956.

164 **UCLA coach John Wooden** *Los Angeles Times*, March 16, 1956.

164 **At one point in the game** Wooden, *They Call Me Coach*, 114–15.

165 **Brown lit up UCLA** *San Francisco Chronicle*, March 17, 1956.

166 **Forward Mike Preaseau** Mike Preaseau telephone interview, April, 18, 2007.

166 **This probably is the greatest** *United Press*, March 20, 1956.

166 **This is a good one** *San Francisco Chronicle*, March 18, 1956.

166 **Woolpert said Utah sneaked up** *San Francisco Chronicle*, March 18, 1956.

166 **K. C. Jones attributed** *San Francisco Chronicle*, March 19, 1956.

167    **Woolpert knew little**    *United Press*, March 20, 1954.

167    **We haven't made any**    *San Francisco Chronicle*, March 21, 1956.

168    **Southern Methodist coach**    *San Francisco Chronicle*, March 17, 1956.

168    **Three days later**    *San Francisco Chronicle*, March 20, 1956.

168    **We didn't play too good**    Terrell, "Victory No. 55: An End to an Era," 43–44.

168    SMU **caught fire**    *San Francisco Chronicle*, March 23, 1956.

169    SMU **coach Hayes**    *San Francisco Chronicle*, March 23, 1956.

169    **Hayes's prediction**    Terrell, "Victory No. 55: An End to an Era," 43–44.

169    **The night before the game**    *Iowa City Press-Citizen*, December 25 2005.

169    **Again Woolpert huddled**    *San Francisco Examiner*, August 8, 1999.

169    **Woolpert as usual**    Lee, "Bill Russell, K. C. Jones, Unstoppable San Francisco," 87.

169    **A picture in *Life* magazine**    *Life*, April 2, 1956.

170    **Someone asked him**    Carl Boldt telephone interview, May 8, 2007.

170    **Iowa pulled out**    Gergen, *The Final Four*, 90.

170    **Jones, in his civilian**    Lee, "Bill Russell, K. C. Jones, Unstoppable San Francisco," 87.

171    **Russell was asked after the game**    Terrell, "Victory No. 55: An End to an Era," 43–44.

171    **We switched our game plan**    Rappoport, *The Classic*, 106.

171    **Perry and Farmer said**    *San Francisco Examiner*, March 27, 1996.

171    **Woolpert said he wasn't worried**    *Chicago Daily Tribune*, March 24, 1956.

171    ***Time* magazine**    Time, http://www.time.com/time/magazine/article/0,9171,862081,00.html, downloaded October 1, 2007.

172    **Said Logan, "You jump**    *Chicago Daily Tribune*, March 24, 1956.

172   **After beating Iowa**   Terrell, "Victory No. 55: An End to an Era," 43–44.

172   **This must be the finest**   *San Francisco Chronicle*, March 24, 1956.

172   **Incredibly the MVP award**   *San Francisco Chronicle*, March 26, 1956.

172   **Woolpert thought the award**   *San Francisco Chronicle*, March 30, 1956.

173   **Peter Bjarkman**   Bjarkman, *Hoopla—A Century of College Basketball*, 106.

173   **Statistics on blocked shots**   Sports Illustrated, http:// sportsil lustrated.cnn.com/2007/writers/ian.thomsen/08/20/ Russell/2.html, downloaded September 13, 2007.

173   **Russell recalled, "We were a great team**   Goudsouzian, "The House That Russell Built," 21.

174   **The day after the championship game**   *Los Angeles Times*, March 31, 2005.

17.   A New Sport for Russell

175   **Russell showed up**   Griffin,   www1.umn.edu/ohr/img/ assets/18007/griffin2.pdf, downloaded February 3, 2007.

175   **A high jumper who also played**   Griffin, www1.umn.edu/ohr/ img/assets/18007/griffin2.pdf, downloaded February 3, 2007.

176   **At his first meet**   *Griffin, www1.umn.edu/ohr/img/ assets/18007/griffin2.pdf*, downloaded February 3, 2007.

177   **Russell enjoyed track**   The Associated Press Sports Staff, *The Sports Immortals*, 213.

177   **Years later Mathis recalled**   *Boston Herald*, July 15, 1998.

177   **Mathis has a picture**   *San Francisco Chronicle*, July 19, 2007.

177   **Sportswriters went nuts**   Griffin, www1.umn.edu/ohr/img/ assets/18007/griffin2.pdf, downloaded February 3, 2007.

178   **Soon thereafter the university's president**   Russell, *Second Wind*, 80–81.

178   **The next meet on a slippery**   Griffin, www1.umn.edu/ohr/ img/assets/18007/griffin2.pdf, downloaded February 3, 2007.

178 **Russell thought he might** *Time*, "Along Came Bill," 37.

178 **One sports writer** *Long Beach Press-Telegram*, February 28, 1956.

179 **Eisenhower came into the room** Linn, "I Owe the Public Nothing," 68.

179 **Russell remembered somebody** Russell, *Go Up for Glory*, 48.

## 18. The Aftermath

181 **Find a way to get this guy** Most, *High Above Courtside*, 90–91.

181 **The selection process** *United Press*, February 28, 1956.

182 **But the college All-Stars lost** Lee, "Bill Russell, K. C. Jones, Unstoppable San Francisco," 87.

182 **The world had never seen** *New York Times Magazine*, February 24, 1957.

182 **In the mid-1990s** *Boston Globe*, December 17, 2000.

183 **Russell said that when he received** *Boston Globe*, December 17, 2000.

183 **Along with the Olympics and marriage** *San Francisco Chronicle*, March 19, 1956.

183 **Globetrotters' owner** *San Francisco Chronicle*, March 1, 1956.

183 **Russell also knew** Linn, "Bill Russell's Private World," 66.

184 **The Globetrotters raised** Russell, "I was a 6'9" Babe in the Woods," 68.

184 **He said Saperstein** Fitzpatrick, *And The Walls Came Tumbling Down*, 61.

184 **Russell believed black players** Tax, "The Man Who Must Be Different," 30.

184 **Woolpert told Auerbach** Most, *High Above Courtside*, 90–91.

185 **Barksdale also worked** Thomas, *They Cleared the Lane*, 131.

185 **Bill Reinhart** Most, *High Above Courtside*, 90.

185 **When Russell played** Linn, "Bill Russell's Private World," 66.

185 **Because of the Olympics** National Public Radio interview, November 17, 2005. http://www.npr.org/templates/story/story.php?storyId=5016616, downloaded July 8, 2007.

186 **Speculation had arisen** *Oakland Tribune*, February 7, 2007.

186 **We thought we could** *Oakland Tribune*, February 7, 2007.

186 **During the season the Dons** *San Francisco Examiner*, March 27, 1996.

186 **When we lost it** *Hartford Courant*, February 1, 2003.

187 **Woolpert said more than twenty years later** Johnson, "Triumph in Obscurity," 77.

187 **All-American forward Mike Farmer** Johnson, "Triumph in Obscurity," 77.

187 **Said teammate Mike Preaseau** Johnson, "Triumph in Obscurity," 77.

188 **After the 1958–59 season** Johnson, "Triumph in Obscurity," 77.

188 **Woolpert said he was going to look** *The Associated Press*, November 28, 1959.

188 **In retrospect, I should have** Johnson, "Triumph in Obscurity," 77.

189 **Woolpert always was modest** Johnson, "Triumph in Obscurity," 77.

189 **The Saints' president** *United Press International*, May 21, 1981.

189 **In 1962 the University of San Diego** *The Associated Press*, October 14, 1969.

190 **My interest in the game** *Sporting News*, March 31, 1986, 12.

190 **About his loss of interest** *The Associated Press*, October 14, 1969.

190 **When he died** *San Francisco Chronicle*, May 7, 1987.

190 **Woolpert's death also saddened** Seattle Times, May 7, 1987.

191 **Bickerstaff said about his time** *Seattle Times*, May 7, 1987.

19. Epilogue

193 **It's just a shame that we haven't** *Los Angeles Times*, April 2, 2007.

193 **When Woolpert resigned** *The Associated Press*, November 30, 1959.

194 **Guidice stepped down in 1960**  *Hayward Daily Review,* March 4, 1960.

195 **Russell has distanced himself**  Russell, *Go up for Glory,* 50.

195 **Lo Schiavo said both sides**  *Los Angeles Times,* April 2, 2007.

196 **Russell noted thirty years**  *San Francisco Chronicle,* November 22, 1985.

196 **About twenty years after Russell left** USF  *San Francisco Chronicle,* November 22, 1985.

197 **At the dedication**  *San Francisco Chronicle,* October 12, 2003.

198 **Perry fondly remembers**  *San Francisco Chronicle,* March 12, 1998.

198 **He returned to** USF  *San Francisco Chronicle,* March 12, 1998.

199 **I had the best view**  Vince Boyle telephone interview, April 17, 2007.

203 **In mid-1985** USF  *Washington Post,* July 30, 1982.

203 **Lo Schiavo admitted**  Deford, "A heavenly game?," 58.

203 **K. C. Jones was shocked**  *Washington Post,* August 1, 1982.

203 **Despite the estrangement**  *Los Angeles Times,* April 2, 2007.

204 **But fifty years later**  *The Union,* November 22, 2005.

# BIBLIOGRAPHY

"All-America Basketball Preview," *Sport*, January 1956, 12+(1).

"Along Came Bill," *Time*, January 2, 1956.

Anderson, Dave. *The Story of Basketball*. New York: Morrow, 1983.

Anderson, Kelli. "In Their Own Style," *Sports Illustrated*, July 3, 2006, 98+(1).

Anderson, R. Bentley. *Black, White, and Catholic: New Orleans Inter-racialism, 1947–56*. Nashville: Vanderbilt University Press, 2005.

Ashe, Arthur R. Jr. *A Hard Road to Glory*. New York: Amistad, 1988.

Associated Press Sports Staff. *The Sports Immortals*, Englewood Cliffs NJ, 1972.

Bjarkman, Peter. C. *Hoopla: A Century of College Basketball*, Indianapolis IN: Masters Press, 1996.

Carey, Mike with Jamie Most. *High Above Courtside*, Champaign IL: Sports Publishing LLC, 2003.

Daley, Arthur. "Educating of a Basketball Rookie," *New York Times Magazine*, February 24, 1957, 22+(3).

Davis, Ronald L.F. *Racial Etiquette: The Racial Customs and Rules of Racial Behavior in Jim Crow America*, http://www.jimcrowhistory.org/resources/lessonplans/hs_es_etiquette.htm, downloaded July 7, 2007.

Deford, Frank. "Defensive wizard revolutionized the college game," *si.com*, 2005.

———. "The Ring Leader," *Sports Illustrated*, May 19, 1999 96+(1).

———. "A heavenly game? (Basketball in Catholic colleges)," *Sports Illustrated*, March 3, 1986, 58+(12).

"Dons on Defense," *Time*, February 14, 1955.

"Dons, Playing 'Em Close, May Go Far in Title Play," *Sporting News*, January 19, 1955, Section 4, p2.

"Dons win again as Russell soars—1956," *tsn.sportingnews.com/archives/ncaa/1956.html*, downloaded September 8, 2006.

Douchant, Mike. *Encyclopedia of College Basketball*, New York: Gale Research Inc., 1995.

Edwards, Harry. *The Revolt of the Black Athlete*, New York: The Free Press, 1969.

Einhorn, Eddie and Ron Rapoport. *How March Became Madness*, Chicago: Triumph Books, 2006.

Fay, Bill. "All American Team," *Colliers*, March 16, 1956, 35+(2).

Feinstein, John. *Last Dance*, New York: Little, Brown, 2006.

Fitzgerald, Ray. *Champions Remembered*, Battleboro VT: Stephen Green Press, 1982.

Fitzpatrick, Frank. *And The Walls Came Tumbling Down*, New York: Simon & Schuster, 1999.

George, Nelson. *Elevating the Game: Black Men & Basketball*, Lincoln: The University of Nebraska Press, 1992.

Gergen, Joe. *The Final Four*, St. Louis MO: Sporting News Publications, 1987.

Giethschier, Steve. "San Francisco Dons win 60 consecutive games," *sportingnews.com/archives/sports2000/numbers/143117.html*, downloaded August 12, 2006.

Goudsouzian, Aram. "The House That Russell Built," California History, Fall 2007.

Goldstein, Joe. "Explosion: 1951 scandals threaten college hoops," *espn.go.com/classic/s/basketball_scandals_explosion.html*, downloaded January 29, 2007.

Griffin, Edward M. "Hoops & Hurdles: How I Learned How I Learn,"

*www1.umn.edu/ohr/img/assets/18007/griffin2.pdf*, downloaded
February 3, 2007.

Grimsley, Will. *101 Greatest Athletes of the Century*, New York: The Associated Press, 1987.

Grundsman, Adolph. "The Images of Intercollegiate Sports and the Civil Rights Movement: A Historian's View," *Arena Journal 5*, No. 3 (1980), 77+(8).

Heinsohn, Tommy and Joe Fitzgerald. *Give 'em the Hook*, Englewood Cliffs NJ: Prentice-Hall, 1988.

Isaacs, Neil. *All the Moves*, Philadelphia: Lippincott, 1975.

Jenkins, Bruce. *A Good Man: The Pete Newell Story*, Berkeley CA: Frog, 1999.

Johnson, William. "Triumph in Obscurity," *Sports Illustrated*, April 22, 1968 68(8)

Jones, K. C. with Jack Warner. *Rebound*, Boston: Quinlan Press, 1986.

Keith, Larry. "The magic numbers were 6 and 60," *Sports Illustrated*, January 31, 1977, 28.

Kerkhoff, Blair. *The Greatest Book of College Basketball*, Lenexa KS: Addax Publishing Group, 1998.

Klein, Dave. *Pro Basketball's Big Men*, New York: Random House, 1973.

Knapp, Ron. *Top 10 Stars of the NCAA Men's Basketball Tournament*, Berkeley Heights NJ: Enslow Publishers, 2001.

Kornheiser, Tony. *Bill Russell: Nothing but a Man*, Chicago: Rare Air Media, 1999.

Krause, Jerry and Ralph L. Pim. *Basketball Defense Sourcebook: Lessons from the Legends*, Chicago: Triumph Books, 2005.

Lee, Bruce. "Bill Russell, K. C. Jones, Unstoppable San Francisco," *Sport*, April 1974, 37+(6).

Linn, Ed. "Bill Russell's Private World," *Sport*, February 1963.

———. "I Owe the Public Nothing," *Saturday Evening Post*, January 18, 1964.

Lucas, Adam. *The Best Game Ever*, Guilford CT: Lyons Press, 2006.

Masin, Herman L. ed. *The Best of Basketball from Scholastic Coach*, Englewood Cliffs NJ: 1962.

McGuire, William. *The Final Four*, Mankato MN: Creative Education, 1990.

McTaggart, Lynne. "The Power of Intention," *Ode Magazine*, January/ February 2007.

Miller, Patrick B. and David K. Wiggins, eds., *Sport and the Color Line*, New York: Routledge, 2004.

Minsky, Alan. *March to the Finals*, New York: Metro Books, 1997.

NCAA. *NCAA March Madness: Cinderellas, Superstars, and Champions from the NCAA Men's Final Four*, Chicago: Triumph Books, 2004.

NBA. *The Perfect Team*, New York: Doubleday, 2006.

Nelson, Murry R. *Bill Russell: A Biography*, Westport CT: Greenwood, 2005.

Newell, Pete. *Pete Newell's Defensive Basketball: Winning Techniques and Strategies*, Lincolnwood IL: Masters Press, 2000.

——— and Dan Berger. *Basketball: The Sports Playbook*, Garden City NY: Doubleday, 1976.

O'Donnell, Chuck. *Basketball Digest*, December 2000.

O'Liam, Dugal. "They Make Rules to Stop Russell," *Sport*, April 1956, 37+(4).

Packer, Billy and Roland Lazenby. *College Basketball's 25 Greatest Teams*, St. Louis: Sporting News, 1989.

———. *Golden Moments of the Final Four*, Dallas TX: Jefferson Street Press, 1989.

"Picked for the Pros," *Time*, January 16, 1956.

Rappoport, Ken. *The Classic: The History of the NCAA Basketball Championship*, Mission KS: NCAA, 1979.

Richardson, Ben and William F. Fahey. *Great Black Americans*, New York: Crowell, 1976.

Russell, Bill with William McSweeney. *Go Up for Glory*, New York: Coward-McMann, 1966.

——— and Taylor Branch. *Second Wind: The Memoirs of an Opinionated Man*, New York: Simon & Schuster, 1991.

——— with Alan Hilburg and David Falkner. *Russell Rules*, New York: New American Library, 2001.

———. "We are grown men playing a child's game," *Sports Illustrated*, November 18, 1973, 75+(3)

———— with Al Hirshberg. "I was a 6'9" Babe in the Woods," *Saturday Evening Post*, January 18, 1958.

———— with Bob Ortum, "The Psych and My Other Tricks," *Sports Illustrated*, July 16, 1965, 32+(2).

Rust, Art, Jr. and Edna Rust. *Art Rust's Illustrated History of the Black Athlete*, Garden City NY: Doubleday, 1985.

Schneider, Bernie. "1948–49: Pete Newell's NIT Championship," *usfdons.cstv.com/trads/newell.html*, downloaded August 12, 2006.

————. "1953–56 NCAA Championship Seasons: The Bill Russell Years," *usfdons.cstv.com/trads,Russell_years.html*, downloaded August 12, 2006.

————. "1956–57: Return to the Final Four," *usfdons.cstv.com/trads/return_final_four.html*, downloaded August 12, 2006.

"Scientist in Sneakers," *Boston Magazine*, February 1989.

Shapiro, Miles. *Bill Russell*, New York: Chelsea House Publishers, 1991.

Smith, Dean with John Kilgo and Sally Jenkins. *A Coach's Life*, New York: Random House, 1991.

Smith, Jessie Carney, ed. *Notable Black American Men*, Detroit: Gale, 1999.

Spivey, Donald. "The Black Athlete in Big-Time Intercollegiate Sports: 1941–1968," *Phylon 44*, June 1983, 116+(9).

Taylor, John. *The Rivalry*, New York: Random House, 2005.

Tax, Jeremiah. "The Man Who Must Be Different," *Sports Illustrated*, February 3, 1958, p. 29+(3)

Terrell, Roy. "The tournaments and the man who," *Sports Illustrated*, January 9, 1956, 39+(1).

————. "Victory No. 55: The End of an Era," *Sports Illustrated*, April 2, 1956, 42+(1).

————. "It's Dayton and the Dons," *Sports Illustrated*, March 10, 1956, 21+(1).

————. "Even the loss of K. C. Jones may not cost San Francisco the NCAA title—but it will make the Dons' job tougher," *Sports Illustrated*, January 23, 1956, 45.

————. "The Big Surprise of 1955," *Sports Illustrated*, March 28, 1955, 17+(2).

Thomas, Ron. *They Cleared the Lane*, Lincoln: University of Nebraska Press, 2002.

Thomsen, Ian. "Ruminating with Russell," *http://sportsillustrated.cnn.com/2007/writers/ian.thomsen/08/20/Russell/2.html*, downloaded September 13, 2007.

Urban, Hal. *Life's Greatest Lessons*, New York: Simon and Schuster, 1992.

Vancil, Mark, ed. NBA *at 50*, New York: Park Lane Press, 1996.

Whalen Thomas J. *Dynasty's End: Bill Russell and the 1968–69 World Champion Boston Celtics*, Boston: Northeastern University Press, 2004.

Wolff, Alexander. *100 Years of Hoops*, Birmingham AL: Oxmoor House, 1991.

Wooden, John with Jack Tobin. *They Call Me Coach*, New York: McGraw-Hill, 2003.

———— with Steve Jamison. *Wooden on Leadership*, New York: McGraw-Hill, 2005.


Interviews*

Balchios, Steve. May 9, 2007

Baxter, Warren. April 9 and April 28, 2007

Boldt, Carl. March 15, 2007

Boyle, Vince. April 17, 2007

Braghetta, Bob. April 9, 2007

Briare, Vince. May 12, 2007

Brown, Eugene. April 24 and May 5, 2007

Buchanan, Stan. May 15, 2007

Bush, Bill. Feb. 27, 2008

Farmer, Mike. October 9, 2006

Guidice, Ross. March 20 and May 8, 2007

King, Jack. May 15, 2007

Kirby, Gordon. May 7, 2007

Koljian, John. May 7–8, 2007

Lawless, Dick. April 3, 2007

Lo Schiavo, John. April 9, 2007

Mulholland, Bill. May 6, 2007

Nelson, Tom. April 17, 2007
Payne, Hal. May 10, 2007
Perry, Hal. June 19, 2007
Preaseau, Mike. April 18, 2007
Wiebusch, Bob. May 9, 2007.
Zannini, Rudy. March 20, 2007

*All interviews were conducted by telephone,
except the one with Mike Farmer.*